GE 195 .S683 2002
Spowers, Rory.
Rising tides

MHCC WITHDRAWN

AF681530

Rising Tides

Rising Tides

A History of the Environmental Revolution and Visions for an Ecological Age

Rory Spowers

CANONGATE

This edition published simultaneously in Canada
and the United States of America in 2003 by
Canongate Books Ltd

First published in Great Britain in 2002 by
Canongate Books Ltd, 14 High Street,
Edinburgh EH1 1TE

10 9 8 7 6 5 4 3 2 1

Copyright © Rory Spowers, 2002
The moral right of the author has been asserted

British Library Cataloguing-in-Publication Data
A catalogue record for this book is available on
request from the British Library

Extracts from E.F. Schumacher are © Verena Schumacher,
and used with permission

Tables on p277 and p278 are from *Something New Under the Sun: An Environmental History of the Twentieth Century* by John McNeill, Penguin Books/W.W. Norton and Company, 2000. Permission sought.

Graphs on p279 and a slightly different version of the accompanying text appeared in *Contraction and Convergence: The Global Solution to Climate Change* by Aubrey Meyer, Green Books, Totnes, Devon, 2000. Reproduced by permission.

Graph on p280 appeared in *Sharing Nature's Interest: Ecological Footprints as an Indicator of Sustainability* by Nicky Chambers, Craig Simmons and Mathis Wackernagel, Earthscan, 2001. Reproduced by permission.

The sections entitled 'The Ecology of Hollywood'
and 'Auto-addiction' first appeared in
Geographical magazine as 'The Ecology of
Hollywood' and 'Dream Machines'.

Printed on acid-free paper from a renewable source

ISBN 1 84195 357 1

Typeset by Palimpsest Book Production Limited,
Polmont, Stirlingshire, Scotland
Printed and bound in the United States of America
by R.R. Donnelley

www.canongate.net

For my father

We modern people think we can just trample on something in our way as you trample on an ant, and it will not make the slightest difference to the universe; but it is not true. Somewhere it has an impact, and it does affect us, no matter how small or insignificant. In meaning there is no quantity, only quality; size and amount and distance do not apply, position and direction of spirit is all. That is why it is important that we recover this sense of belonging and the responsibility as individuals of being a good neighbour to all forms of life.

LAURENS VAN DER POST
A Walk with a White Bushman

Contents

Preface

After leaving university, I was lucky enough to spend a year cycling through Africa with three friends. Six years later, I spent six months walking through India. These journeys forced me to redefine my notion of concepts like 'wealth', 'development' and 'progress', influencing the direction my life has taken ever since.

I consumed books about the environmental crisis and the 'new world-view', made a film in India about pollution in the Ganges, worked for an environmental film-maker and contributed to magazines which documented the issues which threaten us all. Throughout this time I was continually amazed by the lack of interest that most people displayed towards these ideas, ranging from total apathy to polite indifference. As far as I could see, we were all heading for a global melt-down but hardly anybody seemed to be even remotely concerned.

Twelve years later and the situation is only slightly different. Most of us now recognise that there is a problem but find it hard to know what to do about it. I began to realise just how little of the revolutionary thought which I had come across in those years had percolated through to the mainstream; that the media hardly ever reported the full story and that many of the solutions to these escalating problems were stuck within the rarefied domains of an eco-academia and rarely presented to a wider audience in an accessible way. There seemed to be a lot of talk and little action, while the brilliant minds behind the 'new world-view' were often preaching to the converted. With a few notable exceptions, it seemed that progressive environmental solutions were not making the cross-over to the general public.

Hence this book; an attempt to distil these ideas and communicate them to a wider readership in a concise manner. It has not been written for those who have been involved in the environmental movement for many years, rather for those who find themselves waking up to the horrors of what we are doing to the planet. I am not a qualified historian, or an ecologist. I am purely a concerned individual, and a writer, and acknowledge that much of what is presented here is a distillation and a synthesis of other people's work. However, I hope that the reader will use this as a springboard to pursue some of these radical concepts in more detail. The bibliography, the notes and the directory in Appendix 1 are intended to facilitate that process, so that we can collectively make the Environmental Revolution a reality.

As Zac Goldsmith said to me, 'I often wonder why everyone isn't an environmentalist.' I have been asking myself the same question for twelve years. Why isn't everyone concerned about the state of the planet that we are dependent upon? I hope that this book will convince a few more to feel the same. We are all engaged in a planetary race between two rising tides. On one side we have the literal rising tide of world sea levels caused by global warming, Nature's response to Man's interference with the carbon cycle. On the other side we have the rising tide of opposition confronting the economic machine responsible for raping our planet. As we enter the twenty-first century, one question confronts us all: which tide will be the first to break down the barriers that we have created?

Acknowledgements

The reader will soon become familiar with the names of those who are the primary inspiration for this book, since they are referred to and quoted from on a regular basis. I am indebted to all those who have contributed to the emerging ecological world-view and am acutely aware that my primary role as the author of this book has been to present a distillation of their ground-breaking work.

I would like to thank Teddy Goldsmith, Zac Goldsmith, Helena Norberg-Hodge and James Lovelock for the time they put aside for me, Fritjof Capra for our discussion about the convergence of the anti-globalisation movement, Tony Juniper at Friends of the Earth and John May for his help on the history of Greenpeace. Special thanks to Herbie Girardet for all his support, Jamie Byng at Canongate for believing so passionately in the book, Mairi Sutherland for doing such a skilful job as editor. I would also particularly like to thank my wife Yvette for helping me to maintain a sense of optimism while digesting information about the state of the planet.

Abbreviations

AEC	Atomic Energy Commission
ALF	Animal Liberation Front
BSE	Bovine Spongiform Encephalopathy
CAP	Common Agricultural Policy
CAT	Centre for Alternative Technology
CBC	Canadian Broadcasting Corporation
CEO	Chief Executive Officer
CFC	Chlorofluorocarbon
CJA	Criminal Justice Act
CJD	Creutzfeldt-Jakob Disease
CND	Campaign for Nuclear Disarmament
CPRE	Council for the Protection of Rural England
CSA	Community Supported Agriculture
DTI	Department of Trade and Industry
EDF	Environmental Defense Fund
EF!	Earth First!
EIS	Environmental Impact Statement
EPA	Environmental Protection Agency
EPC	Environmental Policy Centre
EPEA	Environmental Protection Encouragement Agency
EU	European Union
FBI	Federal Bureau of Investigation
FDA	Food and Drug Administration
FoE	Friends of the Earth
GATT	General Agreement on Tariffs and Trade
GDP	Gross Domestic Product
GM	Genetic Modification
GMO	Genetically Modified Organism
HGDP	Human Genome Diversity Project
IMF	International Monetary Fund
IPCC	Inter-Governmental Panel on Climate Change
IWC	International Whaling Commission
LETS	Local Exchange Trading System
LSD	Lysergic Acid Diethylamide
MAD	Mutually Assured Destruction

MAFF	Ministry for Agriculture, Fisheries and Food (now DEFRA: Department of the Environment, Food and Rural Affairs)
MAI	Multi-national Agreement on Investments
MDMA	Methylenedioxyphenylisopropylamine
MRL	Maximum Residue Limit
NAFTA	North American Free Trade Agreement
NASA	North American Space Administration
NGO	Non-Governmental Organisation
NVDA	Non-Violent Direct Action
OECD	Organisation for Economic Co-operation and Development
PCB	Poly-chlorinated Biphenyls
PTO	Patent Trademark Office
RTS	Reclaim the Streets
SAFE	Sustainable Agriculture Food and Environment
SDS	Students for Democratic Society
SSSI	Site of Special Scientific Interest
SUV	Sports Utility Vehicle
TLIO	The Land is Ours
UNCED	United Nations Conference on Environment and Development
UNEP	United Nations Environment Programme
WEN	Women's Environmental Network
WHO	World Health Organisation
WTO	World Trade Organisation
WWF	World Wildlife Fund (now World Wide Fund for Nature)
ZPG	Zero Population Growth

Introduction

This generation may either be the last to exist in any semblance of a civilized world or it will be the first to have the vision, the bearing and the greatness to say 'I will have nothing to do with this destruction of life, I will play no part in this devastation of the land, I am determined to live and work for peaceful construction for I am morally responsible for the world of today and the generations of tomorrow.'

RICHARD ST BARBE-BAKER[1]

What Went Wrong?

When I started work on this book, I saw myself as an environmentalist. Not a very diligent one maybe, but fairly committed on an ideological basis. The deeper I delved into the roots of the modern environmental movement, the more hazy a term like 'environmentalism' became. We are so deeply embedded in processes of exchange with the natural world, through what we eat, drink and consume, that it seems absurd to think about completely eliminating our impact on Nature. How then do we minimise it and create an ecologically sustainable society? Is this crisis an entirely modern problem, or are there historical precedents for it? What really is the environmental movement? Where did it come from and, perhaps most importantly, why does it even exist?

Before examining the history of environmental thought, it is worth looking at the premise upon which it is based. The environmental movement would not exist unless we saw ourselves as somehow separate from Nature and believed that we should be doing things differently. The aspirations of the movement are based on the assumption that we have lost touch with the natural world and that, through a blind faith in science, technology and expansionist, capitalist economics, we are causing untold damage to the systems that support our very being.

The whole notion of human separation from Nature is full of profound philosophical and spiritual questions. How can we possibly be separate from the Nature from which we came, on which we depend from moment to moment and to which one day we shall return? However, implicit in that question is the whole notion of an individual human ego, which separates itself from the 'concept' of Nature.

There has been much speculation in recent years as to how and when this separation from Nature occurred. There is a prevailing notion that, at some stage of human history, we stopped living 'in tune with Nature' – when we stopped being hunter-gatherers and settled as agriculturalists, when we stopped worshipping the Earth as The Mother, when our species first developed the capacity for self-reflective consciousness, when the human ego was fully developed as a psychological reality, when we started to see Nature as obeying mechanical laws and no longer viewed her in a holistic, organismic way.

However, Nature is just a word – a word with as much cultural baggage as any in the English language. The environmental movement is built upon the notion that the way in which we are treating Nature is fundamentally wrong. But where and when did we start to go wrong? What is the right way to treat Nature? *Is* there a right way to treat Nature? Most importantly, what do we mean by Nature and how has that changed during the course of human history?

Why Should We Care?

The scale and complexity of the environmental crisis provokes a variety of responses. Many of us feel so daunted by the sheer magnitude of the issues that we feel powerless to do anything about them. Psychologists refer to the process of 'psychic numbing', anaesthetising us against the catastrophic implications of an impending ecological melt-down, like the state of shock felt in personal trauma.

Many of the problems that we are confronted with seem so intangible, somehow removed from our daily lives: invisible chemical pollutants in the air we breathe, the water we drink and the food we eat; the hole in the ozone layer above Antarctica, the widespread loss of topsoil in Africa and the long-term effects of radioactive waste. In response, many of us choose to ignore the problems altogether, thinking 'there's plenty more where that came from', placing our trust in science to provide technological fixes, or reassuring ourselves that the only consequence of global warming will be to bring us balmy Mediterranean weather.

The environmental movement itself has often succeeded in alienating the public it hopes to convert. Early projections of impending catastrophe failed to occur and many began to look at environmentalists as hysterical idealists, or just deluded, self-righteous cranks (a label which Fritz Schumacher, one of the gurus of the modern movement, was quite happy to embrace, since a crank is a small, simple, efficient tool 'and it makes revolutions'[2]). The impact of horrifying statistics often precipitates an adverse reaction, seen by many as a direct assault on their way of life. As Theodore Roszak observes, 'it is elementary psychology that those who wish to change the world for the better should not begin by vilifying the public they seek to persuade, or by confronting it with a task that appears impossible.'[3] The result of questioning people's lifestyles, to galvanise collective fear and guilt, has often produced an adverse reaction. Ironically, these tactics played into the hands of the so-called 'greenwash', corporate-sponsored attempts to undermine information provided by environmental groups.

Even if the movement succeeds in making us aware and concerned, we feel there is a limit to which we can involve ourselves and make the difference we would like. Organic produce is too expensive for many of us to afford, or our livelihood is entirely dependent on using the company car. This in turn creates feelings of guilt, making us feel that we are inconsistent, unable to contribute to what we may believe in. Various options then present themselves as a way out, ranging from 'Oh well, it won't happen in my lifetime' to 'The planet will be better off without us anyway.'

These complex psychological reactions have led to some extreme positions within environmental circles, leading some to see drought, famine and the AIDS epidemic as part of Nature's vengeance, a necessary response mechanism to our species spreading like a cancer across the planet. Then there are others who extrapolate James Lovelock's Gaia Theory – which regards the planet and the biosphere as one integrated self-regulating organism – to include the actions of Man as part of a self-correcting process: 'it's all happening as it's supposed to'.

These are all legitimate responses. Maybe, in the 'really big picture', human consciousness is a process within Gaia and it is just another example of our egocentric hubris to suppose that we can somehow control a 'web of life' which is infinitely more complex than we currently suppose. Maybe we shall be driven to extinction as a species and our interaction with Nature will ultimately trigger the final collapse of life support systems on the planet. Maybe Gaia has decided that, if the rest of Nature is to survive, humanity has to go. It would surely be the ultimate human arrogance to assume that the universe operates on principles designed to protect our species above and beyond any other.

However, while we are still here, trying to heal the split that has developed between us and the natural world, our psychological response to the perceived crisis is clearly a crucial point to consider. A whole new area of eco-psychology has developed to address precisely these issues as we work towards a new conception of the Ecological Society and Ecological Self. In order to preserve and protect the Nature we see 'out there', it seems that we need to think long and hard about the Nature we carry around 'in here', so that ultimately they can become one and the same. Maybe then we can develop the humility that a sacred, healthy, harmonious relationship with the living earth demands.

We are not powerless as individuals – a single micro-organism can affect the course of history and change is always propelled by a minority. Each one of us can become an active cell within the green web which now encircles the globe. We are approaching a point of critical mass as, through the sheer scale of the issues we face and the number of people involved, the Environmental Revolution has become essential for our own survival.

Despite the doom-and-gloom statistics that are an inevitable part of any study concerned with the global crisis, this book is intended to be positive and optimistic. In 1970, when environmental problems were first percolating through to the mainstream, few viable solutions were offered by those ringing the alarm bells. The situation is now very different. Over the last thirty years, the environmental movement has produced the political framework, the economic models and the benign technologies which we need to create a sustainable future. Unfortunately, most western politicians, and the multinational corporations which dictate global economic policy, still cling to an antiquated paradigm which promotes infinite economic growth through the exploitation of finite resources. This is not only incompatible with ecological principles, but logically impossible.

At the same time, those who seek to perpetuate a system that is intrinsically flawed continue to insist that the 'green agenda' is naive, idealistic and out of step with 'reality'. But what is this 'reality'? Has money, that artificial human construct which we have devoted our lives to, become the only 'reality' that we subscribe to? Many would argue that money is considerably less 'real' than acid rain, ozone depletion or global warming. Despite incontestable proof from more than a thousand of the world's most distinguished climatologists, there are still those who dismiss the notion of global warming. This is no longer a tenable position. It is like saying that two plus two equals five.

The problem is that one cannot accept the 'reality' of global warming and continue to promote profligate patterns of consumption without appearing inconsistent. The psychological response is to find some way out of accepting this 'reality' so that neither one's conscience, nor one's lifestyle, is in any way compromised. Until the 'reality' of the environmental crisis hits people on a personal level, most of us continue to keep our heads in the sand. However, when your house is destroyed by climatic conditions caused by global warming, you are diagnosed with a cancerous tumour triggered by chemical pesticides, your child dies from variant CJD, or your baby is born with disfigured reproductive organs due to synthetic compounds in the water supply, it is hard to deny the 'reality' of what we are doing to the planet and to ourselves.

The environmental crisis forces us to challenge basic assumptions which have become so deeply ingrained within our psychological conditioning that we rarely stop to question them. Within the political realm this includes the basic role of government and the democratic process itself. Economically, it addresses the notion of 'Better is More' and the whole concept of 'wealth' being purely equated with financial worth. In the world of science, it undermines our faith in the benefits of relentless technological innovation. Philosophically and spiritually it raises fundamental questions about who or what we are and how we relate to the world around us.

Although the word has been become deeply stigmatised within our society, because of its associations with institutional religions or New Ageism, the core issue raised by the environmental movement is spiritual. By spiritual I mean the basic enquiry into the nature of human existence, the relationship between Spirit and Matter, the interaction between the internal processes of the human mind and the external processes of the planet. This has little to do with the dogma that has developed around our religious traditions, all of which have drifted a long way from their original essence, corrupted by social hierarchies to be used as a means of exerting authority and power. The environmental crisis is a spiritual crisis which can only be solved through a deep enquiry into who we are and what it means to be alive. It is about making the transition from an egocentric perspective, which emphasises the individual sense of separation from an external world, to an eco-centric perspective, which recognises the interdependence of all life. It is inclusive rather than exclusive.

The crisis that we face threatens the entire planet. There is nobody for whom it is not relevant. Humanity has never been confronted with a challenge that is even remotely similar. Every one of us is faced with a simple choice. We can either keep our heads in the sand, take the easy option and dismiss the 'reality' altogether, or we can accept and embrace the challenge that we face. We have all the tools that we need to move into an Ecological Age – the political and economic models, the eco-technologies, the philosophical and spiritual wisdom. All we need is the collective vision to implement it. Surely we owe this not only to our children, but to the planet that sustains life itself?

The Environmental Revolution

The environmental movement has become the largest single social movement in British history.[4] When extended to the planet as a whole, it can be seen as the most powerful force for change that the world has ever seen, transcending barriers of race, colour, gender and creed.

The world's first environmental group – the Commons, Footpaths, and Open Spaces Preservation Society – was founded in Britain in 1865.[5] At the start of the new millennium, the movement has grown to encompass 5 million people in Britain.[6] Nearly one in ten of us subscribes to organisations such as Greenpeace, Friends of the Earth (FoE) and the World Wide Fund for Nature (WWF), making the movement larger and more diverse than any political party or social organisation. This tide continues to rise at a rate of 7 per cent a year.[7]

An expanding planetary network, disillusioned with the basic structure of our global economic and political system, has united characters as diverse as Prince Charles, the Dalai Lama and the eco-warrior Swampy. Old age pensioners are linking arms with dreadlocked anarchists to protest against genetically modified crops and new sections of motorway. Around the globe, environmental groups range from grass-roots organisations in tribal villages campaigning against World Bank dam projects, through to swish corporate-style offices advising governments.

Within the last thirty years, this movement has brought such terms as global warming, ozone depletion and biodiversity into our living rooms, while huge international conferences, like the 1992 Earth Summit in Rio de Janeiro, have endeavoured to find political solutions to these burgeoning problems. New issues arise almost daily, bringing us to the top of an exponential curve. Our relationship to the planet has become the most urgent agenda of the age and the twenty-first century will be the last chance we have to resolve the crisis that threatens, not only our own survival as a species, but the very systems that support life itself. The Environmental Revolution has become a necessity.

About 10,000 years ago, mankind took part in the Agricultural Revolution, making the transition from nomadic hunter-gatherer societies to the settled existence of 'civilisations'. As we learnt to manipulate the natural world to our benefit, through the irrigation of the land, the cultivation of crops and the domestication of animals, our relationship to Nature changed at a fundamental level. The Industrial Revolution, which started a mere six generations ago, ushered in a new age of mechanisation and mobility, driven by the use of fossil fuels. We are now witnessing the consequences of the ensuing Industrial Age and the notions of 'growth' and 'progress' that came with it.

While islands in the Pacific disappear beneath the waves, and global climate change turns millions into refugees, a rising tide of opposition is now confronting the economic machine which is destroying the life-support systems of our planet. A green web is spinning itself around the globe, propelling an Environmental Revolution which is not only producing the technological, economic and political systems that will be necessary for us to survive beyond the next hundred years, but also the philosophical and spiritual insight that we need to create an Ecological Age.

The environmental movement has evolved from isolated events and issues to a broad spectrum assault on our entire economic and political system. It is no longer just about saving whales and forests. It is now obvious that a consumer society pursuing a vision of *infinite* growth, while reliant on *finite* resources, is not only unsustainable but, by definition, logically impossible. Capitalism has revealed some fundamental flaws.

What the movement is asking us to embrace is nothing less than a revolution in our world-view, an entirely new social, political and cultural paradigm which is redefining our antiquated notions of 'growth', 'wealth' and 'progress'. A 'high standard of living', gained by 'being successful', is no longer an adequate indication of our 'quality of life'. What is at hand is no less radical than the Copernican Revolution, transforming our value system, our beliefs and our relation to the rest of the natural world in the same way that our perception of the planet was changed in relation to the sun and the solar system.

Information technology is clearly playing a crucial role in this global awakening, connecting pressure groups, grass-roots organisations and concerned individuals from around the world. More and more of us sense that we are suffering from some sort of collective insanity as we learn the truth about the world we now live in; a world in which multinational corporations wield more financial clout than nation states, the ten largest companies turning over more than the hundred smallest countries;[8] a world in which a tiny elite controls the 4 trillion dollars that slosh around the global casino each day while a billion people are denied the basic food, water and shelter that they need;[9] a world in which one billion dollars are spent every day on military weapons and where the combined wealth of the 350 richest people exceeds the net worth of nearly half the human population;[10] a world in which governments tax the things that are supposed to be good for us, like capital and income, and don't tax the things that are bad, like pollution and resource depletion; a world in which road accidents, insurance claims, hospital bills, energy consumption and environmental disasters, all add to our indicators of economic health and prosperity, as presented to us by gross domestic product (GDP); a world in which one company, Shell, controls an area of land larger than Alaska;[11] a world in which our 3.8 billion-year reserve of 'natural capital' – the topsoil, forests and coral reefs which constitute our 'real' wealth – is being eroded at such a rate that we have lost one third of the planet's resources in the last thirty years;[12] a world in which our DNA, the very matrix of life itself, is being bartered over by multinational interests; a world where we can no longer trust the food we buy in the shops or the drugs that are forced upon us by a medical establishment controlled by pharmaceutical corporations with vested interests; a world where we are are losing all faith in our politicians, our business leaders and our religions; a world which has lost all sense of the sacred; a world controlled by those that are best at being greedy.

We have ended up in a terrible muddle, where everything is back to front and upside down. Whether we are treating medical conditions like cancer, societal problems like drug addiction, the threat of international terrorism or the environmental impact of toxic pollutants, we continue to look at the symptoms rather than the causes, applying crude 'band-aid' technological fixes. Unfortunately, however many drugs we develop to combat the spread of cancer, they do nothing whatsoever to reduce the incidence of the disease.

The scale of the symptoms that are now manifesting across the planet provides some disturbing statistics: tropical rainforests continue to be felled at a rate of one football field per second; acid rain has damaged over 31 million hectares of trees in Europe alone;[13] 6 billion hectares of productive land are being lost to desertification every year and 26 billion tons of topsoil are literally washed out to sea;[14] that adds up to a quarter of the world's topsoil and a third of the world's forest cover being lost in the last twenty-five years;[15] despite the warnings of 170 scientists sitting on the Inter-Governmental Panel on Climate Change (IPCC), who unanimously agreed that we need to cut carbon dioxide emissions by 60–80 per cent to avoid climatic catastrophe, world leaders continue to conduct business as usual, while every night when we go to sleep, 40,000 new cars roll off the production line; every year, climate change causes $90 billion worth of damage around the world;[16] this figure is predicted to reach £200 billion by 2005 and environmental disasters have now created 80 million refugees; the insurance industry estimates that economic losses from these trends are growing at 10 per cent per year and will exceed the total value of all human production within two generations; carbon dioxide levels are now 30 per cent higher than at any time registered in the ice-core records and climbing so fast that projections speak of a 300 per cent increase in atmospheric concentrations by 2030;[17] the polar ice caps are melting and one third of humanity lives in areas threatened by a sea level rise of just 25 centimetres. The latest projections made by the Hadley Centre at the UK Meteorological Office point to a situation which is even worse than that predicted by the IPCC, forecasting an average global temperature rise of 8 °C by 2100, well above the IPCC's worst scenario figure of 5.8 °C which would already cause a sea level rise of nearly a metre.[18]

Meanwhile, the average American watches 22,000 television commercials a year,[19] generates 1 million pounds of material waste[20] and consumes five times as much energy as anybody else in the world – if all 6 billion of us adopted similar patterns of consumption, we would need five more planets to provide the resource base; intensive farming monocultures have reduced the genetic diversity of our staple crops to a fraction of what existed just fifty years ago; world fisheries are on the point of collapse, with blue-fin tuna and Atlantic cod joining the endangered species list; in Britain, more than 150,000 miles of hedgerow have been lost since subsidies began and are still being destroyed at a rate of 10,000 miles a year;[21] 20,000 tons of chemicals are applied to UK farming land every year,[22] during which time the average British adult eats his way through 3 pounds of chemical additives;[23] in addition to the 83,000 animals used in British laboratories every week,[24] often in duplicated experiments, it is estimated that we have driven one million other species into extinction in the last decade,[25] while every year we add another 100 million to the human population.[26]

By waging war on Nature, we are waging war on ourselves and heading towards an act of global suicide. As Czech President Vaclav Havel once remarked, 'transcendence has become the only real alternative to extinction'.

Some Basic Terms

There are numerous ideologies within the environmental arena, some of which deserve a brief definition.

Ironically, the word **ecology** shares the same Greek root as economy – *oikos*, meaning house. Both words refer to the management of the household, whereby all is maintained for the mutual benefit of those living there. Ecology was first developed as a science by Ernst Haeckel in 1866 and is concerned with the study of relationships between organisms and their environments. It takes a **holistic** approach, looking at the flow of interconnections within 'the web of life', rather than a **reductionist** approach, which seeks to explain life by looking at the constituent parts.

The origins of environmental ethics, or an **eco-centric** 'land ethic', is often traced to Aldo Leopold, one of the founders of the modern US movement. Leopold famously declared that 'a thing is right when it tends to preserve the integrity, stability and beauty of the biotic community. It is wrong when it tends otherwise'.[27] **Deep Ecology** was developed by Arne Naess, a Norwegian mountaineer, to distinguish it from a more human-centred or **anthropocentric** world-view. Rather than the 'shallow' approach of plain **environmentalism**, which seeks to make incremental improvements to the current system – through the 'wise use' of resources, recycling industries and pollution abatement technologies – deep ecologists seek to replace it with an **ecological world-view**. Deep Ecology sees no distinction in value between mankind and other species, proposing that 'humanity has no right to reduce the diversity of life except to satisfy its own vital needs'.

Eco-feminism attributes the crisis to the predominance of patriarchal, masculine values of aggression and greed in our political and economic systems and argues that a more intuitive, feminine relationship to Nature is needed to heal the division between ourselves and the planet. Similarly, the emerging schools of **eco-philosophy** and **eco-psychology** are concerned with the most fundamental inner relationship that exists between Mind and Nature.

The most significant scientific contribution to the environmental movement is James Lovelock's **Gaia Theory**, in which 'the entire range of living matter on earth, from whales to viruses, and from oaks to algae, could be regarded as constituting a single living entity, capable of manipulating the earth's atmosphere to suit its overall needs and endowed with faculties and powers far beyond those of its constituent parts'.[28] Although similar concepts have existed within the cosmologies of indigenous tribes for thousands of years, Lovelock's theory is the first comprehensive, scientific model to explain the earth and the biosphere as one integrated, self-regulating organism.

When first published, Gaia Theory came under scathing attack from the mainstream scientific community, regarded as some form of animism. It was then seized upon by the New Age and elevated to quasi-religious status. The scale of reaction that it has produced may be a good indication of just how revolutionary Gaia Theory is and there is little doubt that it is playing a crucial role in shaping our new world-view. As Lovelock says, his model provides 'an alternative to that pessimistic view which sees Nature as a primitive force to be subdued and conquered, and that equally depressing picture of our planet as a demented spaceship, forever travelling, driverless and purposeless, around an inner circle of the Sun.'[29] Maybe most importantly, Gaia re-awakens a sense of the sacred in Nature and provides us with a moral purpose to preserve the diversity of our beautiful planet for the generations of tomorrow.

1

Man vs Nature

The history of man's efforts to subjugate Nature is also the history of man's subjugation by Man. The development of the concept of the ego reflects this twofold history.

HORKHEIMER[1]

Genesis: The First Division

The history of the western world-view, which now dominates the globe, runs parallel to an increasing sense of separation between mankind and the natural world. In fact, the rise of human 'civilisation' could be described as synonymous with the attempted conquest of Nature.

This polarisation between Man and Nature is usually cited by those seeking a single root cause for the environmental crisis, a pursuit which others see as inherently flawed since ecology teaches us to recognise the complex inter-relation of countless systemic factors. However, a quick glance at the newspapers is enough to confirm that a deep division has developed between 'the civilised world' and the planet itself. At the same time, if we look at the few indigenous tribes that remain relatively untouched by the relentless march of globalisation, we see that no such separation has occurred. As we shall see, the social organisation of these ancient tribal cultures, which are rapidly being eroded by aggressive mining corporations, logging companies and transmigration policies, may have much to teach us about how to live in harmony with the environment. Despite this, they continue to be systematically eradicated in the name of something called 'progress'.

Before looking at the various forces which have contributed to our separation from Nature, it is worth noting that this is just one example of an inherent dualism upon which our world-view is dependent. It is also important to remember that this distinction is purely conceptual because, ultimately, we cannot be separate from Nature, a fact which is now supported as much by ecology and quantum physics as it is by the core teachings of the so-called Perennial Philosophy, the ancient sacred wisdom which forms the basis of all our religious and mystical traditions. This dualism manifests itself in the many divisions which humanity seeks to heal, between the material and the spiritual, between the cold logic of reason and inner voice of intuition, between science and religion, masculine and feminine, the head and the heart. The processes of the modern western mind are built upon this subject–object divide, unable to comprehend the absolute unity of existence. The whole notion of an individual human ego doing battle with an objective world may be the one obstacle that prevents us realising the balance which we seek.

One of the most powerful forces to have shaped our prevailing world-view is the Judaeo-Christian tradition, regarded by the American historian Lynn

White Jr as 'the most anthropocentric religion that the world has ever seen'.[2] White's 1967 thesis cited the medieval church as a root cause of the environmental crisis and proposed that little could be done to improve the situation 'until we reject the Christian axiom that Nature has no reason for existence save to serve man'.[3] Al Gore has been among those to challenge this as 'a cartoon version of the Judaeo-Christian tradition' and 'one that bears little resemblance to the reality'.[4]

Initially, the Genesis story leaves us in no doubt as to where we stand in relation to the rest of God's creation: Adam and Eve are told to 'be fruitful, and multiply, and replenish the earth, and subdue it' before being given 'dominion over the fish of the sea, and over the fowl of the air, and over every living thing that moveth upon the earth'. However, this is tempered in the following chapter, thought to have come from a different source, when they are left in the Garden of Eden 'to dress and keep it', suggesting a form of stewardship rather than the total subjugation of the non-human world. This is taken even further in a passage from Ecclesiastes, which almost suggests sentiments similar to those of Deep Ecology: 'that which befalleth the sons of man befalleth beasts; as the one dieth, so dieth the other; yea they all have one breath; so that man hath no pre-eminence above a beast'.[5]

However, passages like this are rare. The overall impression is that mankind has the right to exploit the earth for his benefit. What really matters is the relationship between the individual and a transcendent God rather than Nature. After the flood, the sense of Man's superiority is made even more acute: 'The fear of you and the dread of you shall be upon every beast of the earth', while Psalm 8 confirms that 'Thou hast given him dominion over the works of thy hands.' Historian Roderick Nash explains how 'Hebrew linguists have analysed Genesis 1:28 and found two operative verbs: *kabash*, translated as 'subdue', and *radah*, rendered as 'have dominion over' or 'rule'. Throughout the Old Testament *kabash* and *radah* are used to signify a violent assault or crushing. The image is that of a conqueror placing his foot on the neck of a defeated enemy, exerting absolute domination. Both Hebraic words are also used to identify the process of enslavement.'[6]

The sense that the world was created exclusively for Man to conquer and subdue was perpetuated by the Christian Church well into the twentieth century. Only in the recent climate of environmental awareness has there been some capitulation through an emphasis on humanity being the 'stewards' of God's creation. Calvin preached that 'God created all things for man's sake'[7] while Thomas Aquinas proposed a hierarchy, like the Great Chain of Being, whereby man's role was actually to improve upon the divine plan through agriculture and the use of natural resources.

There have of course been exceptions, like St Francis of Assisi, once vilified by the Church for an almost animistic, Pagan love of Nature, but now resurrected as 'a patron saint of ecologists' by religious leaders trying to defend a tradition which is seen as antithetical to the emerging ecological vision. Like the twelfth-century mystic Hildegaard of Bingen, who referred to God as 'the breeze that nurtures all things green',[8] St Francis developed a deep, mystical union with Nature, connecting him to the entire universe; from the sun and moon to birds, ants and worms, from man-eating wolves to the presence of fire and water. In his dismissal of dualistic, hierarchical 'chains of being', St Francis can be seen as a visionary precursor to the emerging world-view. However, as Nash observes, he was 'the exception that proves the rule of Christian anthropocentrism', since a good Christian soul is destined only for heaven and 'a grizzly bear or redwood tree could never be one's late grandmother reincarnated',[9] while Aldous Huxley notes that 'St Francis' attitude towards the brute creation was not entirely unequivocal. True, he converted a wolf and preached sermons to birds; but when Brother Juniper hacked the feet off a living pig in order to satisfy a sick man's craving for fried trotters, the saint merely blamed his disciple's intemperate zeal in damaging a valuable piece of private property.'[10]

During the last thousand years therefore, the prevailing attitude within the Christian tradition has been to look upon Nature as a separate realm, needing to be tamed and controlled. Any sense of Spirit within the organic life that surrounds us was heavily suppressed as Pagan blasphemy. Eastern religions, on the other hand, have tended towards an inherent respect for the diversity and intrinsic value of all living things. Hindu temples are often built around sacred trees, and pilgrimages are undertaken to mountains, rivers and springs. The concept of *ahimsa*, or non-violence, is taken to its absolute extreme within the Jain religion, where every aspect of the organic world, including soil, air and water, is imbued with Spirit. Jain monks often wear muslin over their mouths to prevent them from swallowing flies, while some ascetics stop eating and drinking altogether. Huxley observes how, 'Compared with that of the Taoists and Far Eastern Buddhists, the Christian attitude towards Nature has been curiously insensitive and often downright domineering and violent.'[11] However, over the last 200 years this awareness in the East has been sacrificed in favour of western ideals of economic growth, resulting in some of the most ecologically devastated habitats on earth.

Eco-feminists have highlighted the fact that the male supremacy of the Christian Church was not fully established until the Protestant Reformation in the sixteenth century. There is considerable evidence that the feminine aspect of the divine was held in equal regard to the masculine by early Christians; some of the first priests were women and the Hebrew term for the Holy Spirit, *ruah*, is feminine. Virtually every indigenous culture on the planet worshipped the Mother Goddess, or the Earth Mother, long before the Father God appeared around the time of the Agricultural Revolution. Even now, within the modern Judaeo-Christian tradition, most people regard Nature as alive and feminine. Biologist Rupert Sheldrake draws attention to the fact that, although living plants were evoked by God in Genesis, they were ultimately formed and brought forth by Mother Earth: 'God said: "Let the earth produce growing things; let there be on earth plants that bear seed, and trees that bear fruit, each with its own kind of seed." So it was; the earth produced growing things.'[12]

This distinction may be subtle but, as Sheldrake observes, it illustrates the way in which our world-view has suppressed an intuitive connection with Nature, leading to the position in which most modern business people, politicians and economists assume – at least during office hours – that Nature is 'inanimate and neuter', while 'nothing natural has a life, purpose or value of its own; natural resources are there to be developed, and their only value is the one placed on them by market forces or official planners.'[13]

What forces led to this polarisation between Man and Nature? How did we lose this intuitive, feminine connection to the natural world and separate ourselves to such a degree? Most importantly, is there anything that we can collectively do to transcend this basic contradiction within our world-view?

The Greeks: Ancient Roots

Three major periods of transition stand out when we look at the roots of the modern western mind: ancient Greek philosophy; the Copernican Revolution, which triggered the Enlightenment and the work of men like Francis Bacon; and the foundations of modern science – specifically the paradigm we inherited from Newton and Descartes – which formed the basis for the ensuing Industrial Revolution. A combination of these factors led us to look upon Nature as an enormous machine, obeying mechanical laws, despite the fact that the planet is clearly pulsating with organic life.

Generally, the Greeks saw Nature as being permeated with Mind, which was the source of regularity in the natural world. Mind was regarded as the dominant element, imposing order on everything that was contained within it. Therefore, as the philosopher R. G. Collingwood remarked, 'the world of Nature was not only alive but intelligent, not only a vast animal with a soul or life of its own, but a rational animal with a mind of its own'.[14] Plants and animals were thought to participate 'psychically in the life-process of the world's soul and intellectually in the activity of the world's mind'.[15] Plato's concept of the planet as one living organism seems to echo the belief systems of indigenous cultures and has been compared with the basic premise of the Gaia Theory.

However, this view was far from universal. Aristotle listed fourteen definitions of Nature and various writers concentrated on different aspects of the human interaction with the environment: Hippocrates was concerned with the effects on human health, Thucydides looked to history while Sophocles analysed the impact on the landscape. In the last years of Greek civilisation, Protagoras combined the basic premise of the modern Deep Ecology movement, the unity of all species, with the Eastern concept of reincarnation, or transmigration of souls. Huxley draws attention to the Greek belief in Nature's capacity for divine retribution, that human *hubris* was countered by an avenging *nemesis* and that Xerxes was punished for two offences – 'overweening imperialism directed against the Athenians, and overweening imperialism directed against Nature'.[16]

Despite the germination of an ecological sense, the Greeks rarely translated this into practice, seeing modification of the natural world as a beneficial activity. Although they respected the diversity of Nature, many believed that it was man's duty to manage it. Socrates proposed that Man was on some sort of divine mission which the gods had provided for, while Aristotle proposed an anthropocentric position similar to that of the Old Testament: 'Now if Nature makes nothing incomplete, and nothing in vain, the inference must be that she has made all animals for the sake of Man.'[17] As a result, the Greeks dramatically altered the landscape through mining, agriculture and canal building.

In his *Critias*, Plato actually provides us with one of the earliest records of environmental degradation, through deforestation and consequent soil erosion:

> What now remains compared with what then existed is like the skeleton of a sick man, all the fat and soft earth having wasted away, and only the bare framework of the land being left . . . there are some mountains which now have nothing but food for bees, but they had trees not long ago . . . there were many lofty trees of cultivated species and . . . boundless pasturage for flocks. Moreover, it was enriched by the yearly rains from Zeus, which were not lost to it, as now, by flowing from the bare land into the sea; but the soil it had was deep, and therein it received the water, storing it up in the retentive loamy soil.[18]

The process that Plato describes devastated the coastal regions of the Mediterranean; a combination of deforestation and over-grazing led to widespread soil erosion, resulting in the bare, arid ecosystems we see today.

The Greek conception of Nature as one living organism was maintained in medieval Europe by the animistic tradition of Paganism. Although the Christian Church made efforts to stamp out the worship of springs, streams, groves and mountains, the legacy of Paganism survived well into the Middle Ages and beyond, resurfacing now in New Age spirituality. Within this tradition, every living thing is thought to have a soul and the symbolic figure of the Green Man was revered as a microcosmic image of one vast cosmic organism. Nature was still sacred – living, breathing and imbued with Spirit. However, all that was about to change.

The Secretary of Nature

About 500 years ago, something momentous occurred in the evolution of our species. During the course of a single generation, Christopher Columbus 'discovered' America, Leonardo da Vinci produced detailed plans for flying machines and Michelangelo painted the Sistine Chapel. As Richard Tarnas says in his seminal study of the western mind, 'Compared with his medieval predecessors, Renaissance man appeared to have suddenly vaulted into virtually superhuman status.'[19]

Perhaps the most significant event of the time was the discovery, made by Copernicus, that planet Earth was not actually the centre of the universe but part of a heliocentric solar system which orbited the sun. This in turn led to the realisation that the universe was an infinite expanse of other suns and that there was no centre to it at all. The implications of this were clearly very profound. Combined with the subsequent work of Giordano Bruno, Kepler and Galileo, it led to a conception of the universe as a vast, cosmic machine, totally devoid of life, and governed by mathematical laws. 'The universe', according to Galileo, 'is written in mathematical language, and the letters are triangles, circles and other geometrical figures.'[20] Nature was stripped of any inherent intelligence, regarded instead as nothing but dead matter. That which could not be measured and quantified did not really exist. Collingwood describes the Renaissance vision of the universe as an 'arrangement of bodily parts designed and put together and set going for a definite purpose by an intelligent mind outside itself'.[21] With the subsequent spread of machines like the printing press, the windmill and the clock, it became an easy step to accept that the natural world itself was a machine, designed and set in motion by a separate creator, God himself. Nature was denied any creative independence.

In England, this new vision of the universe found its apotheosis in Francis Bacon, celebrated as the source of inspiration for the Enlightenment and praised at the time as the herald of a new world order. He was even entitled 'The Secretary of Nature'. In the light of recent advances, the challenge for Bacon was to disentangle scientific knowledge from its previous associations with alchemy and re-align it with the Christian Church. Having perceived that society was reluctant to embrace scientific innovation, for fear of incurring God's wrath, he proposed that science and religion were engaged in a mutual effort to recover the position that had existed before The Fall, when Adam and Eve were expelled from the Garden of Eden: 'For Man by The Fall fell at the same time from his state of innocence and from his dominion over creation. Both of these losses, however, can even in this life be in some part repaired; the former by religion and faith, the latter by arts and sciences.'[22] Bacon therefore insisted that 'the most innocent and meriting conquest' of Man's intellectual endeavours, was 'the conquest of the works of Nature'.[23] In fact, he believed that the total control of the natural world was the ultimate goal of our species: 'Only let the human race recover that right over Nature which belongs to it by divine bequest, and let power be given it; the exercise thereof will be governed by sound reason and true religion.'[24]

To add moral weight to this position, Bacon drew a parallel with Adam's naming of the animals in Genesis, making the conquest of Nature appear to be the recovery of power originally bestowed on Man by God. As the biologist Rupert Sheldrake points out, he drew 'an ingenious distinction between the innocent knowledge of Nature, which was beyond good and evil, and morality, in which Man should submit to God's commands'.[25] In the process, Bacon reinforced the split between Man and Nature which was inherent in the Bible: 'The world is made for Man, not Man for the World', and 'Man, if we look to final causes, may be regarded as the centre of the world, insomuch that if Man were taken away from the world, the rest would seem to be all astray, without aim or purpose.'[26] He proposed that machines do not 'merely exert a gentle guidance over Nature's course; they have the power to conquer and subdue her, to shake her to her foundations'.[27]

This emphatically anthropocentric world-view became the basis, not only for Bacon's own work, but the entire history of mainstream modern science. In his *New Atlantis*, published in 1624, Bacon describes his utopian society, a sort of institutional technocracy ruled by a scientific priesthood; a world which is not dissimilar to that which exists today. There are references to vivisection and manipulation of new life-forms, pre-empting the science of genetic engineering. For Bacon, this new science would usher in a 'blessed race of Heroes and Supermen'.[28] This is the ethic that propels most scientific research today, trying to provide simple solutions for problems which are inherently complex.

The Cartesian Split

One day in November 1619, while living in the German town of Neuberg, a twenty-three year old mathematician had a visionary experience as he sat beside the Danube. Reducing the universe to separate, inanimate, mechanical objects, and thus giving birth to dualistic, western philosophy, René Descartes felt that he had 'discovered the foundations of a marvellous science'.[29] (Ironically, the young Descartes regarded this insight as being inspired by the Holy Mother of God and, three years later, made a pilgrimage to the Shrine of Our Lady in Loreto to thank her for the mystic vision which was to influence the entire mechanistic world-view which has suppressed our spiritual connection to Nature ever since.)

The ramifications of Descartes's famous maxim, *cogito ergo sum*, have been persistently blamed as the source of our alienation from the non-human natural world. By making this assumption, 'I think therefore I am', Descartes took human separation from the external world to an absolute extreme. Through establishing cognition as the process of a disembodied ego, the subject–object polarisation between Man and Nature, mind and body, matter and spirit, was fully constellated. It is only in recent years that the full implications of this Cartesian Dualism have become apparent.

For Descartes, the entire cosmos was nothing but a vast machine, made of lifeless matter which obeyed a system of fixed mathematical laws: 'I do not recognise any difference between the machines made by craftsmen and the various bodies that Nature alone composes.'[30] The animistic concept of the soul was sucked out of the living world once and for all, including the human body itself, now reduced to the status of a mere robot. The mind was seen as separate from, and transcendent to, the body, leading Descartes to conclude that the connection between the two was located in the pineal gland. Although this idea was subsequently ridiculed by Spinoza, and many others since, modern mechanistic science still upholds a similar theory, focusing the attention two inches away in the cerebral cortex, convinced that consciousness is a phenomenon which is generated within the human head rather than seeing the brain as an instrument through which consciousness is made manifest.

The Cartesian split became the basic tenet of the mechanistic world-view and the reductionist methods which have dominated western science ever since. Like Galileo, Newton felt that 'there exists an infinite and omnipresent spirit in which matter is moved according to mathematical laws'.[31] For Descartes and Newton, and those that followed them, the role of science was 'to render ourselves the masters and possessors of Nature'.[32] Animals were now seen as inanimate brutes and 'the cry of a beaten dog no more proved that it suffered than the sound of an organ proved that the instrument felt pain when struck'.[33] This position of empirical and objective detachment was given the moral and philosophical basis which typifies the hubris of many modern scientists.

There is no denying the success of mechanistic science in reducing the universe to sub-atomic particles but, in the process, it has transcended itself and triggered the demise of materialism. Modern physics now tells us that everything is made of fields of energy, which sometimes behave like waves and sometimes behave like particles. In addition, the role of the observer is now understood to have an impact on that which is being observed. Consequently, the hard, inert atoms of Newton's solid, material and objective universe, which could only be explained by taking it apart like a machine, have been replaced by energetic fields of vibratory activity.

Simultaneously, revolutionary advances in modern science, which are contributing to a new and ecological world-view – Gaia Theory, Chaos Theory and General Systems Theory – have developed from a more holistic approach, which recognises the interconnections and inherent complexity of living systems and seeks to understand them through looking at the whole rather than individual constituent parts. The vision that is being presented to us is of a dynamic, living web of relationships, an organic intelligent world in which we are implicitly involved, rather than a cold and lifeless universe which we are here to harness and control.

The 'Progress' Myth

In Aldous Huxley's utopian novel *Point Counter Point* (1928), Lord Edward mocks the absurdity of talking about infinite growth while relying upon finite resources: 'Progress! You politicians are always talking about it. As though it were going to last. Indefinitely. More motors, more babies, more food, more advertising, more money, more everything, forever . . . You think we're being progressive because we're living on our capital. Phosphates, coal, petroleum, nitre – squander them all. That's your policy.'[34] Nine years later, George Orwell raised similar issues in *The Road to Wigan Pier*: 'In every country in the world the large army of scientists and technicians, with the rest of us panting at their heels, are marching along the road of "progress" with the blind persistence of a column of ants. Comparatively few people want it to happen, plenty of people actually want it not to happen, and yet it is happening.'[35] In *The Perennial Philosophy*, Huxley observed how faith in the locomotive had convinced people that they were travelling 'at full speed towards universal peace and the brotherhood of man', until it turned into 'a four-motored bomber loaded with white phosphorus and high explosives'.[36] Despite this, most of humanity held fast to the notion of 'Inevitable Progress – which is, in the last analysis, the hope and faith (in the teeth of all human experience) that one can get something for nothing'.[37]

Like the indigenous cultures that survive today, the ancient world had no notion of 'progress'. In fact, many believed that the Golden Age had already been and gone and mankind was destined to live in a fallen state for the rest of time. For thousands of years, primitive societies had existed on what they hunted and gathered; they had no concept of land ownership and what few possessions they had were shared by the community as a whole. The rise of mechanistic science, and the innovations which developed from it, paved the way for the Industrial Revolution and the economic systems that we have inherited today. Like the Agricultural Revolution which came before, allowing man to store surplus food and thus turn to a settled existence, industrialisation led to a dramatic rise in the human population and the process of urbanisation. London grew from about 60,000 inhabitants in the 1520s to 400,000 in 1650. By 1700 it was the largest city in Europe and was the first city in the world to reach one million.[38]

This rapid expansion was fuelled by one resource – coal. At the turn of the century, the world consumed more coal in two years than it had in the whole of the eighteenth century, the equivalent of annually burning down a forest three times the size of Britain.[39] The horses which transported the raw materials and manufactured products through the Industrial Age were consuming 4 million tons of oats and hay, which took up the production of 15 million acres of land.[40] The internal combustion engine, which replaced the horse less than a hundred years ago, has spawned an industry which now consumes more resources than any other: car production currently accounts for 20 per cent of the world's steel, 50 per cent of the lead and 60 per cent of the rubber.[41]

As Adam Smith realised, the faith that has been instilled into the concept of progress is due to the increase in material wealth which it has brought about. According to Smith, society was 'engaged in a process of continual improvement, brought about by investment, increased productivity and the accumulation of individual wealth'.[42] For Karl Marx, it was 'the great civilising influence of capital . . . that rejects the deification of Nature', so that 'Nature becomes, for the first time, simply an object for mankind, purely a matter of utility.'[43] Human history therefore, was 'the march of progress from tribal through feudal and capitalist societies until its climax in the inevitable victory of the proletariat and socialism'.[44]

* * *

As Huxley's Lord Edward points out, the fundamental problem with this idea is that we are spending all our capital. In fact, we are on a massive binge, burning our way through our 3.8 billion year inheritance of fossil fuels. If everyone on the planet used as much oil as the average American, we would exhaust all known reserves within fifteen years. Our economic systems completely fail to account for this depletion of our 'natural capital', making the assumption that they are somehow inexhaustible, expendable and free. As a consequence, we are exchanging our life-support systems for consumer choice; the fact that we are systematically destroying the environment on which we all depend, in the pursuit of our own well-being, is an indication of just how distorted our world-view has become.

For example, the global food industry is supported by a thin layer of topsoil, of which we have lost a quarter in the last century, and this takes hundreds of years to replace. We know amazingly little about the complex systems that make this process happen. One acre of good topsoil in a temperate region may contain up to 125 million small invertebrates while a typical handful will hold one million bacteria of a single type, 100,000 yeast cells and 50,000 fungus mycellium.[45] Lester Brown, President of the Worldwatch Institute in Washington, points out that topsoil is 'the foundation not only of agriculture, but of civilisation itself', and that 'the loss of soil is, in some ways, the most serious of the threats that civilisation faces'. We may well 'survive the exhaustion of oil reserves, but not the continuing wholesale loss of topsoil'.[46]

Notions of 'growth' and 'progress' have become so enshrined in our cultural systems that we are ignoring the total desecration of our 'real wealth'. We have become slaves to our own machines, forgetting that we cannot eat cars, televisions and computers. Porritt highlights the fact that we have distorted language itself to accommodate these errors in our logic, so that 'productivity' is now a measure of our destruction and 'rationality' a reference to the absurd. As a consequence, it has become more 'economic' to tear down forests than to recycle paper. 'Wealth' now means visible symbols of affluence, 'the accumulation of consumer durables and credit cards, or being rich enough to have a huge overdraft'.[47] The environmental economist Hazel Henderson observes that this world-view 'has enthroned some of our most unattractive predispositions: material acquisitiveness, competition, gluttony, pride, selfishness, short-sightedness and just plain greed.'[48]

Aldous Huxley was one of several writers to notice the extent to which science has replaced religion and how we have placed our faith at the altar of high technology: 'Technological idolatry is the religion whose doctrines are promulgated, explicitly or by implication, in the advertisement pages of our newspapers and magazines – the source from which millions of men, women and children in the capitalistic countries derive their working philosophy of life.'[49] The social critic Lewis Mumford also remarked that 'Western society has accepted as unquestionable a technological imperative that is quite as arbitrary as the most primitive taboo: not merely the duty to foster invention and constantly to create technological novelties, but equally the duty to surrender to these novelties unconditionally, just because they are offered, without respect to their human consequences.'[50]

A classic example of this 'technological determinism', in which solutions emerge from scientists and corporations before anyone has identified a problem, is what the 1960s 'counter-culture' called the 'military-industrial complex'. Lord Zuckerman, a former Chief Scientist to the British Government, once remarked that 'it is he, the technician, not the commander in the field, who starts the process of formulating the so-called military need.'[51] As a result, we have accumulated such 'benefits' as the nuclear bomb, anthrax and cruise missiles. The entire nuclear energy industry, which was supposed to give us unlimited amounts of virtually free energy by 2000, has actually yielded a negligible amount when off-set against the costs and subsidies for developing it. Now the reactors are being de-commissioned, again at huge expense, and all we are left with is radioactive waste which will be a hazard to the planet for at least 250,000 years.

This blind belief in the miracles of science and technology has created a vicious circle. As Marx wrote in *Das Kapital*, by seeking to transform Nature, man 'opposes himself to Nature as one of her own forces, setting in motion arms and legs, head and hands, the natural forces of his body, in order to appropriate Nature's productions in a form adapted to his own wants. By thus acting on the external world and changing it, he at the same time changes his own nature.'[52] By elevating it to a position of domination over our internal and external world, Cartesian Dualism gave rise to the tyranny of the ego. The entire universe became a tool of the ego and, in turn, 'the ego plus tools'[53] led to the exploitation of the natural world. The scientist Werner Heisenberg saw that Man's relationship to Nature changed from the contemplative to the pragmatic: 'One was not so much interested in Nature as it is; one rather asked what one could do with it. Therefore, natural science turned into technical science; every advancement of knowledge was connected with the question as to what practical use could be derived from it.'[54] Ironically, through the process of globalised competition which has evolved from this transition, we have become enslaved by the very technology which was designed to facilitate our own conquest of Nature.

We have now reached a position where the momentum of technocratic society has developed a life of its own, which cannot be controlled by even the most powerful political systems on the planet and is starting to outstrip our human ability to keep pace with it – witness the current furore over genetically modified food and the Human Genome Diversity Project (HGDP). The human experience of being dominated by Nature has been replaced by the hollow expectation of achieving domination over Nature. Therefore we are told that the only remedy for the environmental and social problems of the age is said to be increasing amounts of scientific and technological innovation, failing to see that the medicine feeds the disease. The philosopher Hegel recognised this basic flaw in our world-view: 'Man uses Nature as a means to defeating Nature; the nimbleness of his reason enables him to protect and preserve himself by pitting the objects of Nature against the natural forces which threaten him and so nullifying them. Nature itself, as it is in its universality, cannot be mastered in this manner however, nor bent to the purposes of Man.'[55] As the authors of *Natural Capitalism* observe, our collective myopia prevents us from acknowledging one basic fact: 'Nature bats last, and owns the stadium.'[56]

Change – The Only Constant

Media coverage of environmental issues often creates the impression that they are unique to the modern world. There is no doubt that the scale of our impact on Nature has been increasing at an exponential rate ever since the Industrial Revolution, while some ecologists say that we have 'changed the rules' and stepped outside the system, becoming the first and only species to generate more waste than can be recycled by the natural processes of the planet.

At the same time, it would be naive to see issues such as pollution, food adulteration and climate change as entirely limited to the late twentieth century. The classical writers Xenophon and Lucretius noted how noxious fumes from silver mines in Attica were injurious to human health. The philosopher Maimonides described urban air as 'stagnant, turbid, thick, misty and foggy', causing 'dullness of understanding, failure of intelligence and defect of memory'.[57] Core samples drilled from the ice in Greenland reveal significant deposits of airborne lead during the Roman era; aqueducts were lined with lead, thus leaching into the water supply, and lead poisoning is thought to have played a significant role in the decline of the Empire.

In Britain, Eleanor of Aquitaine was driven from Nottingham Castle in 1257 by the smoke from surrounding coal fires and it was only thirty years later that the first commission began to investigate complaints about pollution levels in London. Elizabeth I stayed out of the capital in 1578 because of the 'noisome smells' and for hundreds of years the first sight of the city was the cloud of overhanging smog.[58] During the seventeenth century, Parliament debated about the smell of brick kilns, the inhabitants of Aldgate complained about fumes from an alum factory killing fish in the Thames, and the Duke of Chandos said he was 'poisoned with the abominate smells which infect these parts'.[59] The London sewage system was only introduced when the stench from the river became too severe for Parliament to convene: as an emergency measure, strips of burlap soaked in lime were hung over the windows to protect MPs' nostrils. Unfortunately, the linear sewage system that was adopted, mixing waste with water and diverting it into the Thames, was replicated all over the world, thus ensuring the gradual loss of soil fertility by depriving the land of nutrients which a cyclical system would have preserved.

By 1900, London was the world's largest city, with 6.6 million inhabitants burning coal in several hundred thousand chimneys. The smog was often so dense that people were known to walk into the Thames, unable to see where they were going. In the early part of December 1952, over 4,000 people died from smog-related illnesses, leading to the Clean Air Act of 1956 which regulated domestic coal use.[60]

Recent historians have suggested that the depraved excesses of the Roman Emperors Caligula and Nero might have been due to their penchant for acidic fish sauces, which dissolved the lead in their cooking vessels and tableware, administering them with toxic doses and triggering a gradual descent into madness. In Britain, the introduction of laboratory tests in the nineteenth century produced some alarming results, finding iron sulphate in beer, acorns in coffee and brick dust in cocoa.[61] A study from the time cites sawdust and chalk as regular ingredients in British bread baking, together with the use of heavy metals as colouring agents. The author itemises the cocktail of poisons that a gentleman of the day might have enjoyed:

> with the potted meats, anchovies, red sauces or cayenne, taken at breakfast, he would consume more or less bole Armenian, Venetian red, red lead, or even bisulphate of mercury. At dinner, with his curry or cayenne, he would run the chances of a second dose of lead or mercury; with the pickles, bottled fruits and vegetables, he would be nearly sure to have copper administered to him; while if he partook of bon bons at dessert, there is no telling what number of poisonous pigments he might consume . . . if he were a snuff-taker, he would be pretty sure to be putting up his nostrils, small quantities of either some ferruginous earth, bichromate of potash, chromate of lead, or red lead.[62]

This sort of adulteration is not entirely a thing of the past; in 1969, an ambitious Italian trader was convicted of selling Parmesan cheese made from grated umbrella handles.[63]

The Swedish scientist Svante Arrhenius first speculated about the 'greenhouse effect' in the late nineteenth century. He noticed that industrialisation was 'evaporating our coal mines into the air' and concluded that the average global temperature would rise by 5 degrees Celsius if carbon dioxide levels were allowed to double from pre-Industrial Revolution levels, thus causing the polar ice caps to melt and the sea levels to rise.[64] A hundred years before that, Jean-Baptiste Joseph Fourier had proposed a similar theory, which even used a hothouse as the metaphor.[65] Their predictions have now become reality. By altering the atmosphere and changing the planetary climate, the American writer Bill McKibben believes that we have deprived the non-human world of its independence and that this heralds 'the end of Nature'.[66]

Within the 3.8 billion year evolution of our planet, there have been climatic disturbances which have been considerably more dramatic than what we are witnessing now. The American biologist Lynn Margulis, who has collaborated with James Lovelock and his work on Gaia Theory, points out that 'the greatest pollution crisis that the earth has ever endured' occurred 2 billion years ago, when the spread of bacteria increased atmospheric oxygen from 0.0001 percent to 21 per cent, thereby creating the conditions comfortable for life as we know it.[67] It is perhaps the supreme irony that the human activities which are disrupting the composition of the atmosphere, thereby undermining the biological systems we are dependent upon, are supposed to be making our lives more comfortable.

Global warming is a good example of how hard it is to draw a line between acceptable and unacceptable levels of human impact within the complex systems of the natural world. In addition to car exhausts and manufacturing processes, such disparate factors as termites, paddy fields and farting cattle all contribute to global warming through generating methane. Our meat-intensive diet may be to blame for the number of cattle, but even more methane is added to the atmosphere from rice paddies in the developing world. There are numerous 'positive feedback loops' which can be added into the equation so that, as the planet warms, other processes are implicated. Billions of tons of methane are stored as hydrates in the tundra and continental shelves. Should the permafrost melt, another 6 billion tons of methane would be added to the atmosphere every year, warming the planet still further and releasing even more methane. Some scientists have proposed that there are 'negative feedback loops' which might counteract this process and maintain homeostasis, the balanced conditions that life requires. The long-term repercussions of the Fossil Fuel Age, the massive uncontrolled experiment that we have been conducting, may still be speculative. However, the most recent study by the IPCC scientists suggests that global warming is happening much faster than previously imagined. Carbon dioxide in the atmosphere has increased from 285 parts per million to 365 since 1850[68] and, over the course of just a few generations, we have irreversibly interfered with an incredibly complex system which has supported life on the planet for 2 billion years.

At the same time, we only have to look at the history of the British Isles to see that the climate, and the landscape, have changed quite significantly over the last few thousand years. A mini Ice Age occurred between the early fifteenth and mid nineteenth centuries.[69] The Thames froze over twenty times.[70] There was pack ice off the coast of England, many of the glaciers in the Alps moved over a mile and the sea actually froze in Marseilles.[71] For the previous few hundred years, the tree line was 500 feet higher than it is today, grape vines were grown as far north as the Severn and the upland parts of Dartmoor were being farmed.[72] The British Isles actually originated south of the equator and rising sea levels only separated us from the rest of Europe about 8,000 years ago. David Sinclair highlights the fact that 'the conifers so hated by conservationists of today were one of the most important features of the scenery, along with birch and willow'.[73] The much revered English oak and elm were actually imports from the south, while reindeer, rhinos, hippos, bison and elephants all once roamed the land we now live on. A perfectly preserved tropical forest was recently discovered in the coal seams of South Wales.

Although Man is thought to have existed here 35,000 years ago, in a landscape that would have mostly resembled the bleak highland regions of Scotland, it was not until about 5,000 years ago that our species started to leave an indelible mark on the landscape. It is now known that Neolithic man deforested significant parts of Britain, such as the coastal plain of south-west Cumberland, which was transformed from oak, elm and birch woods into open heath and moorland. Large areas of forest were burnt to the ground. As one historian points out, the idea that our 'Neolithic, Mesolithic or Palaeolithic ancestors were purely "green" is as naive and ill-informed as the idea that contemporary indigenous people are "primitive" and want "progress"'.[74] The construction of the vast Neolithic site at Avebury involved cutting down more trees and moving more earth and stone than building some of the Egyptian pyramids, while various sites have been identified in North America where large mammals were stampeded over cliffs, killing far greater numbers than could have been consumed.

The development of tools during the Bronze Age accelerated the process of deforestation while the Romans diversified the impact on the landscape through such practices as draining the fens and constructing roads. By the time of the Domesday Book in 1086, most of the virgin forest in the country had been cleared to make way for the pattern of rural settlement which has typified the British countryside ever since. Most of what was maintained after the Norman Conquest was set aside for royal hunting and, despite vigorous efforts at replanting, the percentage of the British Isles covered with woodland is now lower than any other country in Europe: a paltry 9 per cent compared with 30 per cent in Germany and 27 per cent in Italy.

Human evolution has clearly developed in symbiosis with the rest of the natural world. The landscape has changed as we have changed. Some of these changes are directly related to human interaction with Nature, like the felling of trees for firewood and the cultivation of crops, while others are the result of complex processes like the Little Ice Age. Some of these changes may be beneficial to one species but disastrous for another, whether it be the wolf, the small-pox virus or humanity itself. In fact, the one thing that does not change is change itself – the constant of the universe.

The Romantic Tradition

There is an enduring image of the British countryside as a rural arcadia of gentle rolling hills and lush green fields, of ancient oak forests and crystal streams. This pastoral vision is both the product of a nostalgic preoccupation with an idyllic past and an intrinsic part of the modern British psyche, instilled by the Romantic tradition. Our collective subconscious has been fashioned by the poetry of Wordsworth, Coleridge and Blake, the paintings of Turner and Constable. The agrarian landscape of neatly partitioned fields, which forms part of this archetype, has its roots in ninth-century Saxon England, but what we see today is the result of 4,000 private Enclosures Acts in the eighteenth and nineteenth centuries, when the expanding Industrial Age turned farming into business and took vast areas of common land away from the people.

One feature of this British attitude to the countryside is what George Trevelyan called 'the harsh distinction between urban and rural life'.[75] This split has been perpetuated over the centuries by that particular genre of British writers, from Thomas Hardy to James Herriott, who have sustained this image of a blissful existence in the country. For Stephen Pile, 'what this love of the countryside is really all about is our refusal or inability to deal with cities' and is 'based upon the notion that the city is a bad place full of unhappy people, while the countryside is a good place, packed with happy, honest, decent folk'.[76] This romanticisation of 'the good life', and the gulf that separates the urban and rural citizen, has become increasingly pronounced, leading to the political divide we see today. As a consequence, a group of Welsh farmers and truck drivers succeeded in bringing the country to a halt in a reaction to rising oil prices, while the Countryside Alliance has united a previously disparate group of people to protest about a ban on fox-hunting. Since 80 per cent of the British population is now urbanised, while 80 per cent of the land mass is devoted to agriculture, it is easy to see why those who live in the countryside, and depend on it for their livelihood, should feel resentment about decisions being made in London and Brussels by people whom they believe are out of touch with the realities of rural life.

Part 4 will examine the complex issues surrounding British agriculture in more detail but, to understand these modern attitudes, we must travel back a few hundred years and examine the various changes in the way that the British people, from every social level, have perceived and classified the natural world around them. Within the prevailing mechanistic paradigm, attitudes towards animals, plants and the landscape have changed dramatically over the last 400 years. The historian Keith Thomas observes that 'the relationship of man to other species was redefined; and his right to exploit those species for his own advantage was sharply challenged'.[77] In his detailed study of these changing sensibilities, Thomas shows how an anthropocentric world-view was being instilled in our political and economic systems while the seeds of the emerging ecological awareness were germinating at the same time.

The legacy of Descartes and Bacon was deeply ingrained in the majority of the educated population by the late seventeenth century. In correspondence to the Secretary of Nature himself, John Beale spoke of the 'Empire of mankind' and how the whole purpose of studying Nature was so that 'it may be master'd, managed and used in the services of human life'.[78] According to Isaac Barrow, vivisection was 'a most innocent cruelty', while Archbishop King saw no problem in slaughtering cattle for the benefit of 'a more noble animal'.[79] At the time, half the population of the country was eating an average of 150 pounds of meat per year, while the list of creatures deemed suitable for the dinner table included 'squirrels, badgers, seals, owls, hedgehogs, otters, tortoises, rooks, lapwings, puffins and curlews'.[80] The Royal Society encouraged the rise of the natural sciences, such as zoology and botany, so that it could be determined whether certain animals and plants 'might be of any advantage to mankind, as food or physic; and whether those or any other uses of them can be further improved'.[81] In 1734, one member of the Royal Horticultural Society observed how it was now possible 'to govern the vegetable world to a much greater improvement, satisfaction and pleasure than ever was known in the former ages of the world'.[82] This belief in the superiority of man over the rest of creation was even extended to our own species; at least two ministers in the late sixteenth century are known to have preached that women had no souls![83]

However, by the end of the seventeenth century, a few dissenting voices were challenging these assumptions with words that still seem pertinent today. John Ray, whose three-volume *Historia Plantarum* was superseded some fifty years later by Linnaeus's standardised classification of species, wrote this in 1691: 'It is generally received opinion that all this visible world was created for Man; that Man is the end of the Creation, as if there were no other end of any creature but some way or other to be serviceable to Man. But though this be vulgarly received, yet wise men nowadays think different.'[84]

Nearly fifty years before that, Thomas Edwards proposed that 'God loves the creatures that creep on the ground as well as the best saints and there is no difference between the flesh of a man and the flesh of a toad,'[85] while John Bulwer disputed whether 'if it were possible for man to do so, it were lawful for him to destroy any one of God's creatures, though it were but the species of toads and spiders, because this were taking away one link of God's chain, one note of his harmony'.[86] In 1683, Thomas Tryon went so far as to say that lions and tigers were 'not more savage and cruel, geese and asses not half so stupid, foxes and donkeys less knavish and ridiculous, wolves not more ravenous, nor goats more lascivious, than that abundance of those grave, bearded animals that pride themselves with the empty title of rational soul'.[87] The philosopher John Locke admitted that 'the busy mind of Man could carry him to a brutality below the level of the beast when he quit his reason', while Thomas notes that 'scores of commentators pointed out that beasts did not get drunk or tell lies, were not sadistic and did not make war on their own species'.[88]

This new sensibility flourished during the eighteenth century, while the foundations for the Industrial Revolution were being laid. Dr Johnson, seen by some as a Nature-lover because of his fondness for feeding oysters to his cat, now described vivisection as the work of 'a race of men that have practised tortures without pity and related them without shame and are yet suffered to erect their heads among human beings'.[89] Although the English had previously been noted for their love of cock-fighting and bear-baiting, those that travelled to Spain in the late eighteenth century were horrified by bull-fighting; Robert Southey spoke of 'a most damnable sport', while the Earl of Clarendon reacted to the 'rudeness and barbarity'.[90] A hundred years earlier, Robert Houghton had noted that bull-baiting was 'a sport the English much delight in; and not only the baser sort, but the greatest ladies'.[91] Cock-fighting, which had been a popular national sport, was then banned throughout the country in 1835. Daniel Defoe deplored the methods of meat production which have been intensifying ever since: 'What rapes are committed upon Nature, making the ewes bring lambs all the winter, fattening calves to a monstrous size, using cruelties and contrary diets to the poor brute, to whiten its flesh for the palates of the ladies,'[92] while the physician William Lambe saw the castration of domestic animals as a 'shocking outrage on the common rights of Nature'.[93]

This new-found love of Nature extended beyond the animal kingdom. The classification, propagation and cultivation of exotic plants and flowers became a national pastime. Mountains, which had been described as 'barren deformities', 'monstrous excrescences' and 'Nature's pudenda', were now esteemed for their wild solitude and romantic attraction.[94] Forests, previously regarded as deep, dark, primal wildernesses, became 'Nature's cathedrals', sources of spiritual renewal and inspiration.

Following the publication of John Evelyn's *Sylva*, commissioned after the Navy consulted the Royal Society about the timber shortage, various intensive tree-planting programmes were begun all around the British Isles. Between 1740 and 1830, three successive Dukes of Atholl are said to have planted a staggering 14 million larches.[95] (The motivation for this feat seems to be in direct opposition to that which propelled one energetic individual from Durham who claimed to have felled 30,000 oaks in his lifetime.)[96] Under the influence of landscape gardeners like Lancelot Capability Brown, the formalised style of tree-planting gave way to random groupings, designed to imitate Nature. By the nineteenth century, trees had become an upper-class obsession; Washington Irving noted how English gentlemen 'spent hours discussing the shape and beauty of individual trees, as if they were statues or horses'.[97]

The gradual erosion of an emphatically anthropocentric position was also linked to scientific advances. The discovery of the microscope had revealed a whole new universe of miniature beings, 'protozoa and bacteria, pursuing their existence in utter indifference to human concerns, occupying a world of beauty and intricacy on which no man had previously set eyes'.[98] In 1683, a Dutchman called Anton van Leeuwenhoek declared that he had used his microscope to discover over 8 million living creatures in a drop of water and that there were 'more animals in my mouth than people in the United Provinces'.[99] At the same time, British explorers were travelling to uncharted and uninhabited parts of the globe: vast jungles, mountains and deserts, 'swarming with hitherto unknown forms of life for which there was no obvious human use'.[100] Back at home, the naturalist and clergyman Gilbert White published the *Natural History of Selborne* in 1789, observing that 'the most insignificant insects and reptiles are of much more consequence, and have much more influence in the *oeconomy* of Nature, than the incurious are aware of'.[101] White's study of the ecosystems in his parish became the fourth most published book in the language, was a major influence on Darwin and is still regarded as 'seminal for the modern study of ecology' because it 'grasped the complex unity in diversity that made of the Selborne environs an ecological whole'.[102]

When the Cumbrian Quaker Thomas Story observed that the strata of cliffs near Scarborough were 'of much older date than the time assigned in the Holy Scriptures',[103] the anthropocentric illusion inherited from the

Old Testament was dealt a further blow. By 1830, geologists knew for certain that the pre-history of the planet had to be measured in millions not thousands of years and Charles Lyell realised that Man's arrival on the planet was really quite recent: 'at periods extremely modern in the history of the globe, the ascendancy of Man, if he existed at all, had scarcely been felt by the brutes'.[104]

The final blow to the Genesis myth was dealt by Charles Darwin's theories of evolution, presented in *On the Origin of Species* (1859) and *The Descent of Man* (1871). The biological separation between Man and the rest of Nature, previously reinforced by the hierarchy of Lovejoy's Great Chain of Being, was now completely undermined; not only had humanity evolved from a species further down the ladder, but the whole evolutionary concept removed any distinction between levels within the chain. 'My object', wrote Darwin, 'is to show that there is no fundamental difference between man and the higher mammals in their mental faculties.'[105] Evolution also removed the possibility that Nature behaved mechanically since machines could not evolve once they were created. However, it was not long before ideas like 'survival of the fittest' were being applied to the economic systems of the Industrial Revolution by men like Adam Smith, later attacked by Marx, who accused Darwin of comparing the natural world to English society with 'its division of labour, competition, opening up of new markets, "inventions" and the Malthusian "struggle for existence"'.[106] Darwin's influence can therefore be seen to have simultaneously strengthened and undermined the separation between Man and Nature. Throughout this period, one of the most powerful influences on the British attitude to Nature was the Romantic tradition, in which the concept of improving on Nature was an aberration in itself. 'A gentleman's park is my aversion,' claimed Constable in 1822; 'It is not beauty because it is not Nature.'[107] In contrast to Henry More, who believed that only those 'as stupid as the basest of beasts' would not glory in the sight of geometrical fields in the landscape,'[108] and William Gilpin, who thought that there were 'few who did not prefer the busy scenes of cultivation to the greatest of Nature's rough productions',[109] Wordsworth spoke of the Ground of All Being at the heart of the Perennial Philosophy: 'And I have felt a presence that disturbs me with the joy of elevated thoughts; a sense sublime of something far more deeply interfused, Whose dwelling is the light of setting suns, and the round ocean and the living air, and the blue sky, and in the mind of man: A motion and a spirit, that impels all thinking things, all objects of all thought, And rolls through all things.'[110]

Wordsworth actually maintained that most of the population were unable to cultivate a true appreciation of Nature due to their social position, that for 'thousands and tens of thousands, a rich meadow with fat cattle grazing on it, or the sight of a heavy crop of corn is worth all the Alps and Pyrenees in their utmost grandeur'.[111] He opposed the Kendal to Windermere railway line because it opened up his beloved Lake District to 'the whole of Lancashire and no small part of Yorkshire',[112] and even suggested in his *Guide to the Lakes* that the urban masses should begin their education by making Sunday excursions to the outskirts of the city.

Although Wordsworth wrote about the 'outrage done to Nature' and his wish to 'avenge her violated rights', his vision of the natural world was often based on nostalgic remembrances from his youth. In contrast, the man whose vision most closely parallels the emerging world-view was the poet, engraver and mystic William Blake, who staunchly opposed the reductionist, mechanistic science of Newton: 'May God us keep/ From Single vision and Newton's Sleep.'[113] While Keats lamented the way in which Newton had destroyed the beauty of the rainbow with scientific theories – 'Do not all charms fly/ At the mere touch of cold philosophy?'[114] – Blake's mystic vision spoke of that ineffable, nameless, formless energy which science could never grasp. In his excellent biography of Blake, Peter Ackroyd draws attention to the beginning of a poem entitled *Europe*, where the poet is shown a world in which 'each eternal flower' and 'every particle of dust breathes forth its joy'.[115] These particles are not the hard, inert atoms of Newton's universe, but rather 'jewels of Light' which are also 'Human formd'. In Blake's eyes, the Newtonian world-view was 'Petrifying all the human Imagination into rock and sand' and shortly before his death he lamented the fact 'that a great majority of Englishmen are fond of The Indefinite which they Measure by Newton's Doctrine of the Fluxions of an Atom, A Thing that does not exist'.[116]

Blake not only pre-empted the conclusions of many modern scientists, seeing the material universe as a projection of consciousness itself, but also echoed the teachings of the Perennial Philosophy. His rhetorical question to a fly, 'Am not I A Fly like thee Or art not thou A man like me', is reminiscent of the Taoist sage Chuang Tzu, who wondered whether he had been dreaming that he was a butterfly during the night, or whether he was now a butterfly dreaming that he was Chuang Tzu. Rather than merely empathising with the rest of creation, Blake and Chuang Tzu are suggesting that the sense of separation between Man and Nature is actually an illusion, created by the identification of the ego. Blake's 'Robin red-breast in a Cage', which 'Put all Heaven in a Rage', can be seen as a warning to humanity about waging war on Nature. Similarly, when he tells us to 'Kill not the moth or butterfly, For the last Judgement draweth nigh', Blake was warning us of the consequences of destroying Nature's diversity. While Wordsworth claimed that he 'would not strike a flower as many a man would strike a horse', the impression is of a sentimental attachment to Nature's beauty. When Blake affirms that 'Every thing that lives is holy', there is a sense of ecological awareness which resonates with the new world-view.

The paradigm which had evolved from Bacon, Descartes and Newton, and the 'satanic mills' which were now scattered over 'England's green and pleasant land', subsequently became the subject of Blake's 'awful vision' for the future:

> I see the Past, Present and Future existing all at once
> Before me. O Divine Spirit, sustain me on thy wings,
> That I may awake Albion from her long and cold repose;
> For Bacon and Newton, sheath'd in dismal steel, their terrors hang
> Like iron scourges over Albion: Reasonings like vast Serpents
> Infold around my limbs, bruising my minute articulations.
> I turn my eyes to the Schools and Universities of Europe
> And there behold the loom of Locke, whose Woof rages dire,
> Wash'd by the Water-wheels of Newton; black the cloth
> In heavy wreathes folds over every nation: cruel Works
> Of many Wheels I view, wheel without wheel, with cogs tyrannic
> Moving by compulsion each other, not as those in Eden, which Wheel within
> Wheel, in freedom revolve in harmony and peace.[117]

Blake's prophetic words rang true for the ensuing Industrial Age.

The legacy of the Romantic imagination flourished during the nineteenth century and has been with us ever since. In contrast to Dr Johnson, who had described the Scottish Highlands as a 'wide extent of hopeless sterility',[118] we find that Queen Victoria now loved the solitude and inspiration to be found in wild, untarnished Nature.[119] While William Camden had thought that the landscape of Radnorshire was 'hideous after a sort to behold, by reason of the turning and crooked by-ways and craggy mountains',[120] the philosopher John Stuart Mill now believed that 'solitude in the presence of natural beauty and grandeur is the cradle of thoughts and aspirations, which are not only good for the individual, but which society could ill do without'.[121]

However, there was a dilemma that confronted this new ethic, illustrated in microcosm by the Duke of Marlborough's approach to wildlife at

Blenheim. While the servants were forbidden to disturb the birds in the shrubbery, they were instructed to shoot them if they entered the kitchen garden.[122] As Keith Thomas observes in *Man and the Natural World*, this is the basic tension which has existed within the mind of every conservationist since – how do we preserve wild Nature, yet keep it out of the kitchen garden? Where do we draw the line between mass extinctions of other species and Jain ascetics refusing food and water for fear of imbibing other life-forms? Are there any practical ways in which we can make the transition from a society based upon a separation from Nature to a society which fulfils an integral, symbiotic function within the complex systems of the planet?

The Romantic imagination suggests that we *can* find the answers to these problems and perhaps the greatest value of the whole tradition is the way in which it helps us aspire to a better world, to cultivate our sense of vision. As Herbert Girardet, a leading environmentalist, told me: 'Hope is the great motivating force of humanity.'[123] Without being able to believe in the possibility of a better world, we are unlikely to make much progress in creating it.

The Perennial Philosophy

The philosophical perspective that overcomes a conceptual separation between Man and Nature has existed for thousands of years. This strand of sacred Truth forms the background to all the great mystical and religious traditions of the world, from Taoism to the Old Testament, from the Hindu Vedas to the primal belief systems of indigenous tribes. Often referred to as the Perennial Philosophy, or *philosophia perennis*, it was described by Aldous Huxley as 'the metaphysic that recognises a divine Reality substantial to the world of things and lives and minds; the psychology that finds in the soul something similar to, or even identical with, divine Reality; the ethic that places man's final end in the knowledge of the immanent and transcendent Ground of all Being'.[124]

At the core of this ancient Truth is the knowledge that all sense of duality is an illusion, created by an ego which is nothing more than a psychological construct, the product of our mental conditioning. In the absence of the ego, all is one; the distinction between 'me' and 'you', or 'us' and 'the world', or 'Man' and 'Nature', completely disappears. All that is left is the pure silent awareness of existence, the sense of 'I am' that it is shared by every conscious being on the planet, our own self-luminous background and the only absolute Truth that is available to us all – consciousness itself. However, the fundamental problem with discussing this basic Truth is that, once it has been articulated, either mentally or verbally, it loses its non-dual nature. This is emphasised by the very first line of the *Tao Te Ching*: 'The Tao that can be named is not the true Tao.'

Within the Judaeo-Christian tradition, the Perennial Philosophy frequently appears in the Old Testament with the words: 'I am That I am.' (Yahweh, the Hebrew term for God, literally translates as 'I am'.) In the New Testament, it appears within the Gospel of St Thomas, when Jesus is asked 'When shall the kingdom of God come?' and replies: 'When the two shall be one, when that which is without is as that which is within, and the male and female shall be one.' The instruction 'Be still and know that I am God' is a pointer to the same basic insight.

The Perennial Philosophy forms the basis for all the non-dualist teachings; in the Hindu system of yoga, it appears as *advaita*, an intellectual method for bringing about fusion of the individual ego, the *jiva*, with one universal Absolute, *Brahman*; it is the essence of Taoism, the ancient Chinese philosophy developed by Lao Tzu and often cited as a model for the emerging worldview; it can be found in the teachings of the Buddha, who equated the ego with the bondage of desire and consequent suffering, as well as the prophet Mohammed and the mystic vision of Sufism. Transcending all the conceptual boundaries which have been created by religious dogma, social–political conditioning and barriers of race, gender and colour, it is the one basic truth that every sage and mystic from every part of the globe has always agreed upon – that consciousness is the substratum of the material universe, the Ground of all Being, the screen on which our world movie is projected.

Ilya Prigogine, the Nobel prize winning Russian scientist, believes that 'today the world we see outside and the world we see within are converging. This convergence of two worlds is perhaps one of the most important cultural events of our age.'[125] Prigogine recognises the fact that modern physics is now confirming the basic insights of the non-dual traditions, observing that the material world is composed of fields of energy and cannot be studied in isolation from consciousness itself. In the process, the conceptual separation between Man and Nature, between consciousness and the rest of the universe, is gradually being eroded, precipitating the evolution of a new world-view.

This thread of holistic, ecological thought which has its roots in the Perennial Philosophy, can be traced through history: from Plato's conception of the earth as one living organism, throughout the Romantic reaction to The Enlightenment, as expressed in the poetry of Blake, Shelley and Wordsworth, or finding modern expression with Emerson, Whitman and the beat generation, precursors to the sixties counter-culture and the alternative society which has been growing ever since. The dialectic that continues between Romantics and Rationalists is the extension of a dualistic tension that exists, to a greater or lesser degree, within each one of us; this conflict between reason and intuition ensures that Romantics continue to accuse Rationalists of being too rational, while Rationalists accuse Romantics of being too romantic. This is evident today in the gulf that divides reductionist, mechanistic scientists like Richard Dawkins and Stephen Hawking from holistic scientists like Fritjof Capra, Rupert Sheldrake and James Lovelock. This ecological vision therefore, can be found in an eclectic range of poets, scientists, writers and philosophers, identified by Theodore Roszak twenty years ago: 'Anarchist philosophers, pietist Christians, Taoist sages, somewhere, mixed up in the lot, a number of Romantic poets and nature mystics . . . How many of these often cantankerous artists and thinkers could so much as share a conversation with one another? Yet I am sure they belong together. Not as an ideology, but as a sensibility – for the sacred, the organic, the personal.'[126]

For example, we find the following in Oscar Wilde:

With beat of systole and of diastole,
One grand great life throbs through earth's giant heart
And mighty waves of single Being roll
From nerveless germ to man, for we are part
Of every rock and bird and beast and hill . . .[127]

And this in Swinburne's *Hertha*:

One birth of my bosom; one beam of mine eye;
One topmost blossom that scales the sky;
Man, equal and one with me, man that is made of me, man that is I.[128]

D. H. Lawrence saw that 'a bird is rooted in earth as surely as a tree is';[129] Ralph Waldo Emerson, founder of transcendentalism and source of inspiration for early American conservationists, wrote: 'I become a transparent eye-ball; I am nothing; I see all; the currents of the Universal Being circulate through me; I am part or parcel of God.'[130]

In his notebooks, Leonardo da Vinci maintained that 'Nothing grows in a spot where there is neither sentient, fibrous or rational life. The feathers grow upon birds and change every year . . . the grass grows in the fields, the leaves upon the trees, and every year these are renewed in great part. So then we may say that the earth has a spirit of growth; that its flesh is the soil, its bones are the successive strata of the rocks which form the mountains, its muscles are the tufa stone, its blood the springs of its waters.'[131] This Gaian vision of a living, breathing planet is echoed by Shelley in *Prometheus Unbound*:

> She within whose stony veins, to the last fibre of the loftiest tree
> Whose thin leaves trembled in the frozen air,
> Joy ran, as blood within a living frame.[132]

Even politicians have been known to sympathise with the idea. The South African Jan Smuts wrote in the preface to a book about ecology in 1935:

> The world is a closely interwoven system of patterns. Such is reality – a vast pattern of patterns. And to trace these patterns or wholes is to discover the lineaments of beauty in all its forms, whether we call them beauty or truth or good. They are but holistic harmonies in the nature of things. Nothing exists for itself alone; there are no isolated units, but only structured patterns and inter-relations, from the primordial electrons to the most developed physical or moral or social complexes in the universe.'[133]

Increasing numbers of people now resonate with the basic idea of the earth as one living organism, with humanity playing a role within an interconnected 'web of life'. It is not surprising that Gaia Theory has ignited such interest in a public which is disillusioned with a scientific establishment intent on reducing the living world to a collection of minuscule particles, subservient to mechanical laws which drain all sense of the sacred from the non-human world. Reawakening a sacred dimension in our relationship to Nature clearly affects the way in which we interact with the world. If we see the planet as a living extension of our own bodies, then the way in which we treat the natural world will inevitably be more harmonious than if we see everything external to us as somehow separate, inanimate, expendable and to be exploited.

The Taoists have a concept called *wu-wei*, loosely translated as 'non-action' and frequently misinterpreted as an apathetic form of passivity. In reality, it points towards a way of life which is in harmony with Nature, The Tao itself, the *dharma* of the Hindus and The Way of indigenous cultures. It implies living without the imposition of the ego, learning to be like Nature itself, flowing like water in a river and following the course of least resistance. The ego, that part of us which thinks itself to be separate from an objective, external world, is the product of our genetic inheritance and our socio-environmental conditioning. It usually forms as a psychological reality about the age of two and a half, when we make the transition from referring to ourselves in the third person to talking about 'I', 'me' and 'mine'. However, according to mystics, sages and many modern scientists, this ego is nothing but a collection of thoughts, ideas, and memories, instilled by habitual patterns of repetitive mental activity – it has no independent existence. Ultimately it is an illusion, a conceptual object, a fictional entity which usurps the subjectivity of consciousness and superimposes itself, creating the sense of autonomy and individual volition.

Taoism has also been aligned with the political tradition of anarchy, again the subject of considerable misinterpretation. As Jim Dodge says, 'Anarchy does not mean out of control, it means out of their control.'[134] The etymology of the word anarchy can be traced back to the classical world, literally translated as 'without a leader'. However, Peter Marshall parallels the anarchist tradition with the concept of *wu-wei*, highlighting the fact that anarchy does not imply chaos and disorder, merely the removal of external authority and control; the best form of government being that which does not govern at all.[135] Tolstoy proposed that 'the abolition of government will merely rid us of an unnecessary organisation which we have inherited from the past for the commission of violence and for its justification'.[136] In this sense, government can be seen as the extrapolation of individual human bondage, enslaved by the ego, but extended to society as a whole. True anarchists are not necessarily concerned with disruption of the social order, rather the removal of centralised power and authority. Marshall highlights two stock anarchist slogans: 'Whichever way you vote, the government still gets in,' and 'If voting changed anything, they'd make it illegal.'[137] Laurens Van Der Post was another to see the limitations of our current political system and the need to replace the hierarchy of power with co-operative networks: 'There is a very profound reason why there are no great leaders any more. It is because they are no longer needed. The message is clear. You no longer want to be led from the outside. Every man must be his own leader. He must follow the light that's within himself, and through this light he will create a new community . . . we are the bridge between the community we've left and the community which doesn't exist yet.'[138]

The anarchist vision of a de-centralised society has been equated with Gaia Theory, proposing a system of self-regulating government which operates along much the same lines as the processes of the planet. In the *Tao Te Ching* itself, which was ostensibly a series of guidelines about how a king should rule in a just and honourable fashion, it is said that 'When the world has the Tao, ambling horses are retired to fertilize fields. When the world is without the Tao, war-horses are reared in the suburbs.' Therefore, when the doctrine of *wu-wei* is embraced, and the ego is merely observed and accepted for what it is, Man and Nature can live in harmony. However, if the ego is given authority and a sense of power, the balance disappears. 'The truth is, of course, that we are all organically related to God, to Nature and to our fellow-men,' wrote Huxley.

> If every human being were constantly and consciously in a proper relationship with his divine, natural and social environments there would be only so much suffering as Creation makes inevitable. But actually most human beings are chronically in an improper relationship to God, Nature and some at least of their fellows. The results of these wrong relationships are manifest on the social level as wars, revolutions, exploitation and disorder; on the natural level as waste and exhaustion of irreplaceable resources; on the biological level, as degenerative diseases and the deterioration of racial stocks; on the moral level, as an overweening bumptiousness; and on the spiritual level, as blindness to divine Reality and complete ignorance of the reason and purpose of human existence.[139]

Jonathan Porritt draws attention to another Taoist concept, that of *wei-chi*, translated as both crisis and opportunity. Psychologists say that the most likely time for the individual to make the quantum leap to maturity and psychological health is just when he feels that his world is falling apart. If we extend that to our society and the human condition as a whole, it brings with it a sense of optimism. The collective disillusionment that forms the backbone of the global environmental movement can then be seen as a wave of positive change, shaking the current paradigm apart so that we can make the quantum leap to the maturity of an ecological world-view. Only when enough people realise that the happiness and security which we seek can never be found in material objects, that More does not always equal Better, can the illusions of 'civilisation', 'progress' and 'infinite growth' be replaced with visions for sustainability.

What I hope to show is that a new vision of the human Self, which resonates as much with modern science as the core teachings of the most ancient philosophical Truth, is implicitly involved within this transition to an Ecological Age. We are being forced to question the most basic assumption of all, the individual identification that we make with consciousness itself. An Ecological Self can no longer be limited to the three-dimensional object which we believe ourselves to be, but is inextricably connected to the rest of the universe. For a truly sustainable society to emerge, we have to re-discover our own deep, intuitive, mystical connection with the planet. This has never left us, but is persistently denied by an antiquated perception of who and what we are.

2

In the Land of the Free

The American way of life is not up for negotiation.

GEORGE BUSH[1]

The Pioneers and the Wilderness

Fossil fuels and new technologies opened up the globe to myriad possibilities for overseas trade, the British Empire being the ultimate expression of rapid economic expansion. Historically, this process was known as colonisation. Now we call it globalisation.

The speed at which mankind pushed the frontiers of 'civilisation' was most pronounced in America. Thomas Jefferson's recti-linear grid rolled out across the continent, from East to West, imposing its sense of moral order on 'the wilderness' with the straight lines of urban planning and geometrical parcels of private land. No provision was made for the existing native American cultures that had lived in harmony with their environment for thousands of years. Instead, they were systematically eradicated from the landscape, and the pages of history books, as if they had never even existed. In the 1860s, General William Sherman wrote to his brother about the native people he was engaged in obliterating: 'The more we can kill this year, the less will have to be killed the next war, for the more I see of these Indians the more convinced I am that all have to be killed or maintained as a species of pauper. Their attempts at civilization are simply ridiculous.'[2]

The annihilation of tribal culture, exonerated by the values of the 'civilisation' which would replace it, had been unleashed upon indigenous peoples around the globe, from the Inuit of Alaska to the Aborigines of Tasmania. Although the language may not be so explicit, the corporations of today are still engaged in the same process, homogenising our cultural diversity into a global population of consumers, destroying the fabric of communities and the balance of ecosystems in pursuit of profit.

The first Americans to raise doubts about the sustainability of this policy included George Perkins Marsh, a self-trained lawyer from Vermont, and the poet Ralph Waldo Emerson. In 1864, Marsh published the first book to question the myth of super-abundance, *Man and Nature*, subtitled *Physical Geography as Modified by Human Action*.

Born in Woodstock in 1801, Marsh was the quintessential Renaissance man: he bred sheep, ran a wool mill, built roads and bridges, sold lumber, edited a newspaper, speculated in real estate, helped found the Smithsonian Institute, could read in twenty languages and served as the US ambassador in Turin, Florence and Rome from 1861 until his death in 1882. Near his home in Vermont, he noticed the effects of dam building, forest clearance, soil erosion and how disease and insects had decimated the wheat harvest. When farmers turned their attention to sheep, he witnessed the further degradation of the hills, while his time in the Mediterranean supported his theories about over-grazing and desertification. Although he knew little about resource use, or the emerging science of ecology, he surmised that these processes were the root cause of the Roman Empire's decline.

Marsh's book was an immediate success, described by *The Nation* as 'one of the most useful and suggestive works ever published', and by Lewis Mumford as 'the fountainhead of the conservation movement'. Gifford Pinchot, the first Director of the US Forest Service, thought that it was 'epoch-making', while it convinced the geologist Charles Lyell that Man's impact on the planet far exceeded that of other animals. However, this position led Marsh to reinforce a sense of separation between Man and Nature, declaring that 'nothing is further from my belief, that man is a "part of Nature", or that his action is controlled by the laws of Nature; in fact a leading spirit of the book is to enforce the opposite opinion, and to illustrate the fact that Man, so far from being a soul-less, will-less automaton, is a free moral agent working independently of Nature.'[3] At the same time, Marsh acknowledged the power of Nature to subdue the efforts of Man – 'Wherever he fails to make himself her master, he can but be her slave'[4] – and his book has influenced modern environmentalists, being rediscovered in the 1930s and 1960s.

Ralph Waldo Emerson was the founder of Transcendentalism, an American extension of the Romantic sensibility, and the product of his journey to England in 1833, where he met with Carlyle, Wordsworth and Coleridge. In his essay *Nature*, published in 1837, Emerson set forth his vision for a new relationship between Man and the natural world, proposing that America could become the embodiment of humanity's reconciliation with the environment rather than another battleground for conquest. However, Emerson saw that 'things are in the saddle and ride mankind,' already noticing the dominance of technological innovation.

One of those inspired by Emerson was Henry David Thoreau, the radical pioneer of American conservation. Thoreau called for moderation and restraint, not only from the developers and logging companies which were already using an expanding railway network to facilitate their exploitation of the landscape, but also on a personal scale of individual lifestyles. His seclusion in the woods near Walden Pond during the late 1840s, the subject of his most famous work, was partly conducted to prove how little man actually needed to live on; he spent little over sixty dollars in eight months, including the cost of building his house.[5]

Like Emerson, Thoreau's perception of his place in Nature converged on the core insights of the Perennial Philosophy, asking himself: 'Shall I not have intelligence with the earth? Am I not partly leaves and vegetable mould myself?'[6] Rather than seeing the work of a transcendent creator, Thoreau saw that the divine was immanent in Nature and inseparable from her at all times: 'God himself culminates in the present moment, and will never be more divine in the lapse of all the ages. And we are enabled to apprehend at all what is sublime and noble only by the perpetual instilling and drenching of the reality that surrounds us.'[7] Like other radical thinkers who shaped the foundations of the modern environmental movement, Thoreau espoused classic anarchist ideals, believing 'that government is best which governs not at all'.[8]

The Sierra Club, the first active environmental organisation in America, was founded by the Scotsman John Muir in 1892. Muir was the product of a strict Scottish Presbyterian family and his father used to whip him with a leather belt to make him memorise the scriptures. Reacting against the rigidity of his Christian upbringing, Muir was able to express his pronounced mystical disposition by immersing himself in wild Nature, in particular his beloved High Sierras where he was instrumental in establishing Yosemite National Park in 1890. A few years later, his time spent hiking in the mountains with Theodore Roosevelt is thought to have been the catalyst for the President's belief in conservation. Muir subsequently became involved in one of the first and most famous environmental conflicts in American history, centred on the Hetch Hetchy dam, which would supply San Francisco's water but was situated within the boundaries of Yosemite National Park. The split that subsequently developed between Muir and Gifford Pinchot illustrates the division that has existed ever since between preservation of wilderness *per se* and a managerial approach towards the development of resources.

Muir was spiritually nourished by wilderness. Dodging the military draft when he was twenty-six, he had wandered into a swamp near Lake Huron and wept with joy at the sight of wild orchids which had only just flowered and no man could have previously set eyes on. This experience proved pivotal, convincing him that Nature existed first and foremost for itself. Like Thoreau, his connection with the landscape expressed the sense of unity with creation which is the hallmark of all mystic experience:

> We are now in the mountains, and they are now in us, making every nerve quiet, filling every pore and cell of us. Our flesh-and-bone tabernacle seems transparent as glass to the beauty around us, as if truly an inseparable part of it, thrilling with the air and trees, streams

and rocks, in the waves of the sun – a part of all Nature, neither old nor young, sick nor well, but immortal.[9]

At times, Muir pre-empted the contemporary Deep Ecology movement, placing intrinsic value in every aspect of Nature and mankind on a level with other species: 'Would not the world suffer by the banishment of a single weed?' and 'Why should man value himself as more than a small part of one great unit of creation?'[10]

Despite their moments of enraptured oneness with Nature, both Muir and Thoreau helped to establish a basic dualism in the American conservation ethic, a source of tension ever since. 'In wildness is the preservation of the world,' declared Thoreau, casting in stone a fundamental attitude to Nature. However, by elevating the non-human wilderness to such a degree, establishing it as some sort of ideal towards which we must strive, Thoreau unwittingly left humanity out of the equation. In effect, he purely reinforced the separation between Man and Nature. As William Cronon observes, the concept of 'wilderness' is itself the product of 'civilisation' and 'could hardly be contaminated by the very stuff of which it is made'. The problem with the concept of preserving pristine wilderness is that the whole notion of it dies as soon as mankind is a part of it. Cronon goes on to point out that we are unlikely to make much progress in solving the environmental crisis, 'if we hold up to ourselves as the mirror of nature a wilderness we ourselves cannot inhabit'.[11]

Our modern perception of 'the wilderness experience', of untarnished Nature as a source of spiritual renewal, is precisely that – a modern perception. Three hundred years ago, people did not rush off into mountains and deserts to 'find themselves' and 'be close to Nature'. Wilderness was a place to be feared, the void into which Adam and Eve were expelled. Indeed, in total opposition to our current attitude towards protecting the non-human world, wilderness used to be seen as the very opposite of Paradise. However, this changing sensibility is something within us, a fashionable boundary drawn between ourselves and the rest of Nature. As the poet Gary Snyder says, wilderness 'is a quality of one's own consciousness' because 'the planet is a wild place and always will be'.[12]

Thoreau and Muir may have experienced a deeply personal relationship with Nature, but their vision lacked the deeper understanding of modern ecology and was still tinged with anthropocentric views. Ultimately, Muir could not have opposed the Hetch Hetchy dam on principle since he suggested other sites further downstream, while he saw Yellowstone as 'a public park and pleasuring ground for the enjoyment of the people'. In fact, towards the end of his life he seemed to contradict his earlier perspective, believing that the primary value of Nature was for the benefit of Man. This can be explained by his entry into politics and his belief that the only way to save the wilderness was to persuade the American people of its intrinsic worth. Muir may have set a precedent for the country's national parks, but by doing so he helped to reinforce the division between protected 'wild' Nature – a place to go and visit – and 'resources', an area to be used and exploited.[13]

Both men also believed that parts of the biosphere would always be safe from the activities of our species; Thoreau thought that, although deforestation would leave the country 'so bald that every man would have to grow whiskers to hide its nakedness', at least 'the sky was safe', while Muir wrote in his diary that 'the forests too, in time, may be destroyed' and 'only the sky will then be safe'.[14] As we now know, the pattern of climatic change has intensified ever since and the hard evidence of humanity's impact on planetary systems can be traced in every part of the biosphere.

Thoreau and Muir's emphasis on the preservation of wilderness has remained a theme in American environmentalism until the present day and still forms the crux of one of the most divisive splits in the movement. Extremists like Dave Foreman, founder of the radical group Earth First!, believe that 'preservation of wildness and native diversity is the most important issue', while 'issues affecting only humans pale in comparison'.[15] By putting mankind on a level footing with other species, Foreman and others within the Deep Ecology movement are often perceived as misanthropic, or suggesting that we can only live in harmony with the natural world by returning to the life of hunter-gatherers. However, by making mankind separate from wilderness, this position would seem to be guilty of the very thing that it seeks to heal, perpetuating a conceptual boundary between our species and the natural world. While we perceive an intrinsic difference between the wild 'natural' Nature of empty open spaces and the domestic 'artificial' Nature of our own back gardens, it seems impossible to overcome the inherent dualism which a truly ecological consciousness must absorb. If we keep concentrating on that which separates us from Nature, we are unlikely to realise the unity which is always there.

Thinking Like a Mountain

Much of the American wilderness that Muir and Thoreau hoped to protect had already succumbed to intensive farming practices. Surrounded by wide empty spaces, the early settlers felt little need for sustainability, depleting the soil through cultivation of nutrient-thirsty crops like cotton and tobacco. After a few seasons, when the crop yields started to drop, the farmers abandoned the land and moved further west, leaving a trail of scarred dead soil to be washed away by wind and rain.

One area that was neglected, being covered in shallow compacted topsoil and thick, tough grasses, was the Great Plains. However, the advent of the steel plough in the mid-nineteenth century opened up vast new possibilities for agriculture, with 40 million acres of wheat planted in Oklahoma alone. After the First World War, with Russian grain no longer available on the world market, the scale of production increased still further.

Then, in the early 1930s, there was drought. Despite the US Bureau of Soils' assertion that 'the soil is the one indestructible, immutable asset that the nation possesses . . . the one resource that cannot be exhausted',[16] the Great Plains were plunged into one of the most dramatic ecological disasters of the century – the 'dust bowl'. Literally millions of tons of loose dry topsoil were scooped up by the wind and deposited across the country. The first major storm, in May 1934, deposited some 350 million tons of topsoil over the eastern states with an estimated 12 million tons falling on Chicago alone.[17] There are references to dust detected on ships 300 miles into the Atlantic. By 1938, 10 million acres had lost the top 5 inches of soil and another 13.5 million acres the top 2½ inches.[18]

The situation has hardly improved since then. By the 1970s, one third of the topsoil in the country had been lost, dissipating at a rate of 5 billion tons a year, eight times faster than it was forming and six times more than a hundred years previously.[19] As climatic change continues to accentuate catastrophic weather patterns, the agricultural base of America – the fulcrum of its economic power – looks increasingly jeopardised: hydrologists predict that the Ogallala Aquifer, which supplies water to farms from the Texas Panhandle to South Dakota, will run dry within twenty years, while some estimates suggest that there will be no more topsoil left in fifty years.[20] Since we do not have the ability to manufacture soil or water, the future of American farming is far from certain.

* * *

One of the most celebrated figures in American environmental history emerged from the dust bowl years. In the desolate sand country of central Wisconsin, Aldo Leopold and his family undertook one of the first modern experiments in ecological restoration, gradually transforming ravaged, depleted soil into productive farmland. Leopold's *A Sand County Almanac*, first published in 1949, contains a series of sketches outlining a 'conservation ethic' which has been cited as a precursor to Deep Ecology and been elevated to sacred status by many environmentalists; the ecologist Rene Dubos called it 'the Holy Writ of American Conservation'; Wallace Stegner labelled it 'one of the prophetic books, the utterance of an American Isaiah'; Dave Foreman, with characteristic restraint, called it 'the most important book ever written'.[21]

Leopold graduated from Yale's School of Forestry in 1909, at a time when Theodore Roosevelt and Gifford Pinchot had seized upon 'conservation' as a new idea and the 'keystone of Progressive politics'. Like many conservationists, Leopold started life as a hunter, managing forests in Arizona and New Mexico, committed to exterminating every last mountain lion and wolf. However, one pivotal event was to pave the way for an entirely new perspective towards the natural world – the ability 'to think like a mountain'. Out hunting one day, he shot a wolf with her cubs, reaching the animal in time 'to watch a fierce green fire dying in her eyes. I realised then, and have known ever since, that there was something new to me in those eyes – something known only to her and the mountain. I was young then, and full of trigger-itch; I thought that because fewer wolves meant more deer, that no wolves would mean hunter's paradise. But after seeing the green fire die, I sensed that neither the wolf nor the mountain agreed with such a view.'[22]

From this time, Leopold came to value the intrinsic role played by every part of the 'biotic community', proposing that conservation should extend beyond 'spectacular scenic resources' for 'mass recreation', to include areas like 'low altitude desert tracts, heretofore regarded as without value for "recreation" because they offer no pines, lakes or other conventional scenery'. Although he continued to see hunting as an acceptable pursuit, so long as it preserved an ecological balance, he maintained that 'the cowman who cleans his range of wolves does not realise that he is taking over the wolf's job of trimming the herd to fit the range. He has not learned to think like a mountain. Hence we have dust-bowls and rivers washing the future into the sea.'[23] The wolf's role as a predator was thereby seen as integral to the health of the ecosystem: 'you cannot love game and hate predators' because 'the land is one organism'.

* * *

Leopold's conclusions were shaped by a surprising influence – the Russian philosopher Peter Ouspensky. (Nash suggests that the concept of 'thinking like a mountain' had been inspired by Ouspensky's reference to 'the mind of a mountain'.)[24] With language which again seems to echo quantum physics, holistic science and the Perennial Philosophy, Ouspensky proposed that the 'phenomenal' appearance of everything in the universe was inseparable from its 'noumenal' essence, that the static objects we perceive are part of dynamic, fluid processes and that the whole is greater than the sum of its parts. Cells create limbs and organs within organisms, which are in turn part of super-organisms like ecosystems, bioregions or Gaia itself. Since there is a noumenal essence to each level within the increasing complexity of creation, it is impossible to remove a single element without disturbing the entire biotic balance: 'Take away the heart, for example, and you kill the greater life of the wolf. Remove the wolf from the ecosystem and you alter the noumenon of the biotic community of which it was a part.'[25]

The ability to 'think like a mountain' therefore, which Leopold hoped to foster, points to a new way of seeing, transcending our entrenched egoic structure and placing mankind on a level with other species: 'Only the mountain has lived long enough to listen objectively to the howl of a wolf.'[26] By dissolving the boundaries between Man and Nature, Leopold pre-empted Arne Naess and Deep Ecology, while Dave Foreman has extended this position to suggest that drought, war, famine and disease are part of a planetary mechanism, designed to bring human populations back into balance with their surroundings. However, it would be unfair to attach misanthropic sentiments to Leopold himself, just because he saw humanity as 'fellow-voyagers with other creatures in the odyssey of evolution'. Seeing our species as any *less* important than others is guilty of the same polarisation as elevating ourselves into a position of superiority.

The basis of Leopold's famous ethic was that an action is 'right when it tends to preserve the integrity, stability and beauty of the biotic community' but 'wrong when it tends otherwise'.[27] Although this formula may still be seen as anthropocentric, since it appears to depend on a human code of morals and aesthetics to distinguish what is integral, stable and beautiful, Leopold displays a deeper understanding of ecological principles than his predecessors. Despite this apparent affinity with organic life however, he continued to use mechanical metaphors throughout his work:

> The last word in ignorance is the man who says of an animal or plant, 'What good is it?' If the land mechanism as a whole is good, then every part is good, whether we understand it or not. If the biota, in the course of aeons, has built something we like but do not understand, then who but a fool would discard seemingly useless parts? To keep every cog and wheel is the first precaution of intelligent tinkering.[28]

Similarly, Leopold foresaw errors in the assumption that 'economic parts of the biotic clock will function without the uneconomic parts'; noticed that the native Indians had neither disturbed the land, nor the diversity of species; realised that humanity was entering 'a race between the emergence of new pests and the emergence of new techniques for their control' and that we collectively imagine that industry supports us while 'forgetting what supports industry'.[29] He also warned of the spiritual impoverishment that threatens a society which presumes that 'breakfast comes from the grocery and . . . that heat comes from the furnace',[30] warning that our failure to respond to the environmental crisis puts us into 'the biological category of the potato bug which exterminated the potato, and thereby exterminated itself'.

The most poetic expression of Leopold's vision of an interconnected universe, obeying eternal cyclical patterns rather than linear human time-scales, is his story of X, an atom which

> had marked time in the limestone ledge since the Palaeozoic seas covered the land. In the flash of a century the rock decayed, and X was pulled out and up into the world of living things. He helped build a flower, which became an acorn, which fattened a deer, which fed an Indian, all in a single year . . . Between each of his excursions through the biota, X lay in the soil and was carried by the rains, inch by inch, downhill. Living plants retarded the wash by impounding atoms; dead plants by locking them to their decayed tissues . . . One year, while X lay in a cottonwood by the river, he was eaten by a beaver, an animal that always feeds higher than he dies. The beaver starved when his pond dried up during a bitter frost. X rode the carcass down the spring freshet, losing more altitude each hour than heretofore in a century. He ended up in the silt of a backwater bayou, where he fed a crayfish, a coon, then an Indian, who laid him down to his last sleep in a mound on the riverbank. One spring an oxbow carved the bank, and after one short week of freshet X lay again in his ancient prison, the sea.[31]

It is in the conclusion of this story that Leopold conveys the philosophical depth of his world-view, pointing towards the pure subjectivity that 'thinking like a mountain' implies. In the same way that 'an atom at large in the biota is too free to know freedom', while 'an atom back in the sea has forgotten it',[32] an individual ego that dissolves within the background of consciousness has transcended duality and merged with the unity of an absolute source. Ecologically, Leopold knew that 'for every atom lost to the sea, the prairie pulls another out of the decaying rocks', because 'the only certain truth is that its creatures must suck hard, live fast, and die often, lest its losses exceed its gains'.[33] In this passage, Leopold's vision is in total harmony with the ancient perennial wisdom, reminding us, like the philosopher Alan Watts, that 'we do not "come into" this world, we come *out* of it, as leaves from a tree'.[34] In the same way that Leopold traced the cyclical evolution of X, an individual expression of the whole universe, so Watts reminds us that 'as the ocean "waves", the universe "peoples"'. In the same way that X made the transition from rock to flower to beaver, so each individual is 'a unique action of the total universe'.

This fundamental understanding, that everything is simultaneously involved with and connected to everything else, is shared by quantum physics, modern ecology and the Perennial Philosophy, converging now to create our new world-view. Consequently, we now refer to the connection between a butterfly flapping its wings in Sumatra and a cyclone starting on the other side of the world; to sharing the same particles of air that sustained Buddha and Christ, or our basic DNA being formed from material which took part in the Big Bang. However, as Watts concludes, the reason why so few of us ever experience this Truth, even if we accept it, is that we continue to see ourselves as nothing but 'isolated "egos" inside bags of skin', rather than the infinite, eternal consciousness which both modern science and ancient wisdom tell us we are.

The Chemical Age

The alteration in the American landscape during the nineteenth century was not so much seen in the agricultural base as in the proliferation of industrial urban areas which it supplied. The advent of fossil fuels had given birth to numerous associated industries, which would become the focus of twentieth-century environmental problems: waste disposal, pollution, the occupational hazards of dealing with poisonous materials and their by-products. The industrial process ensured that all social and environmental considerations had been subordinated to the welfare of the factory, rather than the people that worked there or the land on which it stood. In addition, poor sanitation meant that epidemics of yellow fever, typhoid and cholera were still frequent throughout American cities until the 1890s. Lewis Mumford refers to one description of an urban river of the time, where 'steam boilers discharge into it their seething contents, and drains and sewers their fetid impurities; till at length it rolls on . . . considerably less a river than a flood of liquid manure'.[35]

The most toxic compounds released into both agricultural practice and the manufacturing process were provided by an expanding petro-chemical industry, challenged at different stages by two remarkable women. From her home in Chicago, Alice Hamilton became the first American environmentalist to confront heavy industry and raise questions about the effects of many of the chemicals involved, from carbon monoxide poisoning to 'phossy jaw' from phosphorus. Her campaigning led to legislation which effectively banned white phosphorous in 1912 and she went on to investigate the industrial uses of other toxic materials, criticising Thomas Midgeley for introducing tetraethyl lead to petrol in the 1920s. Since he also invented CFCs (chlorofluorocarbons), Midgeley has the dubious distinction of having 'had more impact on the atmosphere than any other single organism in earth history'.[36]

Several decades before the environmental agenda had even surfaced in public consciousness, Hamilton recognised that there was no such thing as an 'acceptable level' for toxic substances and was warning factory workers about being used as guinea pigs by industrial chemists. As well as raising awareness in an urban–industrial context, in contrast to the wilderness preservation and land ethics espoused by Thoreau, Muir and Leopold, she touched on issues relating to class, race and gender. Her book, *Industrial*

Poisons in the United States, paved the way for another woman's work, seen by many to signal the birth of the environmental movement.

Rachel Carson was a marine biologist from Springdale, Pennsylvania. *Silent Spring*, her 'clarion call' to the public about the dangers of chemical pesticides, was first serialised in the *New Yorker* before being published in the autumn of 1962. Combining scientific research with a lyrical flair for writing about Nature, Carson connected with a wide public readership. American historian Stephen Fox described *Silent Spring* as 'The Uncle Tom's Cabin of modern environmentalism', while Max Nicholson, founder of the British Nature Conservancy, called it 'probably the greatest and most effective single contribution to informing public opinion on the true nature and significance of ecology'.[37] In his history of the American environmental movement, Richard Gottlieb suggests that Carson's mission was 'to create a new environmental consciousness',[38] while Kirkpatrick Sale observes that there was 'no such thing as an environmental "movement" before the publication of *Silent Spring*'.[39]

Carson wrote her first book, *Under the Sea Wind*, in the late 1930s, while working for the US Bureau of Fisheries and teaching biology. This was followed in 1951 by *The Sea Around Us*, a distillation of the latest oceanic research. The book was a surprising success, winning a National Book Award, selling 2 million copies in thirty-two languages and staying on the bestseller list for eighty-six weeks.[40] By this time, pesticide use was already widespread in American agriculture, following the development of chlorinated hydrocarbons like DDT. The pesticide industry had been expanding at a phenomenal rate during the post-war years, boosting sales by $300 million in a decade.[41] By the late 1950s, chemicals had replaced virtually all other types of pest control and, in states like California, the 'agri-business' had become inextricably fused to the petro-chemical industry. Although there had been cases of food contamination traced to insecticides in the 1920s, the safety of the pesticide revolution, which was being touted as a 'scientific miracle', had never really been questioned.

In 1958, as part of an attempt to eradicate mosquitoes, DDT was sprayed across Duxbury in Massachusetts. Shortly afterwards, Carson came to visit a friend who lived in the area and heard about the 'agonising deaths' of the birds in a private sanctuary. She immediately started researching the products which were being welcomed with open arms, rapidly concluding that the chemicals were far from being as safe as both government and industry claimed. Carson discovered that children had been killed by the drifting spray of insecticides and that farm labourers were suffering from exposure to chemicals like chlordane, dieldrin and parathion.

Before *Silent Spring* was even launched, Carson was being attacked by the corporations whose products she sought to expose. Veliscol tried to prevent publication with a lawsuit, their lawyer, Louis A. McLean, complaining that

> in addition to the sincere opinions by natural food faddists, Audubon groups and others, members of the chemical industry in this country and western Europe must deal with sinister influences, whose attacks on the chemical industry have a dual purpose: 1) to create the false impression that all industry is grasping and immoral, and 2) to reduce the use of agricultural chemicals in this country and in the countries of western Europe, so that our supply of food will be reduced to east-curtain parity. Many innocent groups are financed and led into attacks on the chemical industry by these sinister parties.[42]

Despite these attempts, the book went straight to the top of the *New York Times* bestseller list and immediately became the centre of national controversy. Carson was not only labelled a lesbian and a communist, but by nature of being a woman, incapable of having a grasp on the science which she had presented. She was accused of 'a mystical attachment to Nature', of being 'an hysterical fool' and an 'emotional female alarmist'. Gottlieb quotes Edwin Diamond, a Senior Editor and former Science Editor at *Newsweek*, who said that 'Thanks to a woman named Rachel Carson, a big fuss has been stirred up to scare the American public out of its wits', and then likened the book to the 'paranoid fears' of 'such cultists as the anti-flouridation leaguers, the organic-garden faddists, and other beyond-the-fringe groups'.[43]

As we now know, Carson did have a firm grip on the science and the prospect of a spring without bird song seems to come closer each year, with many bird populations down over 70 per cent in the British Isles. We will never know how many human lives have been cut short by exposure to these chemicals but the list of cancers and other modern diseases which can be attributed to them grows longer every year. Carson was battling with cancer herself while trying to finish the book and she died eighteen months after *Silent Spring*'s publication.

Some commentators have noted that her writing was still tainted with traditional anthropocentrism – dividing the insect word into 'friends' and 'enemies' and 'keeping the balance of nature firmly tilted in our favour' – but Carson probably did more than anyone in the last hundred years to expose the inherent fallacy of pursuing the 'control of Nature', a phrase which she regarded as 'conceived in arrogance, born of the Neanderthal age of biology and philosophy, when it was supposed that nature exists for the convenience of man'. Her book will be remembered as one of the most influential texts of the twentieth century, a source of inspiration for the emerging counter-culture and instrumental in persuading policy-makers to fund new research and introduce legislation. A report by the Presidential Scientific Advisory Committee validated the claims made by Carson, culminating in the Pesticide Control Act of 1972 and the Toxic Substance Control Act of 1976.[44]

Carson not only confronted some of the most powerful corporations in the world, but bravely raised questions about the role of science in our society, highlighting the fact that research had been corrupted by the vested interests of a governing elite. In a speech she made after receiving the National Book Award, she spoke about how we assume that scientific knowledge is 'the prerogative of only a small number of human beings, isolated and priest-like in their laboratories', when 'the materials of science are the materials of life itself'.[45] Carson advocated a de-mystified science, thereby exposing the 'new priesthood' of corporate scientists creating markets for the toxic chemicals they are developing. Her message may have awakened millions to the dangers of pesticides, but the corporations which Carson attacked continue to sell banned chemicals like DDT to the Third World and are now using 'technological determinism' to convince us of the need for genetically modified crops. Of all the pioneers cited by the modern environmental movement, the legacy of Rachel Carson remains amongst the most prophetic. Her conviction that 'no civilisation can wage relentless war on life without destroying life itself', is even more poignant today than it was in 1962.

Murray Bookchin: The Anarchic Prophet

Although she enlightened public opinion, Carson was not the first to become aware of the dangers of chemicals in our environment. Reports about the potential horrors of DDT had been published as early as 1946 and, five months before the publication of *Silent Spring*, a book appeared called *Our Synthetic Environment*, written by a Lewis Herber. This book not only acknowledged the link between chemical pesticides and cancer, but pointed the finger at several other carcinogenic compounds and radioactive substances which were being introduced to the environment unchecked. Through his presentation of a 'human ecology', the author was one of the first to address the complex psychological problems of urban living.

The man behind the pseudonym Lewis Herber was Murray Bookchin, a radical thinker with roots in anarchist philosophy and Marxism. Born in 1921, to Russian Jewish immigrants in New York, Bookchin grew up in the shadow of the Russian Revolution. By the early 1950s, disillusioned with the limitations of communism, he was exploring new possibilities for a co-operative society, combining some of Marx's basic ideas with anarchist philosophy: 'Life itself compels the anarchist to concern himself increasingly with the quality of urban life, with the reorganization of society along humanistic lines', while 'the future of the anarchist movement will depend upon its ability to apply basic libertarian principles to new historical situations'.[46]

Social Ecology, the name that Bookchin gave to this synthesis, traces the roots of the environmental crisis to the hierarchical structure of human society: 'The imbalances man has produced in the natural world are caused by the imbalances he has produced in the social world' and 'the domination of Nature by Man stems from the very real domination of human by human'.[47] Bookchin believed that healing our relationship to the planet depended on healing society first, suggesting that the domination of Nature first flowed from the male domination of women in patriarchal society and now continued in the hierarchies of social organisation.

Ten years before the publication of *Silent Spring*, Bookchin recognised the inherent dangers of introducing chemicals to the food chain: 'Within recent years, the rise of little known and even unknown infectious diseases, the increase of degenerative illnesses and finally the high incidence of cancer suggest some connection between the growing use of chemicals in food and human diseases.'[48] Like Carson, Bookchin observed the insidious manner in which these chemicals were being introduced, 'shaped neither by the needs of the public nor by the limits of nature, but by the exigencies of profit and competition'.[49] While he realised that society's ecological health was being undermined by the very forces of capitalism, Bookchin also saw that environmental destruction caused by expansionist policy would ultimately produce a social movement calling for radical change.

Like the environmental movement of today, Bookchin called for massive decentralisation, creating a non-hierarchical network of communities using human-scale eco-technologies and sustained by renewable energy sources: 'In decentralisation exists a real possibility for developing the best traditions of social life and for solving agricultural and nutritional difficulties that have thus been delivered to chemistry. Most of the food problems of the world would be saved today by well-balanced and rounded communities, intelligently urbanized, well-equipped with industry and with easy access to the land.'[50] As early as 1962, with the technologies still in their infancy, Bookchin was aware of the intrinsic need for alternative energy sources within an ecological society:

> To maintain a large city requires immense quantities of coal and petroleum. By contrast, solar, wind and tidal energy can reach us mainly in small packets. To use solar, wind and tidal power effectively, the megalopolis must be decentralized. A new type of community, carefully tailored to the characteristics and resources of a region, must replace the sprawling urban belts that are emerging today.[51]

By 1964, Bookchin was making projections about global warming which have already rung true:

> It can be argued on very sound theoretical grounds that this growing blanket of carbon dioxide, by intercepting heat radiating from the earth, will lead to rising atmospheric temperatures, a more violent circulation of air, more destructive storm patterns, and eventually a melting of the polar ice caps (possibly in two or three centuries), rising sea levels, and the inundation of vast land areas.[52]

Janet Biehl observes that in 1971, the year before Arne Naess made the distinction between 'deep' and 'shallow' ecology, Bookchin highlighted the difference between 'environmentalism' and a non-anthropocentric approach:

> I speak, here, of ecology, not environmentalism. Environmentalism deals with the serviceability of the human habitat, a passive habitat that people use, in short, an assemblage of things called 'natural resources' and 'urban resources.' Ecology, by contrast, interprets all interdependencies (social and psychological as well as natural) non-hierarchically. Ecology denies that nature can be interpreted from a hierarchical viewpoint.[53]

By stressing the role of humanity within the evolutionary process, Bookchin's social vision has since clashed with Deep Ecology. Peter Marshall draws attention to Bookchin's contemplation of 'controlled thermo-nuclear reactions', of a 'landscape totally transformed and dominated by humans' and how 'he waxes lyrical about air-conditioned tractors'.[54] At the same time, Marshall believes that the rift that has developed between Social and Deep Ecology is 'both destructive and unnecessary', calling for a synthesis in a 'libertarian ecology' which is both 'deep in the sense of going to the roots of the ecological crisis' and 'social in recognizing that the human domination of nature begins in society and that its freedom will necessarily involve the freedom of humanity as a whole'.[55]

These differences are a recent development. Throughout the 1960s, an increasingly disillusioned sub-culture started to resonate with Bookchin's agenda and the 'legacy of domination'. His influence extended from radical left-wing student groups to the various beatniks, anarchists, feminists and peace protesters which formed the political wing of 'the counter-culture', a mass social reaction to 'the affluent society' and the ideological background from which a cohesive environmental movement would emerge.

The Counter-culture

In 1958, J.K. Galbraith coined the term 'the affluent society' to describe the post-war economic boom. With a proliferation of new technologies, the American Dream seemed to have actually happened: suburban houses, with their own plots of land, housed bulging refrigerators while leviathan automobiles, with long, sleek tail-fins, sat parked on the drive.

The Age of Affluence made few concessions to concepts like recycling or fuel economy. Theodore Roszak notes how 'Today we ponder the mysteries of sustainability. But the ideal of the forties, fifties and sixties was disposability.'[56] This was the time for 'the plastic revolution', for the values of 'the martini generation' lampooned in *The Graduate*, for the birth of the 'use it up and throw it away' culture which we have inherited today. This faith in technology had been instilled at a time when nuclear power was going to give us an endless safe supply of virtually free energy and the pesticide industry was promoted as 'Better things for Better Living through Chemistry'. A time before nuclear catastrophe was narrowly avoided at Three Mile Island and the chemical industry was exposed by *Silent Spring*. However, as the 1960s progressed, the values and assumptions upon which this society was based would be questioned by an increasingly vocal alternative, first identified by Roszak as 'the counter-culture'.

The political roots of 'the counter-culture' have been traced to left-wing groups like Students for a Democratic Society (SDS), influenced by Bookchin and the work of social critics like Herbert Marcuse and Paul Goodman. Marcuse was born in Berlin in 1898 and had been part of the famous Frankfurt School of Critical Theory with Martin Horkheimer. Like Bookchin, Marcuse and Horkheimer fused Marxist philosophy with the politics of ecological concern, observing the way in which scientific advances had 'made humanity the servant of blind forces'.[57] Books like Horkheimer's *The Eclipse of Reason* became standard texts for those seeking to undermine the prevailing world-view.

Marcuse fled Germany when Hitler came to power, and found a position at Columbia University. *One Dimensional Man*, published in 1964, made him an intellectual hero of the political underground and a 'guru of the student rebels'.[58] By attempting to conquer Nature with science and technology, argued Marcuse, consumer society had produced a way of life which was based on 'one-dimensional thought and behaviour'. Similarly, the New York intellectual Paul Goodman attacked the foundations of 'the affluent society', seeing cities as little more than giant department stores and describing science as the 'chief orthodoxy of modern times', financed by corporations that 'rush into production with neat solutions that swamp the environment'.[59] Goodman's progressive thought was way ahead of its time, promoting ways of reducing the distances that people travelled between home and the work-place, methods for decentralising government and even calling for a ban on cars in Manhattan.

In their 1962 Port Huron Statement, the SDS addressed civil rights issues and built on the growing anti-nuclear sentiments which were developing on both sides of the Atlantic. While governments continued to deny any risk from radiation exposure, nuclear atmospheric testing had raised serious concerns about the danger of materials like Strontium 90. Rather than fading away when the Partial Nuclear Test Ban Treaty was signed in 1963, the protest movement turned its attention towards the Vietnam War and the whole 'military-industrial complex' which supported it. By the end of the decade, this new political left was challenging the automobile, aerospace and chemical industries with slogans like 'Where there's pollution, there's profit.'[60]

Although the New Left was often aligned with 'the counter-culture', there were times when 'hippie' philosophy clashed with the social activism espoused by Jerry Rubin and members of the protest movement. While Abbie Hoffman and others persuaded hundreds to try and levitate the Pentagon, or 'expand the consciousness' of politicians, the activists campaigned to redistribute wealth until everyone enjoyed a middle-class standard of living, a concept tainted by the rampant materialism which the counter-culture intrinsically opposed.

The search for alternative lifestyles and institutions led to the foundation of maverick organisations on both sides of the Atlantic; FUNY, the Free University of New York, and the Antiuniversity of London, of which Roszak was a founder, attracted 'transient students with little more to their names than guitars, begging bowls and a stash of magic mushrooms to study the teachings of Timothy Leary, anarchist politics, and Tantric Sex'.[61]

Slightly more constructive experiments occurred with ecological lifestyles, leading to the infamous 'hippie commune', a thousand of which were believed to have developed in New York alone. However, as Gottlieb observes in *Forcing the Spring*, these were mainly 'ad hoc experiments rather than strategically defined alternatives' and the populations were often itinerant. The 'free town of Christiana', on the outskirts of Copenhagen, proved to be a prominent exception; a continuing communal project since 1971, this self-styled community grew to over 1,000 members, including artists, potters, blacksmiths, weavers and bakers.

Although 'hippie' philosophy has become a source of ridicule for the modern media, much of what we value in today's culture can be traced to those pursuing an alternative vision for society in the late 1960s and early 1970s. Herbie Girardet, an environmental writer and film-maker, remembers first coming to live in the multi-racial diversity of London's Notting Hill in

1963. After seeing two small children run over in the street, he became an active member of a community action group called the People's Association, campaigning to remove barbed wire fences which denied the community any access to gardens in a nearby square. Dressed as animals in hired theatre costumes and armed with wire cutters, the group 'liberated Powis Square'. The *Evening Standard* carried a front page picture of the police arresting the 'gorilla' and the 'zebra', and the local council were obliged to open up the green space. Herbie and his friends then took over four squatted houses in nearby Talbot Road, opened a cafe, workshops, a playground and recycling centre, in what became the first offices for the Notting Hill Carnival.[62]

Adding a quirky edge to protests, and thus attracting media attention, was a winning formula which would be replicated by groups like Greenpeace throughout the coming decades, using 'guerilla theatre' tactics to devastating effect. For sheer humour, few of these escapades can match one demonstration by the members of Christiana, when 100 of them dressed up as Father Christmas, entered a huge department store and started giving things away to customers. The genuine in-house Father Christmas then appeared in court, trying to plead his innocence, while sitting amongst his imposters.

The most famous attempts at creating the alternative society centred on Haight-Ashbury in San Francisco, the epicentre for the Psychedelic Revolution and the focus of hippie culture. A combination of rising rents, police harassment and intrusive tourists had driven the beatnik community out of North Beach and into the Haight, likened to 'the delta of a river' by social historian Helen Perry, in which 'all the uprooted sediment of America was washing ashore'.

In December 1964, the Free Speech Movement gave the sub-culture its first taste of political power, when 400 people seized Sproul Hall at Berkeley University, holding it until 'they were dragged out singing by hundreds of helmeted riot police'.[63] This peaceful form of direct action was replicated by similar 'Be-in' and 'Love-in' protests across the country, the most famous occurring at Golden Gate Park in January 1967.

Self-help groups sprang up in urban pockets, like the Diggers in Haight-Ashbury, hoping to provide a support network for those trying to implement an alternative tribal society. Groups like Abbie Hoffman's 'Yippies' combined civil rights issues with an environmental agenda while, on New York's Lower East Side, Gottlieb draws attention to 'The Motherfuckers', a synthesis of Black Power consciousness, the counter-culture and the New Left. During the garbage strike in the winter of 1967–68, they moved hazardous waste from the streets to the front of the Lincoln Centre, a prominent performing arts venue.

Perhaps the most poignant event with a 'green agenda' was conducted at People's Park in San Francisco. Protesting against the construction of a car park, students at the University of California planted trees and erected picnic tables in the vacant lot, declaring that it was 'liberated for Nature'. Gary Snyder saw it as a positive attempt to highlight the 'non-negotiable demands of the Earth'.[64] Ronald Reagan, Governor of California of the time, saw it as subversive in the extreme, calling in the National Guard and precipitating a confrontation in which hundreds were injured and one person killed by a tear gas cannister. People's Park has since been described as a 'symbolic turning point for those whose concern with democracy and Nature led them into direct confrontation with the forces of the State'.[65]

To a large extent, the legacy of the counter-culture was corrupted by a media intent on reducing the 'Summer of Love' to an orgiastic frenzy of sex and drugs. While Charles Reich's *The Greening of America* announced a 'new revolutionary form of consciousness', and Roszak's *The Making of a Counter-culture* spoke about a 'stance of life which seeks not simply to muster power against the misdeeds of society, but to transform the very sense that men have of reality', the polarisation that developed between 'alternative' and 'straight' society led to traditional forms of confrontation. The Haight turned into a battlezone, forcing the counter-culture into 'heightened rhetoric and more desperate actions'.[66] LSD was made illegal, and psychedelic heroes like Timothy Leary, Ken Kesey and the acid chemist Owsley, were hounded by media, police and the establishment in general, many of them ending up behind bars.

The fact that Richard Nixon saw Timothy Leary as 'the most dangerous man in America' is an indication of just how threatening the values of the 'counter-culture' were deemed to be. However, few people in 'straight' society had even glimpsed the extraordinary power of the revolutionary tool which Leary and others were propagating. As Jay Stevens observes in his seminal study of the drug, even the activists of the New Left had overlooked 'the role LSD was playing in redefining the Counter-culture's thrust'.[67] For the beat poet Allen Ginsberg, 'technology had produced a chemical which catalyzes a consciousness which finds the entire civilisation leading up to that pill absurd'.[68]

Aside from the controversial politics which Leary's 'tune in, turn on and drop out' philosophy seemed to advocate, individual psychedelic experience was perhaps the most subversive social experiment that the counter-culture was engaged in. Anthropologists and ethnobotanists have shown that, through the shamanic use of hallucinogenic plants in traditional tribal cultures, the psychedelic experience reveals itself as the earliest form of communication between Man and Nature. In virtually every culture of the world, the very notion of transcendence, of access to different levels of consciousness, of the existence of a spiritual realm in Nature, has been attributed to primitive man's experimentation with various hallucinogenic plants, roots and mushrooms.

Modern psychologists, like Stanislav Grof, have shown that an almost universal quality of the psychedelic experience is a feeling of connection with the natural world, of seeing the objective reality of Nature as not only a projection of consciousness but also as somehow alive. For thousands around the world, the basic revelations of this experience awakened the notion that everything is interconnected, that the planet is one integrated organism and that the concept of an individual consciousness is just part of one universal vision. As Aldous Huxley so famously declared, in the words of William Blake, the psychedelic experience helped to 'cleanse the doors of perception' so that everything could appear as it really is – 'infinite'. By undermining the conditioned processes of the ego, the sacramental use of psychedelic drugs dissolved the social, cultural and psychological boundaries which set Man apart from Nature. On an individual basis, the Psychedelic Revolution may have done as much to give birth to an ecological world-view as the direct actions and political protests with which it was aligned.

Although the counter-culture seemed to dissipate after the early 1970s – 'absorbed into commercialized New Age settings'[69] – the ecological awareness which developed from it led to a new environmental politics. Roszak maintains that the 'environmental movement would surely never have gotten beyond its conservationist orientation if there had not been those who were willing to ponder the limits of urban industrial society' because 'the counter-culture' 'rediscovered human ecology as a critical force that demanded a reappraisal of the economics of growth, the high-consumption lifestyle and anthropocentric science'.[70] By emulating the networks of tribal societies, rather than the hierarchies of the military-industrial complex, 'the young were dignifying the cultures of primary people, finding a wisdom in their capacity to live sustainably in their habitat'. Perhaps most importantly, this 'lent the environmental movement a cultural thrust that reached beyond mere resource management'.[71]

For the first time in western history, the basic values and ethics of a 'civilisation' propelled by principles of unlimited economic expansion, structured around hierarchical social organisations and governed by a political and corporate elite, had been sharply challenged by a significant number of people. From this 'mosaic of unease',[72] the environmental movement now emerged as a sociopolitical force which could no longer be ignored.

Earth Day

On 22 April 1970, an estimated 20 million Americans, including 1,500 schools and 10,000 colleges, took part in Earth Day, a nationwide 'teach-in'. Senator Gaylord Nelson, who first proposed the idea, called it 'an astonishing grass-roots explosion'.[73] One hundred thousand people converged on New York's Fifth Avenue in part of an event which symbolised the transition of environmental issues from rebellious sixties protest to the mainstream political agenda. 'The people cared', said Nelson, 'and Earth Day became the first opportunity they ever had to join in a nationwide demonstration and send a big message to the politicians – a message to tell them to wake up and do something.'[74] After Earth Day, American politicians realised that they had at least to be seen to tackle issues like pollution. President Nixon announced that it was time to start making 'reparations for the damage we have done to our air, to our land and to our water'.[75] *Time* magazine referred to 'Nixon's New Issue' and a national network of waste treatment plants became the most costly programme in American history.

In 1969, a massive oil spill from an off-shore rig near Santa Barbara had released millions of gallons of crude oil along the California coastline. The historian Kirkpatrick Sale believes that this incident 'brought home to a great many Americans a feeling that protection of their environment would not simply happen, but required their active support and involvement'.[76] The establishment of the Environmental Defense Fund (EDF) in 1965 had already shown how lawyers and ecologists could work together in bringing injunctions against polluters and work more effectively than conventional lobbying tactics. Then, in 1969, the National Environmental Policy Act had created the Environmental Protection Agency (EPA), which gave birth to the Environmental Impact Statement (EIS), 12,000 of which would be prepared in the following ten years and signified that 'federal government, as ill-prepared and unwilling as it might have been, was at last irrevocably in the environmental management business'.[77]

In addition to the gurus of 'the counter-culture' and the 'patrician mountaineers' of old-school conservation groups, the movement had begun to produce an eclectic range of leaders, like the biologist Barry Commoner, who proposed more efficient technologies for pollution control and was described at the time as 'the Paul Revere of Ecology'. Meanwhile, the publication of Paul Ehrlich's *The Population Bomb* in 1968 had alerted public opinion about the fundamental discrepancy between diminishing resources and an expanding population. Although it was attacked by politicians and industry for being 'neo-Malthusian' and 'neo-Luddite', the book went on to sell 3 million copies in the next decade and sits alongside *Silent Spring* as one of the most popular and influential environmental books ever written.

By 1970, the media had seized upon the environment as the issue of the day, with front page stories appearing in *Time, Fortune, Newsweek, Life*, the *New York Times* and the *Washington Post*. As Kirkpatrick Sale observes, 'ecology had become a buzz word' and phrases like 'resource depletion' had entered everyday vocabulary, while in the run-up to Earth Day, the *New York Review of Books* admitted that the environmental crisis 'may indeed constitute the most dangerous and difficult challenge that humanity has ever faced'.[78]

The real drive behind Earth Day came from Dennis Hayes, a twenty-five year old Harvard law student. An activist aligned with the New Left, opposing both government and industry, Hayes characterised the inherent contradictions of the event by projecting a less confrontational approach and wanting to 'involve the whole of society'.[79] In *Forcing the Spring* Gottlieb notes how many within the alternative movement felt betrayed by this approach, seeing it as 'further consolidation of power and profit in the hands of those responsible for the present dilemma'. Similarly, the old school conservationists were embittered by the media celebration, which seemed to suggest that the movement was something entirely new and had no historical precedent. It suddenly seemed like everybody had jumped on the environmental bandwagon, including the President himself, who had put the issues at the centre of his State of the Union address some three months before Earth Day. Despite Nixon's aspirations to be seen as the next Theodore Roosevelt – 'a Republican champion of efficiency and technological improvement' who was 'making peace with Nature' – he failed to convince even the most moderate of those attending the Earth Day events.[80]

While some industries appeared to be tackling pollution issues, reluctantly installing new waste treatment technologies, others chose to see Earth Day as evidence of some sinister communist plot, highlighting the fact that it was scheduled to take place on Lenin's one hundredth birthday. One spokesman saw it as 'a broad attack on the entire industrial system' and that the event would 'be used by radicals for revolutionary purposes'.[81] As Hayes remarked at the time, most industrialists and politicians had missed the point altogether – 'talking about filters on smokestacks while we are challenging corporate irresponsibility' – illustrating a basic failure to address root causes rather than just the symptoms. In a way, this gave the impression that the movement had become more anthropocentric, concerned less with the preservation of wilderness than the protection of the human species. One member of the Audubon Society announced that 'There is a new battle to be waged – to keep man's technology in check while promoting the welfare of man himself.'[82]

However, the mass media coverage of Earth Day had helped to set a precedent for both environmental policy and the movement itself; government agencies introduced new legislation to regulate industry, existing conservation groups developed a more professional profile to take their message to the public and a proliferation of small activist organisations were starting to tackle the ever-widening range of issues which would dominate the next three decades. The environmental movement was here to stay.

Greenpeace

Despite the horrors of Nagasaki and Hiroshima in 1945, the four nuclear powers, – the US, the USSR, Britain and France – proceeded to announce a total of 423 nuclear detonations before the Partial Nuclear Test Ban Treaty was signed in 1963. The official line on the environmental consequences of these tests often verged on the bizarre, with one American Senator claiming that fallout is actually beneficial to health. The British government still seems to think that radioactive material is perfectly safe, defending the use of depleted uranium in ammunition while looking for by-products from an ailing nuclear industry.

The realities of fallout proved far more pervasive than originally thought, returning to the earth within months rather than hanging in the stratosphere. Radioactive hailstones fell nearly 2,000 miles from a British test off the coast of Australia in 1952.[83] Two years later, radioactive ash from an American test on Bikini Atoll in the Pacific was caught by the wind and deposited over the inhabited Marshall Islands as well as 7,000 square miles of ocean.[84] Two weeks later, the entire crew of a Japanese trawler returned to port with radiation sickness and many of the fish landed at Japanese ports were found to be contaminated.[85] Prominent international figures, including Albert Einstein, Pope Pius XII, Bertrand Russell and Albert Schweitzer, all joined the global outcry and denounced the proliferation of tests.[86]

America, Russia and Britain all signed the Partial Nuclear Test Ban Treaty in 1963, thus ratifying what has been seen as 'the first global environmental agreement'.[87] However, they maintained the right to test nuclear weapons underground. America chose to conduct their subterranean tests on the Aleutian island of Amchitka, situated off the north-western tip of Alaska in one of the most seismically active places on the planet. In 1964, a major earthquake in the region had left a trail of devastation across Alaska and precipitated a series of tsunamis which were felt as far away as Japan.

Five years later, the US Atomic Energy Commission (AEC) made the controversial decision to detonate a one megaton atomic bomb 4,000 feet below the surface of Amchitka, prompting 20,000 people to converge on US–Canadian border crossings in one of the largest protests of the decade. Although the blast did not cause the earthquakes or tidal waves which the demonstrators feared, it was followed by plans for another test in 1971, five times bigger than the last. For the anti-nuclear movement, the time had come to confront the military–industrial complex with more radical tactics.

In *The Greenpeace Story*, John May and Michael Brown trace the birth of the group to Canada. Jim Bohlen had served with the US Navy during the Second World War and been stationed in the Pacific when the first nuclear bombs were dropped on Nagasaki and Hiroshima. Disillusioned by American military policy during the Cuban Missile Crisis and the Vietnam War, he had moved to Vancouver with his wife Marie, where they both became involved with the peace movement.

In 1967 they met Irving and Dorothy Stowe, a Quaker couple who had also fled the US, and who introduced them to their religion's concept 'bearing witness', a form of peaceful protest which involved travelling to the actual site of an event which was being opposed. Both couples had become active members of the local Sierra Club but were frustrated 'because they weren't doing anything about the nuclear weapons test'.[88] Then Marie remembered that a crew of Quakers had tried to sail to Bikini Atoll in 1958, to protest against atmospheric testing. Despite being arrested in Hawaii, the protesters had attracted national media coverage. 'Why don't we get a ship and take it up there?' she suggested.[89]

The US Sierra Club did not support the idea so, having joined forces with Paul Cote, a young law student and proficient sailor, Bohlen and Stowe formed the Don't Make a Wave Committee, based on a slogan used during the previous Amchitka protest. Bohlen recalls how, at one of their Vancouver meetings, it was decided that the name 'was a lot of words that didn't mean much'.[90] It was a young Canadian social worker, Bill Darnell, who first suggested the name Greenpeace, combining an ecological stance with the anti-nuclear roots of the core members.

The *Phyllis Cormack*, the boat which the protest crew hired for the voyage, was a battered 80 foot vessel with a top speed of 9 knots and was barely considered sea-worthy: 'The depth sounder had to be hammered with a fist to get it working; the anchor winch was worn out; the fuel tanks were damaged by rust; the reversing gear was badly worn and the engine was in appalling condition.'[91] Hunter recalls how, 'Paint peeling and damp, with ropes hanging like mossy vines from her rigging, she looked too dilapidated to start up, let alone cross the Gulf of Alaska.'[92] Another crew member described it as a 'floating farmhouse' and, the night before they sailed, a local fisherman told Bohlen that the ship had already sunk twice in the Georgia Strait. To make matters worse, they were heading into dangerous waters which, at that time of year, had been known to break bigger boats in half. However, the crew were committed. Joni Mitchell and James Taylor had played a benefit concert which raised most of the funds required and, two weeks before the date set for the test, they set sail for Amchitka.

Most of the publicity for the protest had been orchestrated by Ben Metcalfe, a theatre critic for CBC, and Robert Hunter, a journalist for the *Vancouver Sun* who would play a prominent role in the early years of Greenpeace. On the first day of the journey, Metcalfe made a radio report for CBC, announcing that 'Our goal is a very simple, clear and direct one – to bring about a confrontation between the people of death and the people of life. We do not consider ourselves to be radicals. We are conservatives, who insist upon conserving the environment for our children and the future generations of man.'[93] Hunter realised that 'mass media is a way of making millions bear witness at a time' and would later defend the direct action tactics used by the organisation: 'If crazy stunts were required in order to draw the focus of the cameras that led back into millions and millions of brains, then crazy stunts were what we would do.'

On this, the first of many Greenpeace sea-faring ventures, Hunter introduced the crew to *Warriors of the Rainbow*, a book which detailed 'Strange and Prophetic Dreams of the Indian Peoples'. Hunter recalls that 'It had been given to me, rather mysteriously, by a Jewish dulcimer maker who described himself as a gypsy and predicted that the book would reveal a "path" that would affect my life.'[94] The vision of a Cree Indian shaman told of a time 'when the earth would be ravaged of its resources, the sea blackened, the streams poisoned, the deer dropping dead in their tracks'. However, the Indians would then help some of the white men to revere Nature again, 'banding together with him to become Warriors of the Rainbow'. As Hunter wrote later, 'the older men were less impressed than the youngsters. But rainbows did appear several times the following day and it all did seem somehow magical'.[95] The prophecy would subsequently inspire the name for the most famous Greenpeace boat – *Rainbow Warrior*.

While anchored off the island of Akutan, the crew received news that the test date had been postponed. After making the decision to continue towards Amchitka, they were approached by a US Coast Guard, the commander of which announced that the *Cormack* was under arrest for having failed to notify customs of their arrival in Akutan. With no firm date for the test, deteriorating weather and failing morale, they were left with little option but to retreat. However, the media attention which they had generated enabled Stowe to raise more money back in Vancouver and the *Edgewater Fortune*, a converted minesweeper, was soon heading for Amchitka with a new crew. Despite these efforts, the bomb was detonated while they were still 700 miles to the south. Four months later, the AEC announced that there would be no more tests in the Aleutians, for 'political and other reasons'.[96]

The following year, similar 'direct action' tactics would be used in the South Pacific. In defiance of international pressure, the French were pursuing their programme of nuclear atmospheric testing on the Moruroa Atoll. David McTaggart, an intrepid Canadian yachtsman, was based in New Zealand at the time, with *Vega*, his 12 metre ketch – one man and a boat that would soon have the French government pulling at their hair.

McTaggart had already led a colourful life. A champion badminton player in the 1950s, he had established his own construction company at the age of twenty-one. Then, in 1969, a gas leak caused an explosion at a ski lodge development which he had recently completed in Bear Valley, a Canadian ski resort. 'Something went out of me then,' McTaggart said later. 'Perhaps the desire to continue fighting for a quality of life I had no taste for; perhaps the rules of the game; maybe the game itself had become meaningless. Whatever the reason, I took what little money I had and boarded a plane for the South Seas. A short while later, *Vega* became my one and only possession.'[97]

While in New Zealand, McTaggart met Ann-Marie Horne, whose father had noticed a newspaper item about 'a group called Greenpeace who were looking for someone to sail a boat to Moruroa to protest the French nuclear tests'.[98] McTaggart had never seen himself as an activist but was incensed by the audacity of the French wanting to 'cordon off thousands of square miles of international waters'.[99] Since the test was scheduled to take place in six weeks' time, and the 7,000 mile trip to Moruroa and back might take up to four months, he realised that 'any fool crazy enough to try it would have to find a crew, stock provisions, and do all the million small things necessary for a voyage of this kind, in two weeks!'[100] However, McTaggart was determined to try. He contacted Ben Metcalfe in Vancouver, who volunteered as radio operator and released funds left from Amchitka to pay for much-needed equipment. The rest of the crew was made up by Roger Haddleton and Nigel Ingram, who had both served with the British Royal Navy, and Grant Davidson, 'a twenty-six year old with no sea experience but who was a good cook and badly wanted to make the trip'.[101]

Word about the impending journey had filtered through to official channels and the New Zealand government, anxious that the protest might upset the country's dairy trade with France, tried their best to prevent the crew's departure; customs officers tore *Vega* apart, seized a handgun that McTaggart carried on the boat for protection, then threw him in jail for a night on smuggling charges after finding several watches that he had purchased in Fiji.

Through a combination of serendipity and shrewd tactics, *Vega* and her crew finally slipped out of Westhaven Harbour, exactly one month before the test date. Strong winds helped them cover the first part of the journey much faster than expected. However, the long-range radio equipment was faulty and tensions began to brew. Metcalfe, who was far from physically fit, was also trying to assume control of the boat. McTaggart decided to detour to Rarotonga in the Cook Islands, where they all came down with fever and Haddleton became too ill to continue. It was then discovered that Metcalfe had issued a press release claiming that the *Vega* was a decoy and that the real protest boat was scheduled to leave from South America. Metcalfe left for Peru and the three-man crew continued, battling their way through heavy seas to arrive in the forbidden zone on the morning that the French had originally scheduled for the test, taking up position 20 miles from the test site and directly downwind of the fallout.

Since leaving New Zealand, the crew had been trying to create confusion by broadcasting false positions. However, *Vega* was being closely monitored by the French Navy and an exhausting process of intimidation began, with planes, helicopters and warships circling the tiny yacht for days that turned into weeks. At one stage McTaggart picked up a French report on the radio, which maintained that *Vega* had been peacefully escorted from the danger zone some eleven days previously. This seemed to indicate that the French were planning to go ahead with the test and deny any knowledge of what had happened to the protesters and their boat. McTaggart recalls how 'it was like having a maniac standing behind you with a sledgehammer' and later described the impact that the French tactics were having on the Greenpeace crew: 'The effect of the preparations was to send grotesque images tumbling through our minds – of scorching walls of heat, blinding unearthly light, shock waves coming across the water like freight trains and showers of heat-cracked rocks and charred wood. I caught myself looking at my own and others' skin, wondering how much laceration it could take. We started wearing sunglasses – just in case.'[102]

However, the presence of *Vega* was making more of an impact than they realised. Eventually the French lost all patience and rammed them with a minesweeper, causing extensive damage. McTaggart and his crew were left with no option but to be escorted into Moruroa, where the French orchestrated photographs to imply that they were all on good terms. These pictures were dispatched with a press release, maintaining that the collision had been McTaggart's fault.

Back in Canada, McTaggart set to work on *Outrage*, his book which detailed the true course of events. An advance from a publisher paid for repairs to *Vega* and, after the French announced plans for another test in 1973, he headed back to New Zealand. Joined by Ann-Marie Horne, Nigel Ingram and Mary Lornie, he set sail for Moruroa again, covering the distance in just three weeks. Two other protest boats had already been forced to leave, while the Australian and New Zealand governments had even sent warships to express their opposition to the tests. However, *Vega* was soon on her own and had been spotted by French aircraft.

What followed was tantamount to piracy and would be the cause of international embarrassment for the French government. Six commandos boarded the yacht, battered McTaggart with truncheons and knocked him unconscious: 'Something crashed into my right eye with such incredible force that it seemed to come right into the middle of my brain in an explosion so that I thought that half my head had been torn off. And then everything went black.'[103] His injuries were so severe that he had to be flown to Tahiti for emergency treatment. Ingram was also attacked, while Ann-Marie managed to photograph the incident and conceal the film from the French. These images would later be seen in twenty different countries and would form the basis of McTaggart's legal battle for compensation from the French authorities, a three-year struggle with the civil courts in Paris. His efforts had not been in vain. In September 1974, at a meeting of the UN General Assembly, the French government announced that all future tests would be conducted underground.

The birth of Greenpeace will always be associated with nuclear issues but, by the mid-1970s, the group was starting to diversify. Robert Hunter joined forces with Paul Spong – a psychologist from New Zealand – to form Project Ahab, an ambitious attempt to confront the international whaling fleets which were driving many species close to extinction: the blue whale population had been reduced from 200,000 to 6,000, hump-backs had declined at a similar rate and the Pacific grey and sperm whales had been cut by half.

Hunter recalls the 'unconventional blend of human talents and skills' that the campaign attracted:

> There were . . . dozens of people who regularly consulted the I Ching, astrology charts, and ancient Aztec tables. Yet for every mystic there was at least one mechanic, and salty old West Coast experts on diesel engines and boat hulls showed up at the meetings to sit next to young vegetarian women. Hippies and psychologists mixed freely with animal lovers, poets, marine surveyors, housewives, dancers, computer programmers, and photographers.[104]

After Irving Stowe died in October 1974, Hunter and Project Ahab effectively replaced the old Greenpeace Foundation with a new agenda. Operating out of a small office in Vancouver, the group launched a sustained attack on the Russian and Japanese whaling fleets that were responsible for most of the trade. After Spong managed to infiltrate the Bureau of International Whaling Statistics in Norway, posing as a researcher, they were able to make an educated guess about the whalers' preferred hunting grounds. The *Phyllis Cormack* and *Vega* were soon back in action, enabling the activists to deploy high-speed Zodiac dinghies which they could position between whale pods and harpoons.

One long-running confrontation was with a vast Soviet 'factory' ship, the *Dalniy Vostok*, which collected dead whales left by the harpoon boats, stripped off the skin and fed blubber directly into vast boilers for rendering into oil. The alternative tactics used by Greenpeace were often greeted with bemusement by their opponents:

> As two of the Zodiacs buzzed around the *Dalniy Vostok*, with cameramen Easton and Weyler filming the whales being fed into the bowels of the ship, blood gushing from a waste outlet in its hull, the *Cormack* pulled alongside. To the astonishment of the Soviet crew lining the deck, the Greenpeace people took up their guitars and sang anti-whaling songs, then serenaded them with tape recordings of the songs of humpback whales, played at full volume through the loudspeakers.[105]

It was straight after this light-hearted exchange that Hunter placed the Zodiac directly between a whale pod and one of the harpoon boats. Despite the presence of cameras, the Russian fired at the whales, missing Hunter's dingy by 5 feet. These images were soon dispatched around the world, aired on TV stations from the US to Europe and Japan. Thousands were inspired by the campaign and Greenpeace factions proliferated across Canada and the US, from Honolulu to Montreal to New York.

The group may have attracted 10,000 supporters at the time but the core organisation was still small, about thirty people, and the Vancouver office was $40,000 in debt. It was time to make Greenpeace more professional, employing accountants, starting a newspaper and selling merchandise. By the middle of 1976, the organisation was in a viable position to launch a new protest against the whalers, chartering the *James Bay*, an ex-Canadian navy minesweeper which was almost identical to the boat that had rammed McTaggart in the South Pacific. With increasing levels of expertise, sophistication and experience, this second campaign was directly able to save about 100 whales and divert the hunters from at least 1,300 others. This sustained pressure certainly caught the attention of the world's media but it was not until 1982 – when the International Whaling Commission (IWC) met in England – that an agreement was made to end all commercial whaling within three years. Inevitably, the four principal whaling nations – Russia, Japan, Norway and Peru – filed objections to the decision and commercial whaling persists to this day, still vigorously opposed by one of the early Greenpeace veterans.

Paul Watson claimed to have had a vision during a Sioux Indian sweat-lodge ritual, in which he was told to save the marine mammals of the world. He was a key player in Greenpeace campaigns against the hunting of whales and baby seals, famously hand-cuffing himself to a load of pelts before being dragged across the ice, dropped into freezing water and then hauled onto the deck of a seal ship. 'It was like being in the Roman Coliseum,' Watson said later. 'They were yelling "drown the bastard" when they pulled me on board and laid me face down in the seal pelts so that I got all bloody.'[106] However, after creating divisions over campaign tactics, Watson was expelled for being too militant. He went on to form the Sea Shepherd Foundation, announcing: 'We don't talk about problems, we act.' His drive and tenacity certainly seemed to reflect the zeal with which he embraced this mission, incapacitating seven illegal whalers with one small boat, putting the plight of baby seals into the international spotlight and exposing dolphin slaughter in Japan.

By drawing Brigitte Bardot into their campaign against the slaughter of baby harp seals, Greenpeace raised their media profile still further, with nearly fifty European journalists following the French actress to Newfoundland. However, the incident which would irrevocably turn the group into a household name was a more sinister encounter with that veteran Greenpeace enemy, the French government itself.

McTaggart was still based in Paris, doing battle with the French authorities over damage done to *Vega*. In collaboration with the embryonic UK chapter of Friends of the Earth, he had helped to establish a London office for Greenpeace, given the task of finding a new protest boat that could tackle whaling in the North Atlantic. A rusty 44 metre trawler was located, 'languishing on the Isle of Dogs'.[107] The first diesel-electric ship built in the UK, the *Sir William Hardy* had been a research vessel for the Ministry of Agriculture, Fisheries and Food (MAFF). During the spring of 1978, a team of volunteers worked against the clock to transform the *Hardy* into the most famous boat ever associated with environmental protest, 'chipping at the rusty hull, overhauling the engines, and fixing the complex and waterlogged electrical system'.[108] At the end of April, the *Rainbow Warrior* began her illustrious career, heading straight into action against Icelandic whalers. Two months later she was hounding the *Gem*, a British ship dumping 2,000 tons of radioactive waste in international waters, and it was the start of another running battle.

After three years of persistent confrontation in Europe and the North Atlantic, *Sirius* joined the Greenpeace fleet, taking the group's international level of protest to new heights. In 1981 they orchestrated fifty separate actions around the globe, highlighting issues both out at sea and back on land. Campaigns exposed the transportation and disposal of nuclear fuels and waste, the continuation of whaling, the toxic pollutants of heavy industry and the impact on rivers like the Rhine in Germany. *Sirius* continued to track the *Gem* and confronted Russian nuclear testing on the Arctic island of Novaya Zemlya. Meanwhile the *Warrior* travelled to Canada and the US, before heading off to tackle objections to the IWC whaling ban, focusing on Peru and then Russian activities off the coast of Siberia. All across Europe, Greenpeace climbers highlighted acid rain issues by scaling industrial smokestacks and leaving banners, while the toxic discharge pipes from chemical factories were plugged from the Humber Estuary to Monsanto's plant in Boston.

After a major renovation in Jacksonville, the *Rainbow Warrior* was back at sea in March 1985, heading to the South Pacific on her most important voyage to date – to bring an end to French nuclear testing once and for all. The boat stopped in Rongelap, one of the Marshall Islands which had been badly affected by US tests during the late 1940s and 1950s. Over a period of ten days, they helped 300 people relocate to a safer island, Mejato, about 120 miles away. During this time, Christine Cabon, a French secret agent posing as an ecologist, was infiltrating the Greenpeace office in New Zealand, supplying her Paris superiors with information about the *Warrior* and its movements. While the boat was docking in Auckland, another ten French agents were converging on the island, bringing explosives, diving gear and, ironically, a Zodiac dingy.

On the night of 10 July, Jean-Michel Bartelo slipped into the waters of Auckland harbour and secured two sets of plastic explosive to the *Warrior's* hull. The leading crew members were attending a regional trustees' meeting at a hotel outside Auckland but a few remained on board. The first bomb blew a hole in the engine compartment. The boat started to sink and the captain, Peter Willcox, ordered everybody off the ship. The second blast trapped Fernando Pereira, a young photographer who had only recently joined the ship. It is thought that he drowned while trying to save his cameras. The news sent shock waves through the organisation and its supporters around the world. At the time, David McTaggart was attending an IWC meeting in England. He immediately assumed the French were involved but then dismissed the notion, thinking 'they couldn't be that stupid'. However, his suspicions were soon confirmed.

The French agents had hardly covered their tracks: two of them carrying Swiss passports were soon exposed and a telephone call they made while in custody was traced to their headquarters in Paris. Bartelo had been seen launching the Zodiac and then loading his diving gear into a van while still dressed in his wetsuit. Investigations by the New Zealand police, the French media and Greenpeace themselves had soon revealed the facts. Two months after the incident, the French Defence Minister resigned and Admiral Lacoste, head of the French secret service, was dismissed. Even President Mitterrand's position seemed threatened. The two French agents in New Zealand were later sentenced to ten years for manslaughter and, in the world media, the arrogance of the French government was the subject of ridicule and embarrassment.

Ironically, the sinking of the *Rainbow Warrior* had drawn even more attention to Greenpeace: membership had risen to 1.2 million and the group spread its web on an increasingly global basis, operating from offices in seventeen countries. Over the next ten years, a whole spectrum of campaigns saw activists trekking through the Nevada nuclear test site, dropping dead fish outside the offices of a polluting paper factory in Sweden and hanging by ropes from bridges across the Rhine. However, like most of their colleagues within the environmental movement, Greenpeace suffered from the 'green fatigue' of the early 1990s. Ironically, this stagnation was displaced by one controversy where the group's good intentions were propelled by questionable research.

In early 1995, Shell announced plans to dispose of an old oil rig, the Brent Spar, by letting it sink to the bottom of the Atlantic, about 150 miles off the coast of Scotland. Greenpeace immediately opposed the idea, claiming that the only acceptable approach was to dismantle the platform on land, allowing the parts to be recycled and any toxic residues to be contained. Two months later, as Shell began towing the Brent Spar out to sea, Greenpeace activists tried to land a helicopter on the platform. They were fended off by water cannons but the episode generated the sensational images required to secure media attention.

Not even Greenpeace predicted the backlash that followed. A boycott spread across Europe as thousands of people protested at Shell petrol stations. The most aggressive demonstrations occurred in Germany, where the company reported a sales drop of 50 per cent and a bomb exploded at a Shell station in Hamburg.[109] Despite the British government's whole-hearted support of Shell's approach, the multinational backed down to consumer pressure after four months, announcing that the Brent Spar would be towed to Norway to be dismantled on land. Humiliated by their decision, John Major publicly referred to the Shell executives as 'wimps' and *The Economist* lamented 'A Defeat for Rational Decision Making'.[110]

Ironically, despite the fact that Greenpeace studies which assessed the ecological impact of the deep-sea disposal had been exposed as inaccurate, the campaign helped to revive the group's image, even rescue it from falling apart. As Naomi Klein observes, the organisation 'had lost credibility because of internal divisions and questionable financial and tactical policies' but the Brent Spar story 'resonated in the public psyche worldwide' because 'here was proof that if multinationals were left to their own devices, there would be no open space left on earth – even the depths of the ocean, the last great wilderness, would be colonized'.[111] The group's membership rose, contributions poured in and Robin Grove-White, the UK Chairman, extolled the significance of the event: 'For the first time, an environmental movement had catalysed international opinion to bring about the kind of change of policy that unsettled the very basis of executive authority. However briefly, the world turned upside down – the rule book had been rewritten.'[112]

Greenpeace has certainly established itself as one of the most prominent organisations within the environmental movement but the high-profile stunts of the early years have given way to more pragmatic solutions like the 'Greenfreeze' fridge, which relies on neither CFCs nor HCFCs, or less-sensational attacks on GM crops. Peter Melchett, who resigned from his leadership in 2000, admitted that it was difficult to 'remain radical in a period where our original methods and objectives are not as relevant as they were'.[113] Melchett, whose great-grandfather was the inventor Alfred Mond and founder of ICI – one of the multinationals which the group has consistently opposed – has been described as 'a Lord who prefers to be called Peter, wears jeans and tee-shirts and commutes to his office by bicycle'.[114] He has since left the organisation to concentrate on his organic farm in Norfolk.

Greenpeace certainly attracted the first wave of 'green' radicals within the environmental movement and pioneered many of the techniques and tactics which are still being used in the field. However, for many within the second wave – the eco-warriors of the last ten years – the organisation has assumed much of the office-bound bureaucracy and corporate identity of the multinationals which they so despise.

The Road of Excess

The first significant international recognition of the environmental crisis was provided by The Club of Rome, a global coalition of scientists, politicians and industralists that convened in Rome during 1968. The initial meeting was inspired by Aureole Peccei, an enterprising Italian businessman, and within two years the organisation encompassed some seventy-five prominent members from twenty-five countries.

In March 1972, The Club of Rome published *The Limits to Growth*, 'a complex computer-model analysis of global economic and environmental trends', edited by Donella Meadows.[115] The book concluded, 'to considerable fanfare in the world press, that the cause of environmental degradation was exponential growth of the global industrial machine and that severe restrictions on population, resource extraction, and agricultural expansion were necessary to avoid catastrophe by the year 2000'.[116] It was a resounding success, selling 9 million copies in twenty-nine languages and precipitating a spate of apocalyptic books whose titles defined the doom-and-gloom agenda of the time: *The Last Days of Mankind*, *The Death of Tomorrow*, *The Doomsday Syndrome*. 'From my point of view as a scientist', Meadows recalls, 'there was nothing more stupidly obvious to say than the earth is finite and growth can't go on forever. I was simply astounded at the number and power and loudness of people who wouldn't accept that.'[117]

Some of the predictions made in these books have failed to occur, much to the delight of those involved in the 'greenwash', the corporations and their employees which seek to undermine the environmental agenda by insisting that the major issues have been brought under control. However, many of the trends, like global warming, have not only been proved correct but now appear to be happening even faster than was first imagined. Events like the oil crisis in 1973 began to press home the point that resources were finite. Meanwhile James Lovelock, who went on to formulate the Gaia Theory, was using his electron capture detector to trace minuscule amounts of synthetic chemicals, from the polar ice caps to the upper atmosphere, and thus proving the link between CFCs and ozone depletion. His findings formed the basis for a report made by two chemists, Sherwood Rowland and Mario Molina, which was first published in *Nature* in 1974 and ultimately led to CFCs being phased out of production.

The first UN Conference on the Human Environment, which took place in Stockholm in the summer of 1972, was prompted by a Biosphere Conference in Paris four years earlier. At the opening session, the British economist Barbara Ward spoke of 'one of those turning points in man's affairs when the human race begins to see itself and its concerns from a new angle of vision'.[118] (Ward first coined the phrase 'Spaceship Earth', the title of her 1966 book which linked economic theory with the environment.

She was the founder of the International Institute for Environment and Development, a dynamic voice at Stockholm and a catalyst for the United Nations Environment Programme, UNEP.) A list of twenty-six principles was formed by 113 national delegations, along with an Action Plan and a monitoring body called Earthwatch.

In *The Green Revolution* Sale describes the conference as a classic example of 'international bureaucratization at its worst' and 'painful evidence that neither individual states nor collective bodies were prepared to alter seriously the long-established systems that led to the crisis and the meeting in the first place'. The fact that the UNEP headquarters was established in Nairobi, completely removed from the decision-making centres of governments and corporations, seemed to undermine the profile of the event and betrayed the way in which political and business leaders were not ultimately prepared to confront the issues. The way in which the conference emphasised the 'protection and improvement of the human environment' highlighted an inherently anthropocentric approach and a failure to incorporate even the most basic ecological principles: issues like biodiversity were not even addressed and it was agreed that all nations had the 'sovereign right to exploit their own resources'.

Following on from an accident at the nuclear power station on Three Mile Island in 1978, mainstream public opinion in America was rocked further by the legacy of Love Canal in New York. A grass-roots campaign, led by a local housewife called Lois Gibbs, revealed that houses and a school had been constructed on the site where the Hooker Chemical Company had dumped toxic waste between 1942 and 1953.[119] Gibbs and the Love Canal Homeowners' Association took grass-roots tactics to new levels, employing external scientists from the Environmental Defense Fund (EDF) to bolster their argument, confronting the State Health Department head-on and catching the media's attention by taking EPA (Environmental Protection Agency) officials hostage.[120] Their efforts paid off. Since 1978 there have been no new hazardous waste dumps in the US. 'Not because they're illegal,' said Gibbs, 'but because people have lobbied at the grass-roots.'[121]

Similar success came to Penny Newman and her McToxics Campaign, drawing mass media attention to McDonald's and their continued use of styrofoam packaging which contained CFCs. Around the country, protesters dressed in styrofoam suits deposited thousands of used burger cartons on McDonald's counters and mailed thousands more to corporate executives. McDonald's denied the problem at first, trying to maintain that styrofoam was 'basically air' and even saying that it helped to aerate the soil.[122] The company finally changed their packaging in 1991, when the EDF's Fred Krupp persuaded Edward Rensi, President of McDonald's, to adopt an alternative.[123]

However, like many triumphs in the environmental arena, the problem was not really resolved, merely shifted to another area.

While the message of the environmental movement was percolating down to conventional sections of society, other groups appeared with more radical ideologies. American exponents of Deep Ecology, like George Sessions and Gary Snyder, had started to advocate ecological equality between all species; bio-regionalism developed in California during the late seventies and saw the planet in terms of topography and biota rather than nation states and their laws; Eco-feminism attacked the patriarchal systems which define western culture, given added thrust by seminal texts like Carolyn Merchant's *Death of Nature*.

The most radical group to emerge during this time was Earth First! Disillusioned with bureaucratic complexity and personal conflict within the Wilderness Society, Dave Foreman and Bart Koehler decided that they 'clearly needed a harder-nosed approach'.[124] After a hiking trip with three others in the Pinacate Desert, down near the Mexican border, Earth First! was formed with a distinctly militant outlook, blending ideological foundations in Deep Ecology with eco-tage (sabotage) tactics inspired by Edward Abbey's novel, *The Monkey Wrench Gang* – the story of radical activists plotting to blow up a dam. The group intentionally avoided any internal organisation, without even a formal membership, and decided that 'in any decision, consideration for the health of the earth must come first'.[125]

Earth First! advocated 'monkey-wrenching', radical techniques for sabotaging bulldozers and spiking trees that were due to be felled. Such confrontational techniques had already been used by 'The Fox', an anonymous activist operating around the Chicago area during the early 1970s.[126] Dubbed the 'ecological Lone Ranger' by the media, 'The Fox' had plugged factory smokestacks and diverted liquid toxic waste from a steel plant into the chief executive's private office. His true identity has never been revealed. In 1978, farmers in Minnesota formed the 'Bolt Weevils', dismantling powerlines and sabotaging construction sites.[127] Earth First! took these tactics to new levels, forming webs in the top of Oregon's old-growth forests and tying the ropes around their own necks. In 1985, Foreman published *Ecodefense: A Field Guide to Monkeywrenching*, giving detailed instructions on topics ranging from Treespiking and Destroying Roads to Decommissioning Heavy Equipment, Trashing Billboards and Leaving No Evidence. 'Monkeywrenching can not only be morally *justified*', believed Foreman, 'but is morally *required*.'[128] Mike Roselle, another one of the group's founders, claimed that monkey-wrenching followed an American tradition – 'Look at the Boston Tea Party' – while others have pointed to the radical measures required for the abolition of slavery.[129]

Meanwhile Murray Bookchin criticised the group for propagating 'eco-fascism' and Foreman alienated many within the movement by making controversial statements about the value of famine, AIDS and even nuclear war in curbing human populations. Foreman believes that 'Environmental groups worry about health hazards to human beings, they worry about clean air and water for the benefit of people and ask us why we're so wrapped up in something as irrelevant and tangential as wilderness. Well, I can tell you, a wolf or a redwood or a grizzly bear doesn't think that wilderness is elitist. Wilderness is the essence of everything. It's the real world.'[130]

By the end of the 1980s, Earth First! had seventy-five groups operating in twenty-four states, causing damage estimated at some $25 million a year.[131] In May 1987, a sawmill operator was nearly decapitated by a piece of blade broken by a spiked log. This led to infiltration by the FBI, who staged an incident, charged Foreman and three others with conspiracy, and filed a lawsuit in July 1989. The following May, two Californian activists were mysteriously killed in a car bombing. The group became divided over Foreman's apparent misanthropy and he split, claiming that it had abandoned bio-centrism in favour of humanism. However, Earth First! lives on in different guises: Julia Butterfly Hill, who recently finished her two-year protest perched in the top of a giant redwood, was affiliated with an Earth First! campaign and many within the UK road protest movement were inspired by the group on this side of the Atlantic.

Earth First! had formed during a difficult time for the environmental movement as a whole. In the summer of 1980, the White House Council on Environmental Quality had presented the then President Jimmy Carter with their Global 2000 Report, a document which warned of 'potential for global problems of alarming proportions by the year 2000'.[132]

Six months later, Ronald Reagan moved into the White House and the report was rapidly consigned to the bin. Sale notes that, despite being the single greatest threat to the global environment, America 'embarked on a decade of unchecked speculative economic growth, fuelled by an unprecedented increase in the national debt, from $4 trillion to $11 trillion' – those are figures with twelve zeros and made the country by far the largest debtor nation in history.[133] Reagan went on to cut the budgets for the EPA and the Council for Environmental Quality in half, scrap programmes in alternative energy sources and appoint the extreme right-winger James

Watt as Secretary of the Interior. Watt made no qualms about intensifying resource use in every part of the economy, from commercial timber use to the agri-business, and famously compared environmentalists to Nazis and Bolsheviks during a speech. His remarks proved so controversial that he was forced to step down in the autumn of 1983.

Five years later, the mid-west and southern states of America were hit by severe drought. Thousands of animals died and a third of the crop harvest was ruined by conditions reminiscent of those which triggered the dust bowl in the early thirties. Forest fires swept through national parks, and the Mississippi dropped so low that boats were left stranded on sand banks. Russia and China also experienced droughts, while major hurricanes struck the Caribbean, fires from the Amazon sent smoke north to the US, and Bangladesh was hit with yet more flooding. In March 1989, the *Exxon Valdez* ran aground in Alaska, spilling 11 million gallons of crude oil and precipitating a 3.5 billion dollar clean-up.[134] Throughout this period, the media were reporting increased acid rain, expanding holes in the ozone layer, species disappearing at a rate of two per hour and rainforests disappearing at the rate of the area of a football field per second. *Time* magazine summed up the feeling of the time: 'This year the earth spoke. Like God warning Noah of the deluge. Its message was loud and clear, and suddenly people began to listen, to ponder what portents the message held.'[135]

George Bush tactfully made the environmental agenda a central part of his campaign but, according to Sale in *The Green Revolution*, 'raised to a new level the art of administrative neglect'. He reluctantly agreed to phasing out CFC production four years earlier than planned, but 'only after presented with incontestable proof that the ozone layer in the northern hemisphere – and over his summer house in Maine – was growing dangerously thin'. After the 1992 Earth Summit in Rio, America became the only country not to ratify the global treaty on carbon dioxide emissions and stood alone in opposing planetary agreements on protecting forests, wetlands and endangered species. Bush countered international pressure by famously declaring that 'The American way of life is not up for negotiation,' illustrating what was becoming increasingly seen as the selfish arrogance of a culture which was contributing five times more to global greenhouse emissions than any other.

The American addiction to oil was the motivating factor during the Gulf War in early 1991, during which some 300 million gallons of it were dumped into Gulf waters, 700 burning wells released 50,000 tons of sulphur dioxide into the atmosphere every day and whole desert eco-systems disappeared.[136] While President Bush continued to push policies that accelerated resource depletion, he still maintained that his administration had 'crafted a new common sense approach to environmental issues, one that honours our love of the environment and our commitment to growth'.[137] Sale refers to another spokesman who was less economical with the truth, saying that 'Americans did not fight and win the wars of the twentieth century to make the world safe for green vegetables,' while the *New York Times* named Bush 'the pillage President'.

The American approach to infinite economic growth, at whatever social or environmental cost, was mirrored by the World Bank, which continued to spend 20 billion dollars a year on projects, displacing an estimated one and a half million people and wiping out entire eco-systems. After organising another national Earth Day in 1990, Dennis Hayes went to the heart of the matter: 'By any number of criteria that you can apply to the sustainability of the planet, we are in vastly worse shape than we were in 1970, despite twenty years of effort.'[138] This trend continues unabated.

Although some believe that Al Gore's influence had an ameliorating impact during the Clinton administration, leading to more land being protected than by any president since Theodore Roosevelt, few environmentalists have welcomed George W. Bush's arrival in the White House. During his tenure as Governor of Texas, the air in the state became the most polluted in the country and oil company executives were appointed to the boards which were supposed to be regulating the industry. Bush promises to allow drilling in Alaska's Arctic National Wildlife Refuge, the last part of the state's northern coast which has been kept off limits for oil exploration and home to a vast herd of caribou, polar bears, wolves and bald eagles. The team chosen to advise the new President on energy issues included fifty experts on energy supply but only one expert on energy efficiency and none whatsoever on renewables.[139] Similarly, those installed in key posts relating to the environment all have reputations as pro-business politicians with unerring faith in the free market. During the electoral campaign, Ann Veneman, now the US Secretary for Agriculture, told Californian farmers that they would be free from 'unnecessary and burdensome' environmental protections under a Bush administration, while Interior Secretary Gale Norton has been described as 'Jim [James] Watt in a skirt'.[140]

However, the most controversial move made by the new President, which made him an international pariah within three months of taking office, was his rejection of the Kyoto Protocol on climate change. The scale of the reaction across the globe has been almost universal, rapidly forcing Bush to modify his position towards the threat of global warming, having first dismissed the scientific evidence as 'questionable'. The 'Toxic Texan', as he was soon branded, defended his position by claiming that Americans 'are now in an energy crisis', predicting that the country would need up to 2,000 power stations over the next twenty years, most of them burning coal. 'Not the cleanest source of energy,' Vice President Dick Cheney conceded, 'but the most plentiful source of affordable energy in the country'.[141] Bush then pushed the point home even further by revealing plans for new nuclear power stations.

The scale of outrage expressed across the globe clearly took the White House by surprise and, when Bush made his first trip to Europe, he was confronted with demonstrations wherever he travelled. Having alienated himself from the negotiations, Bush was even more stigmatised when 186 countries managed to ratify the treaty in Bonn during an intense eleventh-hour session. The US delegation tried to assuage their embarrassment by claiming that US forests would act as 'carbon sinks' and pointing to growing emissions from developing countries. Since the average American creates twenty times the amount of carbon dioxide as the average Indian, and 300 times that of someone from Mozambique,[142] their arguments were merely seen as absurd.

Although Kyoto was euphorically described as a 'historic' event by those involved, it falls a long way short of the necessary targets set by scientists, reducing global warming by just one tenth of a degree over the next hundred years against a projected global rise of nearly six degrees centigrade. As Andrew Simms – head of the New Economics Foundation – points out, there seems to be little point in 'negotiating on how far to build a bridge across a canyon' since 'cutting greenhouse gases is as optional as breathing'.[143] Environmentalist David Suzuki has compared the situation to 'being in a huge car driving at a brick wall at 100 miles an hour and most of the people are arguing about where they want to sit'.[144] Critics of the agreement highlighted the fact that, rather than producing a realistic framework for dealing with the threat of an unliveable biosphere, politicians were celebrating the fact that carbon had become yet another commodity to be traded on financial markets. Michael Meacher, the UK Environment Minister, was busy extolling the virtues of the 'first domestic emissions trading system in the world . . . with the City of London being the major player in the global system of trading carbon',[145] ignoring the fact that carbon trading will become just another area for manipulation by the economic system responsible for the problem itself.

The fact that Bush is President at all has been a source of consternation for observers around the world. There have been well-documented reports about serious manipulation of the electoral process, making a mockery of the entire democratic system. Then there are serious doubts about whether the man is even fit for office; when one learns that the most powerful politician in the world had hardly left the US before he became President, thinks that Greeks are called 'Grecians', Nigeria is 'a very important continent' and 'the great thing about our exports is that more and more of them are going abroad', one cannot help but feel some sense of alarm. The concept of the 'puppet' President has never been made quite so obvious, with George Bush senior apparently spending more time in the White House than he did during his own administration and mounting evidence that the energy corporations are calling the shots with regard to the White House line on global warming. Exxon Mobil, Esso's parent company and the most profitable corporation in history – making $17 billion net income a year – funds the environmental policy project run by Fred Singer, the most vocal sceptic of global warming, and poured $1.2 million into Bush's electoral campaign.[146] The level of corporate manipulation appears more sinister every day, revealing the true extent to which our lives are being controlled by a tiny elite intent on pushing an unsustainable programme of profligate consumption to the four corners of the globe while America's role as the prime generator of global greenhouse emissions continues unchecked.

The tragic events of 11 September 2001 have only accentuated the way in which the American addiction to fossil fuels continues to direct their energy policy on a global stage. The mainstream media persistently seem to ignore the fact that the root cause of the current conflict is oil. As Fritjof Capra points out, the long-brewing hatred for the dominant US military presence in the Middle East stems from 'an extraordinary bargain, concluded in 1945 between President Roosevelt and King Ibn Saud, according to which Saudi Arabia grants the US unlimited and perpetual access to its oil fields (which contain 25% of the world's known oil reserves!) in exchange for protection of the Saudi royal family against its enemies, both external and internal. This bargain has shaped American foreign and military policy for almost half a century, during which we have protected a totalitarian regime in Saudi Arabia that blatantly disregards basic human rights and tramples democracy.'[147]

Through the Bush administration's outright dismissal of alternative energy sources and total reliance on maintaining current levels of fossil fuel use, the American energy crisis that Bush has predicted is very real indeed – hence the drilling in Alaska. Since China's oil consumption is expected to outstrip that of the US within ten years, the scrabble for fossil fuel reserves is accelerating every day. After initiating military action in Afghanistan, it transpires that America has its eye on gas in Turkmenistan – enough to supply the US for thirty years – which it hopes to pipe to the Arabian Gulf. The build-up of US military might near the oil-rich area around the Caspian Sea starts to seem more strategic than purely a war against terrorism. Some maintain that plans for military action in the area had been finalised in July 2000, over a year before the attack on the twin towers took place.[148] One writer has highlighted an article in the Egyptian press which 'maps the relationship between oil, arms and key members of the American adminstration. Not a conspiracy theory, rather a practical acknowledgement that "oil, defence and politics . . . are not mutually exclusive interests."'[149]

Of course, the American media have conveniently overlooked the deeper issues, leaving the population ill-informed about the real reasons why there is such hatred for US foreign policy around the world. Imprisoned by their own media, the majority of the American public are kept in the dark about the role their country is playing overseas. As Gerald Celente, from the Trends Research Institute, has remarked, 'You are dealing with people who are almost child-like as a nation in their understanding of what is going on in the world. It's all: "We never did anything to anybody, so why are they doing this to us."' However, as George Bush and his advisors know only too well, the last thing they really want is a truly informed electorate to start raising too many questions. In the end, 'the global war on terror' becomes a very convenient way to over-shadow the most critical issue which threatens every one of us – global warming.

In the same way that there is a level of ignorance about the consequences of American foreign policy, there is also an unerring faith in the benefits that globalisation brings to the rest of the world, moving hand in hand with what is seen as American cultural imperialism. All around the globe, from small French market towns to villages in Asia, millions of people are making it clear that they do not want their traditional diet to be replaced by hamburgers and milkshakes, that they do not want their culture homogenised into American brand names and their ancient agricultural systems to become conveyor belts for products concocted by biotechnology corporations. Like everywhere else in the world, the implications of the global economic machine have started shifting the emphasis of the US environmental movement towards a more unilateral condemnation of free trade agreements, World Bank policies and the power of multinational corporations. The web has begun to expand, uniting environmentalists with human rights organisations, the women's movement, animal welfare groups and trade unions.

This new agenda peaked in a dramatic crescendo at the end of 1999, when some 50,000 protesters converged on Seattle and effectively brought the World Trade Organisation (WTO) summit to a resounding halt. According to one observer, after a few days of protest at the end of November 1999, 'much of Seattle's shiny veneer had been scratched off, the WTO talks had collapsed in futility and acrimony and a new multinational popular resistance had blackened the eyes of global capitalism and its shock troops.'[150]

Outfits like the Ruckus Society, founded in Berkeley in 1995, ran camps and seminars to train protesters in non-violent civil disobedience, teaching budding activists how to cope with pepper spray, rubber bullets and tear gas, how to form blockades and respond to police intimidation while staying within the law. Similar information was contained in thousands of leaflets which were circulated through the crowds during the demonstrations. An abandoned warehouse formed The Convergence point, later described as 'far more than a meeting place', being 'part factory, part barracks, part command and control centre'.[151] One reporter described some of the elaborate preparations:

> Inside affinity groups were planning their separate direct actions and getting training in non-violence; others were constructing giant puppets, bearing the likeness of corporate titans and politicians, such as Clinton and Charles Hurwitz; while another group, led by Earth First!ers from Eugene, were constructing what one referred to as the Trojan Horse, a twenty foot tall, armoured siege tower on wheels, capable of holding 14 people.[152]

When the demonstration turned into violent confrontation, the warehouse doubled as an infirmary.

Typically, most of the mainstream media tended to focus on the anarchic elements of the protest, ignoring the fact that important new alliances were developing within an expanding movement. The Building Trade Unions left work at ten in the morning to join the demonstration, as did nearly a thousand workers from the Machinists' Union. The Longshore Workers closed down several West Coast ports at the same time. Jose Bove, the charismatic Gallic leader of Confederation Paysanne, the French environmental group which had raided a new McDonald's being built in Larzac, made an appearance with rounds of Roquefort, the cheese which the US had slapped a huge tariff on in response to the EU decision to ban hormone-treated beef from the US. After a rousing speech against the evils of Monsanto, their bovine growth hormone rBST and genetically modified soya, he handed out pieces of cheese as the assembled crowd stormed the nearest McDonald's, breaking the windows and urging customers to join the protest.

This proved to be a pivotal moment – 'the first shot in the battle for Seattle'.[153] A few hours later, the city was deemed to be in 'a state of civic emergency, a step away from martial law. National Guard helicopters hovered over downtown, sweeping the city with searchlights. A 7 p.m. curfew had been imposed and was being flouted by thousands – thousands who had captured the streets, sustained clouds of tear gas, volleys of rubber bullets, blasts from concussion grenades and beatings with riot batons.'[154] The levels of brutality displayed by the police, in their Star Wars stormtrooper-style riot gear, were caught by the world media. As protesters were beaten to the ground with 4-foot clubs, the crowds chanted in the background – 'The whole world is watching. The whole world is watching.' Two days later, television cameras captured the moment when a local resident, entirely unconnected with the protest, was hit in the chest with a baton, kicked in the groin and then shot in the neck with a rubber bullet. Independent witnesses recorded few unprovoked violent attacks by the protesters, most of whom were armed with little more than water bottles or cardboard placards. Far from indiscriminate looting or damage to property, the stores that were vandalised were specifically targeted as prime exponents of the corporate greed that the protest was aiming to expose, 'the boutiques of Sweatshop Row': Adidas, The Gap, Niketown, Banana Republic and Starbucks.

Seattle will be remembered as something of a watershed, a time when the establishment underestimated the forces of opposition and a time when direct action fulfilled its aims. The entire WTO meeting was reduced to a fiasco and the forces of the State had used brutal violence in response. 'Today, the police in Seattle have proved they are the handmaidens of the corporations,' said veteran campaigner David Brower at the time. 'But something else has been proved. And that's that people are starting to stand up and say: We won't be transnational victims.'[155] Environmental writer and activist Helena Norberg-Hodge observes that 'Before Seattle people did not see that trade treaties were having such a disruptive impact' and that business leaders, and politicians have since 'been forced to change their language'.[156] At the same time, a consolidated European movement was delivering hefty blows to Monsanto, whose stock price slumped as a result. The network was expanding and the tide continued to rise against globalisation and its corporate agents.

The Ecology of Hollywood

Los Angeles serves well to illustrate the way in which contemporary American environmentalism is trying to shed its past obsession with wilderness and tackle the complex ecological problems posed by chronic urbanisation. It has always been an unlikely city. Built over a major seismic fault, on the edge of one of the world's most inhospitable deserts, the City of Angels developed like the extension of a Hollywood movie set, a sprawling urban fantasy which many people feel should not really exist. D.J. Waldie, a city official and environmental spokesman, refers to the 'persistent mythology of Los Angeles that doubts its reality, its legitimacy and authenticity as a place'.[157] It has been estimated that land and water in the area could naturally support 200,000 people, not 15 million.[158]

After the 1880s, the Los Angeles basin was transformed from desert chaparral, surrounding a sleepy cattle town with a population of 4,000, into a seething metropolis that now accounts for nearly 1 per cent of total global greenhouse emissions. It is the car culture *par excellence*, with over 30 per cent of the land mass devoted to streets, freeways and parking, while 9 million cars contribute to 18 million pounds of smog and air pollution.[159] It is somewhat ironic that, in a city where smoking cigarettes is almost illegal, 40 per cent of the population suffer from respiratory problems due to vehicle emissions.[160] But Los Angeles is built on contradictions. Regarded as the urban embodiment of the American Dream, the apotheosis of consumerism and material extravagance, the city is often seen as the essence of anti-Nature. Paradoxically, people often move to Los Angeles *because* of Nature, attracted by the climate, the snow-capped mountains, the ocean and the beaches. The movie industry moved there because of the clarity of the light, the 270 days of sunshine per year and the diversity of locations on the doorstep. The fantasy which took shape in the early years, with the introduction of palm trees and orange groves, continues today in Hollywood gardens and the city's few green spaces; native trees are usurped in favour of exotic imports as Nature is moulded to conform to an ideal. The irony continues in the fact that no city in the world is more prone to natural disasters; the earthquakes, floods and mudslides are often interpreted as Nature's vengeance against 'the plastic society'. In his book *Ecology of Fear*, the LA writer Mike Davis portrays a sort of modern-day Sodom and Gomorrah, drawing attention to the forty-nine nuclear strikes, twenty-eight earthquakes, ten plagues, six floods and thirty-five other forms of destruction that the city has been subjected to by Hollywood's writers and film-makers.

The fantasy has always depended on one fundamental resource – water. No metropolis on the planet has looked further afield for its supply and the fact that there are 'no more rivers to bring to the desert' is a cause of much concern. The natural water-table was exhausted in four decades and, when the wells ran dry in the 1890s, watermelons were smashed at the base of trees in desperate attempts at emergency irrigation. In 1913, when the controversial Los Angeles Aqueduct was first opened, diverting water over 230 miles from the Owens Valley, chief engineer William Mulholland proclaimed that it would supply Hollywood's lawns and swimming pools forever.

Within ten years the city needed more. In 1940 the aqueduct was extended 105 miles north to Mono Lake, while the completion of the Hoover Dam the following year allowed southern California to tap into Arizona, reducing the Colorado River to a sad, salty trickle. This was thwarted in the 1950s, when the US Supreme Court settled in favour of Arizona's claim to the supply. Now the city is dependent on all of the above, together with the State Water Project, which brings more than a trillion gallons of water per year along the 450 mile Californian Aqueduct. This effectively removes half the water that would otherwise flow into the San Francisco Bay area, altering the flow of fresh-water and salt-water in the Sacramento Delta but supplying irrigation systems for the vast agricultural base of the San Joaquim Valley, a desert with less than 5 inches of rain per year.

Almost a third of the water feeding Los Angeles is now pumped from underground aquifers. However, a combination of illegal dumping, run-off from commercial fertilisers and leakage from garbage landfills has left some 40 per cent of the wells in southern California contaminated above federal limits.[161] To compound the problem, half of the considerable winter rainfall, which would permeate the soil and re-charge the aquifers, is swallowed by concrete drainage systems and diverted into the Pacific. Since intensive farming methods require an estimated 4,500 gallons of water to produce what an average Californian eats in a day, the issue of water supply is never far away.[162] Desperation has led to some ambitious proposals, ranging from a plastic pipeline from Alaska to towing icebergs up from Antarctica.

What few Los Angelinos are aware of today is that the city is actually built on a river. The basin that surrounds the city itself was originally created by four tectonic river plates and the so-called LA River, which stretches for 58 miles from the Valley down to Long Beach, passing through the Hollywood studios and Chinatown, is the central natural feature of the city. At one time, it was shaded by sycamores, oaks and willows. However, as the city was paved over, the winter floods created a threat to economic expansion and, in the 1930s, work began to erase the river altogether. 'The Army Corps of Engineers built a concrete trough, put the river inside it and fenced it off with barbed wire,' explains Jennifer Price, an environmental writer living in the city. 'The river became the ultimate symbol of LA's destruction of Nature.'[163] Inevitably, the concrete 'flood control system' had disastrous ecological consequences, destroying wetland areas which provided an important staging area for migratory birds on the Great Pacific Flyway. The empty concrete channel is now used as an area for training municipal bus drivers to turn round and it has even been suggested that it be used as a freeway during the dry season. Fittingly, it is best known today as the location for Hollywood car chases.

Plans are now underway to restore the river, to re-create wetland areas to attract birds, establish nature walks, cycle paths and equestrian trails. In true Hollywood style there has even been talk about white-water rafting through the Sepulveda Basin. Led by the Friends of LA River, a pressure group formed by poet and film-maker Lewis McAdams, the project has pulled people together from government agencies, environmental groups and neighbourhood associations, all working together in what is being seen as a symbolic attempt to heal the split between the population and the landscape of the city. 'We're beginning to wake up to the fact that Nature is not something "out there" but "in here",' says Price. 'The population of LA has forgotten that it lives on a river.'[164]

The resulting hybrid river, part concrete and part natural, again seems indicative of the 'fantasy' city and its intrinsic irony. 'The LA River is a social construct in the purest terms', says D.J. Waldie, a prominent campaigner for the project. 'It was designed as a real estate protection device and as a flood control system. It is a quintessentially LA product, a synthesis of reality and artifice. Consequently, its rehabilitation will be an interplay between these two factors, partly real and largely artificial.'[165] Waldie maintains that Los Angeles was always conceived in these terms, as a 'unique interpenetration of Nature and urban development'. The early planners assumed that this would be 'the perfect Arcadian place to build the ideal house and the ideal garden'.[166] Of course, this dream of a Californian utopia has constantly clashed with the realities of the landscape during the last hundred years, creating what has often been cited as the epitome of a *dystopia*.

Perhaps the most prominent feature of this modern urban landscape is 'the grid', first introduced during Spanish colonisation. Colonel Philippe de

Neve, the Governor of Upper California in 1781, laid out plans for the town in strict accordance with regulations derived from Roman models, believed to be part of a divine plan for imposing moral order on the natural world. With the advent of cartography, which coincided with the exploration of the continent, US President Thomas Jefferson divided the country up into a giant grid. However, when the early Anglo-American settlers arrived in California, they found that the Spanish grid was at 45 degrees to the compass points which determined the direction of the Jefferson grid. Consequently, one can still find pockets of LA where the Spanish grid remains, slicing across the modern streets at an angle.

Waldie sees the rigidity of the grid as a way of 'imposing security on a fairly severe and simple landscape', a sentiment which is echoed by William Fox, another environmental writer working in the city: 'When the first settlers came from the mid-West, crossing the vast Mojave desert, they moved from an area in the agrarian rectilinear tradition and, of course, they replicated the grid.'[167] Fox sees the grid as mankind's attempt to control Nature. 'When you over-rule the landscape with a grid of streets, you think you rule over the characteristics of it – the seismic faults, the mudslides and the floods.' This, he believes, is of particular significance in a desert landscape, where there are 'no strong verticals, like trees, to measure our scale and sense of distance.' The grid therefore, is 'connected to the neuro-physiology of human beings' because 'right angles are very easy for us to recognise'. Fox traces the grid back to Mesopotamia and thus draws parallels with another semi-arid landscape: 'The grid evolves out of the desert as a way of coping with large empty spaces.'[168]

The desert has always had a powerful effect on the public consciousness of Los Angeles, not least on Hollywood itself. In keeping with American beliefs about Nature as some redemptive sacred place removed from everyday life, the desert landscape is often aligned with personal transformation. Fox believes that 'Hollywood has this romance with the desert, seeing it as an enormous blank screen on which to create,' but points out that 'if you drive around the area where these people live, you'll see lots of green lawns and tropical vegetation'.

Waldie sees Los Angeles as 'a place where people have always come to fundamentally reinvent their lives'.[169] It therefore seems appropriate that the city has become a forum for redefining American environmental thought. Now that we have become a predominantly urban species for the first time in our history, there seems to be a shift from wilderness preservation towards issues of urban sustainability. 'The idea that Nature can save your soul has always been the underpinning of American environmentalism,' says

Jennifer Price.[170] 'However, people increasingly realise that it's not possible to preserve wilderness without thinking about the areas where we use Nature the most. We need to think about how we're part of Nature in much more material and specific ways. If you define Nature as "out there", you don't have to think about how you use it "in here".'

Being a prime example of Nature's confluence with human culture, Los Angeles clearly provides the perfect platform to examine this interaction and make progress towards a sustainable urban environment. 'If we actually thought about how to retain the water that falls from the sky', says Price, 'we wouldn't be so dependent on water sources hundreds of miles away.'[171] Various initiatives have now been implemented in this vein: a huge waste water recycling plant has recently been developed in Santa Monica while environmental groups like The Tree People are re-designing drainage systems to collect run-off and re-direct it into underground aquifers.

There is a feeling of optimism about the future of Nature in a city which has always been regarded as being in fundamental opposition to it, leading to a more integrated ecological vision for the twenty-first century. 'The idea that LA shouldn't be here is rather like the belief that you either have Nature or you don't,' says Price. 'We stand to gain a lot more by thinking of ourselves as part of Nature.' Therefore, those involved with the restoration of the LA river see it not only as being important for ecological sustainability and a way of linking disparate communities, but also as being of tremendous significance symbolically. 'There is a feeling that if you can fix the LA River, you can fix the city,' believes Price. 'And if you can fix *this* city, it seems possible that you can fix any city.'[172]

3

Anarchy in the UK

Dissent without civil disobedience is consent.

HENRY THOREAU

Enclosure: Our Land is Stolen

For the last thousand years, the majority of the British people have been alienated from the land into which they were born. At the time of the Domesday Book in 1086, more than half the arable land in the country belonged to peasant villagers. By 1876, the New Domesday Book estimated that 2,250 people owned half the agricultural land in England and Wales and that 0.6 per cent of the population owned 98.5 per cent of the country.[1]

Many people feel that the land, like the air we breathe and the water we drink, should be our birthright. Instead, it is owned and managed by an elite which does everything in its powers to conceal the extent to which it controls the shape of our countryside and to deny the public access. The concept of land ownership, which has been adopted by most of the world, was developed within British shores, turning the ecosystems that provide our food, and the labour used to cultivate it, into tradeable commodities. The system was then extrapolated to the four corners of the globe by colonisation.

The very notion of an individual 'owning' a piece of land, and all that is contained therein, was incomprehensible to the native tribal cultures which were systematically plundered by this process. In a tribal network, the land is shared and maintained by the community, providing food and sustaining a symbiotic balance between humans and the physical environment. Within a hierarchical social organisation, the system of property ownership is manipulated by a land-owning elite to generate profit. It almost invariably leads to social injustice, the depletion of resources and the loss of soil fertility.

Modern pollen analysis shows that agriculture was well established in the British Isles some 4,000 years before the arrival of the Romans.[2] The culture that built the Neolithic temples at Avebury and Stonehenge, and countless other burial mounds, monuments and stone circles scattered across the country, was clearly more sophisticated than our textbook historical education would have us believe. The amount of time and energy required to construct these sites, and the sheer scale of the work involved, suggest that their agricultural base was well established, generating surplus crops which could be stored for future use. Similarly, the relatively small numbers of people buried in the long barrow tombs would seem to indicate that a social hierarchy with a ruling class had evolved, creating a further distinction from the hunter-gatherer culture which came before. Far from being the savages dressed in animal skins which history has portrayed them as, this was a culture with advanced engineering skills, detailed astronomical knowledge and plenty of time on its hands to stage dramatic religious rituals.

However, around 1500 BC these people stopped building. Small farming settlements appeared, sharing vast networks of fields which stretched to thousands of acres.[3] We can only speculate about how this land was managed but it has been suggested that the ruling elite which orchestrated the construction of the religious sites had been overthrown and replaced by a network of peasant farmers living in small communities. During the Bronze Age and Iron Age, however, building began again, although this time it took the form of fortified settlements. The advent of metal tools not only led to advances in agricultural productivity, but also to the development of weapons. Settled agriculture within territorial limits generated conflict over resources between neighbouring communities and the concept of land ownership was gradually established. Two thousand years ago this was displaced by the Roman Empire, an extensive centralised powerbase which required intensive farming practices to support it, thus precipitating the desertification of North Africa and the arid ecosystems of the modern Mediterranean. The depletion of this agricultural base, due to factors such as over-grazing, soil erosion and drought, has been well documented as the underlying cause for the collapse of the Roman economy and the subsequent decline of the Empire.

Anglo-Saxon England was owned by independent peasant proprietors known as *ceorls*, with each family farming a smallholding which provided the food they required. By the time of the Norman Conquest in 1066, this system was effectively controlled by the *thegns*, territorial lords who demanded food from the *ceorls* as a form of rent. However, the system of land ownership that existed was restricted to those that cultivated the soil, and much of the country remained as common land, available to all for grazing animals, collecting food or gathering firewood. William the Conqueror then rewarded his knights by distributing vast areas of his new kingdom among them, creating the basic division of land which survives to this day. The present Duke of Westminster, for example, the biggest private landowner in the country, is descended from the Norman knight Hugh Le Gros Veneur who, in exchange for part of Cheshire, was responsible for keeping the unruly Welsh from crossing the River Dee.[4] William abolished independent peasant ownership of the land and most of the English population became ensnared in the feudal pyramid as serfs, forced to work on land which they could never own. At the same time, much of the common land became the royal playground, devoted entirely to hunting – by the time of Henry II, the royal forests incorporated a quarter of the country.[5]

In 1348, the Black Death killed one and a half million people, about a third of the population.[6] This drastic cut in the labour force, and the growth of the wool industry, led some landowners to convert their arable land to sheep pasture and to accept rent in the form of cash rather than feudal dues. Although this gave some serfs more freedom, it created divisions and conflicts within the rural population. The introduction of a new tax, to pay for the Hundred Years War with France, led to the Peasants' Revolt of 1381, when 100,000 people marched on London and took over the city for several days. Led by men like Wat Tyler and John Ball, the rebels demanded the abolition of the feudal system, the disendowment of the Church and a return to the free use of the forests. Although the King ostensibly agreed to the demands, he arrested and beheaded the leaders as soon as the uprising dispersed.

The first Act of Enclosure, the Statute of Merton, was introduced in 1235, but the process did not gather momentum until the fifteenth century. Attracted by the booming market for exported wool, landowners evicted thousands of peasants from their smallholdings and fenced off common land for sheep. In 1552, Bishop Latimer defended those that were dispossessed: 'As for turning the poor out of their holdings, they take it for no offence, but say their land is their own and they turn them out of their shrouds like mice. Thousands in England, through such, beg now from door to door which have kept honest houses.'[7] A traditional rhyme also attacked the hypocrisy of the process:

> They hang the man and flog the woman
> That steal the goose from off the common,
> But let the greater villain loose
> That steals the common from the goose.[8]

The revolution in the mid-seventeenth century gave new power to landowners that would benefit from enclosures, and the system proliferated across the country. Some 4,000 Private Acts of Enclosure were passed between the early eighteenth century and the General Enclosure Act of 1845, during which time 7 million acres were legally transferred from the common people to a land-owning elite.[9] It is estimated that another 7 million acres were enclosed without application to Parliament – essentially stolen from the people. When cotton started to be imported in the nineteenth century, and the wool industry went into decline, landowners looked to new agricultural methods like the complex crop rotations advocated by Arthur Young and 'Turnip' Townsend. Jethro Tull had invented the seed drill, allowing farmers to sow three rows of seeds simultaneously. By amalgamating several farms and introducing these new methods, the landowners found that they could raise the rents by staggering amounts. The government was happy to reap higher taxes as a consequence, helping to pay for the costs of war with France which, in turn, benefited farmers by inflating the price of food.

However, various external social and environmental costs arose as a result: huge areas of heath and forest were destroyed; ancient meadows were ploughed up to take short-term advantage of artificially high corn prices and, when prices dropped again, discarded as degraded pasture; most importantly, it led to the creation of an underclass, thousands of dispossessed labourers who could no longer feed themselves from their own land or afford the high price of corn. In one of the first major protests against the enclosures, John Ket's rebellion of 1549 had drawn 16,000 people to a camp near Norwich, from which they 'scoured the country around, destroyed enclosures, filled in ditches, levelled fences'.[10]

Like the Luddites, who lost their jobs to mechanisation, the landless labourers of the nineteenth century went on the rampage, burning farm buildings and inciting riots across the country. The repeal of the Corn Laws in 1846 alleviated the situation by allowing the importation of cheap American wheat, while the enforced demise of the textile industry in India and other colonies opened up opportunities for factory work in England. However, by the beginning of the twentieth century, the distribution of land in the British Isles remained firmly in the hands of a land-owning elite. Agriculture was in decline and the externalised costs of the enclosure policy – the social and environmental consequences of alienating people from the land and encouraging intensive farming practices – had spread across the globe.

The Diggers: The Birth of Direct Action

The story of Robin Hood and his band of merry men, who stole from the rich and gave to the poor, may be part of one of the first examples of environmental protest in British history. The area around Nottingham, which includes the legendary Sherwood Forest, was one of the first parts of the country to become involved in the expansion of the wool industry. The commonly owned woods were cleared to make way for sheep grazing and it was not long before the great Barnsdale and Sherwood forests had been reduced to a few scattered clumps of conifers and oaks. Kirkpatrick Sale maintains that 'for all the enduring resonance of this tale, in historical fact it was the royal policy of clear-cutting and wool manufacturing over the commons that prevailed'.[11]

The issue of common land was undoubtedly at the core of protests which have been cited as the birth of 'direct action'. One Sunday morning in April 1649, a band of forty men and women made their way on to St George's Hill, near Walton-on-Thames in Surrey. Over the following weeks, they dug and manured the land, planted 6 acres with grain, rye, parsnips and carrots, and built eleven make-shift shelters. Their aim was to 'work in righteousness and lay the foundation of making the earth a common treasury for all'.[12]

The Diggers were led by Gerard Winstanley, the son of a mercer from Wigan. After a chequered career in the London cloth trade, Winstanley worked as a hired labourer and wrote mystical religious pamphlets before turning his attention to 'a system of progressive and democratic rationalism'.[13] He believed that the State kept the poor enslaved through the system of property ownership and proposed that the substantial areas of land in the country that were not properly cultivated should be turned over to the people to be farmed: 'If the waste land of England were manured by her children, it would become in a few years the richest, the strongest and most flourishing land in the world.'[14] By taking over the common land, Winstanley hoped to pave the way for a new utopia; he believed that 'true freedom lies where a man receives his nourishment and preservation, and that is in the use of the earth',[15] and that 'there cannot be a universal liberty till this universal community is established'.[16]

The Diggers were the product of radical times. Throughout the English Revolution, the historian Christopher Hill observes that 'Men felt free: free from hell, free from priests, free from fear of worldly authorities, free from the blind forces of Nature, free from magic.'[17] Hill cites the Diggers and their manifesto as one of the earliest forms of communism, 'a draft constitution for a communist commonwealth', while Peter Marshall sees them as some of the first British anarchists, created from the bands of 'masterless men', who roamed the countryside calling for 'the abolition of all masters'. In true anarchist style, Winstanley saw that external government would be superfluous if people would just 'govern themselves according to their God-given Reason'. He felt that 'the present state of the old world is running up like parchment in the fire' and saw the concept of private land ownership as the source of division and conflict within society rather than blaming human nature itself.[18]

Despite the fact that other factions sprang up across the country, from Cox Hall in Kent to Bosworth in Leicestershire, the Diggers' occupation at St George's Hill did not last long. They were harassed by everyone from the local clergy and magistrates to the landowners and farmers themselves. Their crops were trampled into the ground, their houses torn down and, after a brief attempt to continue their action a few miles away on Cobham Heath, they disbanded one year after they had formed.[19]

Their efforts had not been entirely in vain. The potential for direct action tactics was borne out by the fact that Oliver Cromwell felt sufficiently threatened by their protest to bring the Diggers before General Fairfax, who subsequently sent soldiers to intimidate them. Peter Marshall believes that 'Cromwell was right to see their experiment as profoundly subversive for the motley band of Diggers threatened the very foundations of his totalitarian rule.'[20] Key players in the American Revolution, such as Thomas Paine and Thomas Spence, are thought to have been influenced by Winstanley's vision, and *The Law of Freedom*, his major work, has continued to resurface in the political underground ever since.[21] In May 1996, a pressure group called The Land is Ours took over a 13 acre site next to Wandsworth Bridge in London and started building an eco-village, installing alternative energy systems and building raised vegetable beds. Although they were evicted from the site by the brewing giant Guinness, the group continue to campaign for land reform in Britain, drawing inspiration directly from Gerard Winstanley and his Diggers.

Green Roots

The 'green agenda' of today has been related to the politics of anarchism, which is coherent with many ecological principles and has been upheld throughout British history. Contrary to the chaos and disintegration which the word usually implies, its political exponents believe in society's potential for self-regulation.

As Peter Marshall so comprehensively shows,[22] the basic concepts of this misinterpreted political tradition have been supported by an eclectic spectrum of adherents, ranging from Greek philosophers to the Russian aristocrat Prince Peter Kropotkin, from the ancient Chinese teachings of Taoism to the findings of modern ecology. They suggest that society is a self-regulating order that functions best when least interfered with, that centralised government and a social hierarchy are in opposition to the laws of Nature, that unity can be best achieved through diversity, and harmony through complexity. For anarchists, the whole notion of an external authority, or centralised power, is not only considered responsible for ruining the lives of millions, but is positively disruptive to the social order. Marshall observes how, when asked what they would replace government with, the anarchist answer is: 'What do you replace cancer with?'[23]

Using the mechanical metaphors so beloved at the time, Pierre-Joseph Proudhon, a nineteenth-century French anarchist, saw that society was in 'eternal motion: it does not have to be wound up; and it is not necessary to beat time for it. It carries its own pendulum and its ever-wound up spring with it. An organized society needs laws as little as legislators. Laws are to society what cobwebs are to bee-hives. They only serve to catch the bees.'[24] Like the Hindu, Taoist and Buddhist vision, which sees all life as a dynamic interaction between the polar opposites of shiva and shakti, or yin and yang, anarchists see Nature and society as existing like water in a river, a fluid process which never stagnates. The Greek writer Heraclitus, who would have been a contemporary of the Buddha and the writing of the Upanishads, observed that 'You cannot step twice in the same river.' Over 2,000 years later, Alexander Pope, the eighteenth-century British poet, expressed a similar insight with this zen-like aphorism, 'Whatever is, is right.'[25]

This position is often seen as promoting apathy, passivity, even nihilism. However, the Taoist and the anarchist would regard that as a misconception, a failure to look at the whole. Since the use of force is logically followed by a loss of strength, the Tao does not advocate defeatist submission but the effective use of energy: 'Practise non-action. Work without doing.' The western ego finds it almost impossible to understand this concept, since we are conditioned to believe that goals can only be achieved through the exertion of effort, and that the more energy that is expended in pursuit of something, the more likely it is to be realised. Taoism, on the other hand, exposes the inconsistent logic maintained by the western ego, highlighting the inherent energy of water: 'Under heaven nothing is more soft and yielding than water. Yet for attacking the solid and strong, nothing is better; it has no equal. The weak can overcome the strong; the supple can overcome the stiff.'[26]

William Godwin was lauded by the Romantic poets and has been described as both 'the first great British anarchist' and 'the father of philosophical anarchism'. He inspired the political radicalism of Percy Bysshe Shelley and the gloomy demographic projections made by Thomas Malthus. (Shelley eloped with Godwin's daughter Mary Wollstonecraft, who went on to write *Frankenstein*.) At the time, William Hazlitt claimed that Godwin 'blazed as a sun in the firmament of reputation; no one was more talked of, more looked up to, more sought after, and wherever liberty, truth, and justice was the theme, his name was not far off.'[27]

Born to a family of Dissenters, a group that consciously rejected the Church of England, Godwin's radical streak was to some extent genetically encoded. At an early age, he had modified the predominant Newtonian paradigm of Nature-as-machine, suggesting that not only are all actions determined by previous causes, but that the manifestation of the physical universe was produced by the mind. These assumptions formed the foundation of his world-view and the basis for his most famous work, *An Enquiry concerning Political Justice, and its Influence on General Virtue and Happiness*, published two weeks after Britain declared war on revolutionary France in 1793. Priced at an exhorbitant three guineas, the book was the first detailed proposal for a society without government and made Godwin instantly famous. Some years later, the young Shelley would use the book as the philosophical basis for his revolutionary narrative poetry, much of which contains anarchist sentiments.

For Godwin, government and society were fundamentally at odds; the former is stagnant, unable to evolve due to the inertia imposed by the human creation of an institution designed to be permanent, while the latter is in a state of constant flux, continually shifting and adapting to all that it is intimately involved with as a living system. He believed that capitalist economics encouraged a 'servile and truckling spirit'[28] and looked forward to 'the dissolution of political government, of that brute engine which has been the only perennial cause of the vices of mankind'.[29] While objecting to the de-humanising aspect of factory labour, he endorsed various technologies produced by the Industrial Revolution which alleviated the miseries endured by previous generations. Godwin believed that science might ultimately render matter subservient to the human mind, and even speculated about immortality. His vision for Britain was of a 'decentralized and simplified society consisting of voluntary associations of free and equal individuals', the sort of utopian co-operative society envisaged by early communism. Godwin adamantly believed in the perfectibility of man, that evolution was heading towards the Omega Point defined by the Jesuit theologian Teilhard de Chardin, culminating in a time when 'there will be no war, no crime, no administration of justice, as it is called, and no government'.[30]

If Godwin's maverick ideas seem prescient of hippie idealism within the modern environmental movement, Reverend Thomas Malthus – and his warnings about the expanding human population – can be likened to the misanthropic statements of Earth First! founder Dave Foreman.

Like Foreman, Malthus believed that war, famine and disease were essential natural processes, designed to stabilise the human population – his world-view saw a place for small-pox, slavery and murder. His famous book, *An Essay on the Principle of Population as It Affects the Future Improvement of Society* (1798), inspired Darwin's concept of 'survival of the fittest' and became the first demographic study to predict that an exponential increase in the human population could not be sustained by the limitations of the resource base. Although he had been impressed by Godwin's work, Malthus dealt a devastating blow to the anarchist dream of a harmonious future. He transformed a prevailing optimism to pessimism. Rather than the utopian paradise of a world without 'disease, anguish, melancholy or resentment', he presented a diverging pattern between human consumption and Nature's capacity to provide.

The debate that Malthus began continues to this day. However, the notion that infinite growth might not actually be possible in a finite world only gained significant political credence with *The Limits to Growth* report, published by the Club of Rome in 1972. The editor of the book, Donella Meadows, made the following conclusion: 'We are convinced that realization of the quantitative restraints of the world environment and the tragic consequences of an overshoot is essential to the initiation of new forms of thinking that will lead to a fundamental revision of human behaviour and, by implication, of the entire fabric of present day society.'[31] The study also warned that without 'significant reductions in material and energy flows, there will be in the coming decades an uncontrolled decline in per capita food output, energy use and industrial production'. The only way of avoiding this would be 'a comprehensive revision of policies and practices that perpetuate growth in material consumption and in population', together with a 'rapid, drastic increase in the efficiency with which materials and energy are used'.[32]

Four years earlier, Paul Ehrlich's *The Population Bomb* foretold of a catastrophic future, a global melt-down caused by the proliferation of the human race. Critics have subsequently accused Ehrlich's book of being 'an invitation to genocide' and exposed the way in which certain trends have failed to follow the predicted patterns, highlighting the fact that many countries in the West have actually stabilised with zero population growth (ZPG).

While it is true that birth control and family planning have achieved remarkable results in some countries, the human population continues to expand at an astonishing rate, especially when seen in the historical context of evolutionary time. The human impact on the planet is further intensified as developing nations industrialise and adopt the profligate consumption patterns seen in the west. With most of the world's fisheries on the point of collapse, and 26 billion tons of topsoil being lost every year, the disparity between population growth and resource use does not seem destined to diminish. In 1996, Paul Ehrlich accepted that 'population over the past half century was for a time matched by similar worldwide increases in utilizable resources', but noticed that 'in the past decade food production from both land and sea has declined relative to population growth'.[33] Technologists use the possibility that there might be a limit to the Earth's carrying capacity to support their plans for colonising other planets. Since only a handful of people have so far left the atmosphere, transport plans for this mass migration seem to be somewhat compromised.

Like Gerard Winstanley and the Diggers, a number of anarchic political groups have appeared throughout British history. Some of the most extreme were the Ranters, whose fondness for 'free love' and unrestrained hedonism has been related to the 'hippie' values of 'the counter-culture':

No hell we dread when we are dead
No Gorgon nor no Fury
And while we live, we'll drink and fuck
In spite of judge and jury.[34]

Others can be seen to convey an ideology which has much in common with that espoused by the green politicians of today. These proponents share a common thread, emphasising a decentralised network of self-sufficient communities, and have since been lumped together as the Utopian Socialists.

A number of these alternative communities sprang up around Britain during the nineteenth century, from the New Forest Shakers in the south to the Ruskinite community at Barmouth in Wales. They were mostly aligned with political or religious movements and generally collapsed well before they constructed their social utopia. However, they can be seen to reflect a broader ideological trend towards a form of agrarian socialism, representing a moral challenge to the existing order and united in certain assumptions – that humans were fundamentally good but had been corrupted by the hold of the established Church and an urban-based capitalism. They believed that, by taking production and consumption into their own hands, governed by principles of co-operation not competition, society would slowly be changed by their example, rather than through radical revolution.

Often seen as the father of British socialism, Robert Owen was one of the most famous radicals of the nineteenth century. Born to poor Welsh parents in 1771, he worked as an apprentice to a linen draper until he was eighteen, then set his sights on Manchester, where he started a business making textile machinery before taking control of a large spinning factory. A few years later, Owen acquired a set of mills in the village of New Lanark, where he set up 'a self-employing, self-supporting, self-educating, and self-governing population',[35] who had access to some of the best schools, highest wages and cleanest surroundings of any workers in Britain.

The success of the community made Owen both rich and famous so that, when the Napoleonic Wars left the country deep in recession, politicians of the day turned to him for advice. Owen presented his sweeping vision for reform, eradicating poverty through the formation of Villages of Co-operation, in which up to 1,200 people would form a self-sufficient unit, working together on farms and in factories. The idea was considered too radical and denounced by William Cobbett as a plan for 'communities of paupers'.[36]

Although funding for a trial village was never raised, Owen clung to the concept, convinced that it could turn disadvantaged lives into prosperous ones. His career underwent a dramatic shift, transforming his entrepreneurial capitalism into a philanthropic mission. In 1824, he sold his interest in New Lanark, sailed to America and bought 30,000 acres in Indiana from the Rappites, a religious sect from Germany. He christened the community New Harmony and, on 4 July 1826, inaugurated it with a 'Declaration of Mental Independence – independent from Private Property, Irrational Religion and Marriage'.[37] It proved to be little short of a disaster; inadequate planning bred chaos, and rival communities sprang up under different leaders. Owen lost most of his fortune within two years and was forced to sell the land.

The rest of his life was spent trying to impress his plans on everyone from President Jackson to Queen Victoria, usually greeted with a bewildered but polite indifference. His only real allies were in the British working-class movement and he established the Grand National Moral Union of the Productive and Useful Classes, a precursor to the trade unions of today. Although it had never been fully realised, the concept behind the Villages of Co-operation had permeated certain areas of the country, spawning various workers' co-operatives, some of which even tried to eradicate money in the manner first suggested by Owen. However, since they were ultimately linked to external markets, these attempts always seemed doomed to failure. The only way in which the concept did take hold was a consumer co-operative, created by twenty-eight men known as the Rochdale Pioneers and recognised today as one of the seeds which became the modern Labour Party. Although he had been lampooned as a naive idealist, and labelled 'a gentle bore',[38] Owen had proved himself as a man of action, prepared to try to change the world when others merely talked of it.

The most extreme utopian vision of the nineteenth century was described by the poet and artist William Morris. Reacting against class distinctions conditioned by a social hierarchy, the utilitarianism of the Industrial Age and a 'dull time oppressed by bourgeoisdom and philistinism', Morris imagined a libertarian heaven, 'a society which has no consciousness of being governed'.[39] He reviled London as a 'sordid and loathsome place', and felt that the beauty of the British countryside was threatened by 'the land of decay'.

In his utopian novel, *News from Nowhere* (1890), Morris describes a post-revolutionary twenty-first century Britain, in which there is no crime, no law, no concept of private property, no marriage and no money. Society is made up of self-governing communes, the dreaded factories of mass production replaced by scattered local workshops. In the absence of a need for government, the Houses of Parliament have been turned into a dung market. However, despite his distrust of government, Morris had reservations about full-blown anarchist doctrine, since it 'negatives society, and puts man outside it'.[40]

Contrary to the naivety that many would see in Morris, Marshall sees him as an 'advanced ecological thinker', due to his desire to 'forgo some of the power over nature won by past ages in order to be more human and less mechanical, and willing to sacrifice something to this end'.[41] In his study of *Early Green Politics*, Gould compares the vision presented by Morris to that of the contemporary 'green' politician Jonathon Porritt, seeing them as 'almost identical'. Derek Wall highlights the fusion of the 'Romantic conservatism of Ruskin and Carlyle', with the 'tradition of utopian socialist experiments' like New Harmony.[42] While he was familiar with the work of Marx and Engels, and saw some value in their ideas, Morris told his daughter that 'he would no more accept the tyranny of a Collectivism that would crush individuality than he would accept the tyranny of Capitalism'.[43] *News from Nowhere* has since been described as 'the best ecotopia so far imagined'.[44]

The poet Edward Carpenter was another radical reformer, a close friend of Morris and an early champion of both vegetarianism and gay rights. He saw that the concept of private property had introduced 'slavery, serfdom, wage-labour, which are various forms of the domination of one class over another; and to rivet these authorities it created the State and the policeman'.[45]

Carpenter believed that living 'close to Nature' was essential to human health and happiness, creating a self-sufficiency experiment with the Sheffield Socialist Society. Like the Utopian Socialists, he called for a decentralised society of farms and workshops, and his book, *Non-Governmental Society* (1911), left a deep impression on Gandhi, proposing that, once established, 'a spontaneous and free production of goods would spring up, followed of course by a free exchange – a self-supporting society, based not on individual dread and anxiety, but on the common fullness of life and energy'.[46] Carpenter's vision also incorporated the insights of the Perennial Philosophy, hoping to cultivate a state which absorbed the sense of individual self within one universal consciousness.

Henry Salt left his job as a classics teacher at Eton and became one of the first active campaigners for animal rights. His 1892 study, *Animal Rights in Relation to Social Progress*, examined some of the themes which have since been adopted by the animal liberation movement, such as vivisection, zoos and hunting. For Salt, 'the point at issue is simply whether man is justified in inflicting any form of death or suffering on the lower races for his mere amusement and caprice'.[47]

Gould sees these last decades of the nineteenth century as 'the most fecund and important period of green politics before 1980', during which time 'the philosophy of industrialism, the relationship between the social and physical environment and the functions and excesses of the city received an extraordinary degree of critical examination.'[48] We find the anarchist tradition being kept alive by Oscar Wilde, declaring that

> All modes of government are wrong. They are unscientific, because they seek to alter the natural environment of Man; they are immoral because, by interfering with the individual, they produce the most aggressive forms of egotism; they are ignorant, because they try to spread education; they are self-destructive, because they engender anarchy.[49]

Wilde observed that 'The order of Nature is rest, repetition and peace. Weariness and war are the results of an artificial society based on capital; and the richer this society gets, the more thoroughly bankrupt it really is.'[50] Like those that came before him, Wilde was not afraid to consider the concept of a utopian future, since 'a map of the world that does not include Utopia is not worth glancing at, for it leaves out the one country at which Humanity is always landing. And when Humanity lands there, it looks out, and, seeing a better country, sets sail.' For Wilde, 'Progress is the realization of Utopias.'[51]

As we move into the twentieth century, we find the utopian novel being used by George Orwell and Aldous Huxley to satirise the Industrial Age and its notion of 'progress', while naturalist writers like H.J. Massingham and A.G. Tansley echo the conservation ideals of Thoreau and Muir, advocating the virtues of small rural communities and the sacred quality of a life lived on the land. In *Pan in America*, D.H. Lawrence lamented the fact that the death of the Greek God Pan, at the beginning of the Christian era, had signalled the death of our sacred relationship to Nature, and that 'Humanity hardly noticed.'[52]

However, alarm bells were only ringing for a few. It was not until the aftermath of the Second World War gave way to the abundance of the fifties that a concerned minority began to deconstruct the industrial paradigm and lay the foundations of the modern environmental movement.

Green Shoots

Ever since the post-war years, human consciousness has been given a dramatic new spin by two significant factors. The bombing of Nagasaki and Hiroshima left few doubts about Man's new capacity to destroy himself in ever greater numbers and with ever more devastating efficiency. The spectre of radioactive fall-out, or nuclear winter, had catastrophic implications for the future of all life. For the first time, a generation was born into a world where the complete annihilation of whole countries could be inflicted at the press of a button. Ever since the beginning of the Cold War, much of the human population has had to deal with the psychological fear that this subliminal knowledge brings. Rather than diffusing the situation, the end of the Cold War merely compounded it. Nuclear devices have spread around the world and the time when one is used in the name of international terrorism draws closer every day.

The second factor has been the image of our planet seen from space, taken from Apollo 8 in 1968. The astronomer Fred Hoyle had predicted that 'Once a photograph of the Earth, taken from the outside, is available . . . a new idea as powerful as any other in history will be let loose.'[53] As well as confirming that the Earth is indeed round, the image helps to remind us that national boundaries are just an idea, that our lives are deeply embedded within Nature and that we are all dependent on one beautiful ball of swirling blue, white and green. The image can be seen as the visual embodiment of Gaia and the emerging ecological consciousness, suggesting unity in diversity, harmony in complexity and the capacity for self-regulation. Inevitably, it continues to be used to great effect by hundreds of environmental groups around the world.

Within this new arena, a plethora of social movements emerged, campaigning against war, whale-hunting and all things nuclear, coalescing into the global movement for change which is now converging around the world. However, when a coherent ecological agenda finally emerged, its leading exponents were more right-wing and conservative than the nineteenth-century socialist origins of the movement might imply. As Edward Goldsmith told me, 'There is a common misconception that the Green Party evolved from socialist, working class origins, when in fact it was a middle-class thing.'[54]

* * *

Founder of *The Ecologist* magazine and brother of the late billionaire Sir James Goldsmith, 'Uncle Teddy' is regarded as one of the founding fathers of the modern movement. Descended from a leading European banking family – 'the poorer cousins of the Rothschilds' – Adolf Goldsmith arrived in Britain towards the end of the nineteenth century.[55] Before the outbreak of the First World War, his son Frank, already an established Suffolk landowner and MP for Stowmarket, disappeared to France, where he ran luxury hotels and married Marcelle Moullier. Teddy was born in Paris in 1928, soon returned to Britain and took up residence at Claridges Hotel.

After the Second World War, he went up to Magdalen College Oxford, where he was soon joined by his sixteen-year-old brother Jimmy, already 'bored of life at Eton'.[56] Jimmy gambled, allegedly using real money rather than IOUs, and the brothers soon became friends with John Aspinall, the flamboyant founder of the Clermont Club, lion-lover, friend of Lord Lucan and a prominent mover and shaker within the echelons of Mayfair high society. From an early age, Teddy thought that the world was in a mess and that 'all history did was try to justify it'.[57] Recognising Jimmy's entrepreneurial business skills, he made the astute move of giving him all his money to invest. Then he started to accompany Aspinall on his trips to Africa, where he developed a passion for anthropology, studied tribal groups and realised that economic development was the ultimate cause of environmental destruction.

The Ecologist was launched in 1970. The magazine provided a forum for ecological issues but the esoteric subjects and heavily referenced style had limited appeal, keeping the material within a specialised field and the circulation low. However, in the run-up to the 1972 UN Conference in Stockholm, Teddy collaborated with Robert Allen to produce a special edition which would sell 750,000 copies and later be seen as a landmark publication – *Blueprint for Survival* – warning that 'if current trends are allowed to persist, the breakdown of society and the irreversible disruption of the life-support systems on this planet, possibly by the end of the century, certainly within the lifetimes of our children, are inevitable.'[58] With some degree of irony, this call for economic restraint was launched at the Clermont, the gambling club frequented by some of the most rapacious capitalists in the world. (After a similar meeting the following year, Goldsmith passed the hat round and raised £14,000 as start-up funds for FoE.)

The report was perceived by many to be extremely right-wing, even misanthropic. Aspinall was accused of greeting the recent floods in Bangladesh, which had killed nearly a million people, as being a positive contribution to achieving stable populations. However, it was endorsed by Sir

Julian Huxley and Sir Peter Scott, as well as FoE and Survival International. It also became the springboard which launched the People Party – which became the Ecology Party, and later the Green Party – from which Teddy stood for Parliament in 1974, in his father's old constituency. However, issues like global warming and ozone depletion were far from the minds of most voters and the first 'green' politicians were generally dismissed as eccentric idealists.

Although some have described him as 'cantankerous', 'alarmist', even 'mad', few people can be seen to have campaigned as tirelessly and for so long as Goldsmith. *The Ecologist*, now run by his nephew Zac, has consistently been at the cutting edge for exposing environmental issues, whether it be toxic chemicals in consumer products, the latest research on global warming, or calling for a fundamental review of institutions like the World Bank and policies of globalisation. *The Way*, Goldsmith's detailed study of ecological principles and the emerging world-view, has been described as 'a truly radical analysis of modern science'.[59] His network extends from World Bank officials to activists around the globe, from Sunder Lal Baghuna, leader of the Chipko tree-hugging movement in the Indian Himalayas, to peasant farmers in Sri Lanka, Africa and Brazil. Fritjof Capra remembers passing through Goldsmith's Richmond home in the seventies, sleeping on a mattress in a garden shed while an eclectic band of tribal leaders and hippie idealists passed through the house.[60] Although some have found his views too dogmatic and radical, there is no doubt that Goldsmith's charismatic style and exhaustive research have played a definitive role in shaping the modern environmental movement.

Along with 'Uncle Teddy', Fred Pearce cites Max Nicholson as another leading figure in the birth of the British movement.[61] Born in 1904, Nicholson also went to Oxford before working for the Ministry of War Transport. In 1952 he became Director-General of the Nature Conservancy, the world's first statutory conservation body and the product of his report for the Wildlife Special Committee. Ten years before *Silent Spring* appeared, he was lobbying local councils to limit the roadside application of herbicides. He went on to establish the largest research unit of the time to study the ecological impact of toxic chemicals and pushed for bans on pesticides like aldrin, dieldrin and heptachlor.[62]

In 1961, Nicholson became the inaugural Chairman of the World Wildlife Fund (WWF, now World Wide Fund for Nature), sitting alongside Sir Peter Scott and Sir Julian Huxley on the committee. From this platform, he formed the Ark Club – 'a select world fellowship of champions and defenders of wildlife' – aiming to raise substantial donations from millionaires seeking association with the royal patronage of his conservation projects. The media machine responded, the *Daily Mirror* printing a six-page special to launch WWF and their campaign to save the black rhino. In stark contrast to the great white game hunters responsible for decimating African wildlife, Nicholson and Huxley were the first to persuade leaders, like Julius Nyere in Tanzania, of the benefits that conservation and tourism might bring.

Despite being more closely aligned with the establishment than Goldsmith, and the fact that WWF has played a more moderate role than other major groups like Greenpeace or FoE, Nicholson was equally disillusioned with our economic system and aware of the need for change:

> I think that the Industrial Age has shown its bankruptcy today. People are turning back to find things in the roots of human evolution. Perhaps the environmental movement's uncanny success has been due to this great wellspring. Politicians are not attuned to this, because they are hooked on the modern myths. But many people in the street talk more sense about the environment than people in Whitehall.[63]

Jonathon Porritt is another 'green' with stronger ties to the establishment than working-class socialism. His father held the bizarre title of Baron Porritt of Wanganui and Hampstead, he was educated at Eton then Oxford and has always been brutally honest about the political benefits that he has exploited through his background:

> The fact that I know how the establishment world works, because I was born into it and educated into it, has not been a disadvantage to me or the organisations that I've worked with. At Friends of the Earth, being at ease with the people who were on the inside track, in the corridors of power, it was plain useful for us. I could take this radical message to people who simply wouldn't have listened to others, but who would listen to me.[64]

Porritt became active in the Green Party during the late 1970s, while teaching at a London comprehensive. After becoming the co-chair in 1980, he left the ailing party to become Director of FoE, raising the group's profile considerably over the following years. He has subsequently chaired the UN's Environmental and Development Committee for the UK, presented numerous television programmes relating to the environment and written several books; *Seeing Green* has been cited as a key inspiration for many modern activists and his most recent is a critique of the arrogance, corruption and manipulation perpetrated in the name of science. In 1996, he founded Forum for the Future, a charity campaigning for solutions to environmental problems, attracting the support of high-profile names like Richard Rogers, Will Hutton and Jonathon Dimbleby. His most recent incarnation is Chairman of the Sustainable Development Committee, confronted with the task of scrutinising New Labour's environmental policy. He remains adamant that his position will not be compromised: 'I've never had any internal dealings with the Labour Party. I've always been critical of them. I have not sought to defend this party's record, and I won't be doing that now. I've always been dark green and radical.'[65]

Despite what he says, Porritt is not 'dark green and radical' enough for some. In a debate in *The Ecologist*, George Monbiot, another middle-class 'green' whose father was a Tory MP, attacked Forum for the Future for working with corporations like BP, Blue Circle and Tesco, allowing them to be used 'as a public relations opportunity'.[66] Monbiot accuses Porritt of being naive to think that he 'can persuade corporations to abandon their core business practices, by appealing to the good grace of their directors'. Drawing attention to companies affiliated with the Forum's Business Network, such as the British Airports Authority (BAA), and their plans for Heathrow's Terminal 5 – 'the biggest and most fiercely contested greenfield development in the history of the United Kingdom' – Monbiot insists that Porritt merely helps to 'legitimise and validate the way these companies operate'.[67] In retaliation, Porritt accuses Monbiot of being pious, of ignoring the fact that the success of the environmental movement 'lies in unceasing, undramatic persuasion and pressure, leading to steady, incremental change amongst both politicians and business people'. For Porritt, compromise is not an offensive insult but 'part and parcel of accelerating change'.[68]

This debate, between two of the most charismatic characters within the UK movement, highlights two polarised approaches which are constantly at odds within the green agenda. One is rigidly uncompromising, arguing that no amount of incremental improvement will ever mend something that doesn't work in the first place, suggesting that a new paradigm can only be implemented when the old slate is swept clean; the other sees the only way forward to be to work with large corporations and steer them in the direction of sustainability. It is easy to see why Porritt's position might be seen to compromise his earlier ideals. As Monbiot points out, the fact that a former Director of FoE is now working alongside BAA seems to undermine the current director's opposition to Terminal 5. Porritt has also previously recognised some of the inherent flaws associated with incremental change:

> The fiction of combining present levels of consumption with 'limitless recycling' is more characteristic of the technocratic vision than of an ecological one. Recycling itself uses resources, expends energy, creates thermal pollution; on the bottom line, it's just an industrial activity like all the others. Recycling is both useful and necessary – but it is an illusion to imagine that it provides any basic answers.[69]

Similar to the distinction made between 'shallow' and 'deep' ecology, Andrew Dobson contrasts plain 'environmentalism', which endeavours to solve environmental problems through a managerial approach to issues like pollution and resource use, with what he calls 'ecologism', which 'holds that a sustainable and fulfilling existence presupposes radical changes in our relationship with the non-human natural world, and in our mode of social and political life'.[70] Porritt may be trying to play the seemingly impossible role of straddling both camps, defending the need to work with corporations and government, while simultaneously advocating 'nothing less than a non-violent revolution to overthrow our whole polluting, plundering and materialistic industrial society and, in its place, to create a new economic and social order which will allow human beings to live in harmony with the planet'.[71]

It is hard to see how Porritt's 'compromise' will facilitate this non-violent revolution and lead to anything but incremental change, but he recognises that 'we are all compromised, in one way or another', that despite some consumer pressure, the majority of us continue to buy corporate products, 'regardless of their impact on other people or the planet'.[72] He welcomes the radical absolutism of campaigners like Monbiot, seeing it as a crucial part of the inherent diversity which an effective environmental movement should represent. While others call him an idealist, Porritt prefers to see himself as an optimist: 'You see, I think I can change things – still, even now, I think I can change what is happening.'[73]

Friends of the Earth

In contrast to the high-profile, daredevil tactics used by Greenpeace, Friends of the Earth (FoE) has always been more aligned with the persuasive powers of lobbying government. Greenpeace may have seized the headlines more often, with the glamour of macho media stunts, but FoE's sustained campaign pressure plays an equally important role within the broad front of the environmental movement. Like Greenpeace, the organisation was born in the US, led by one of the most uncompromising, visionary environmentalists of the last century.

David Brower was a charismatic and controversial figure, known as the 'archdruid of environmentalism' – because of his 'shock of white hair and rugged good looks' – and acknowledged as 'unshakably the most powerful voice in the conservation movement'.[74] When Brower died of cancer in November 2000, at the age of 88, Ralph Nader described him as 'the greatest environmentalist and conservationist of the twentieth century' and 'an indefatigable champion of every worthwhile effort to protect the environment over the last seven decades'.[75] Dennis Hayes regarded him as 'the gold standard by which many leaders of the environmental movement judged themselves, and usually came up short'.[76] His biographer believed him to be so radical that 'To his foes in the Department of the Interior and Bureau of Reclamation, David Brower is the Antichrist.'[77]

Born in 1912, Brower's formative years were spent hiking and climbing in America's national parks. He joined the Sierra Club in 1933, becoming editor of the club's magazine after the Second World War. When he took the role of director in 1952, the club had a membership of 7,000, most of whom were hikers and nature-lovers with a belief in conservation. By the time he left, nearly twenty years later, the membership had risen to 70,000 and become the most prominent group within the emerging environmental movement to be confronting national issues on a nationwide scale.[78] Incensed by the proposed construction of two dams which would flood part of the Grand Canyon, Brower launched a series of full-page newspaper ads, including forms and instructions for writing to Congress. Combined with an energetic series of speeches and a massive publicity drive, the Sierra Club succeeded in halting the project and were hailed as 'the gangbusters of the conservation movement'.

The Sierra Club finally proved too restrictive for Brower and, in 1969, he split to form Friends of the Earth (FoE) in San Francisco. This new organisation would tackle issues on a more global basis and move beyond the traditional emphasis on wilderness preservation and resource depletion. Brower was joined by Joseph Browder, an active member of the Audubon Society who had fought to protect the Everglades in Florida. From the start, Brower's vision and individual style clashed with the professionalism of the organisation and, within three years, most of the East Coast staff had left to form the Environmental Policy Centre (EPC). However, Brower brought energy and immediacy to many issues during the 1970s and helped to establish FoE as an international Non-Governmental Organisation (NGO) with affiliated groups in several countries.

Instead of the 'guerilla theatre' and direct action tactics used by Greenpeace, FoE sought to promote new environmental policies by lobbying for new legislation. This became even more official in 1984, when Brower left to form the Earth Island Institute, a radical think-tank, and FoE moved its headquarters to sit alongside government in Washington. For radicals like Brower, FoE had turned into 'just another lobbying group' and the recruitment of new administrators, lawyers and corporate executives into the mainstream environmental groups alienated many of the early campaigners by adopting the hierarchical structure and corporate profile of the very organisations they were opposing. As Sale observes, 'both sides were wearing suits and lugging laptops'.[79]

After being re-elected to the Sierra Club's board in 1982, Brower left in disgust in 1999, complaining that 'The world is burning and all I hear from them is violins.'[80] However, he will be remembered for more than just his uncompromising integrity. He was the author of the 'think global, act local' slogan, published *The Environmental Handbook* to coincide with Earth Day, played a key role at Stockholm in 1972 and was nominated three times for a Nobel Peace Prize. Shortly before his death, he decided that his most famous phrase – 'We do not inherit the Earth from our fathers, we are borrowing it from our children' – did not convey the complete story: 'We're not borrowing from our children', he reflected. 'We're stealing from them – and it's not even considered to be a crime.'[81]

One night in August 1969, while crawling through sand dunes on the coast of Ireland to look at seals, Edwin Matthews, an American lawyer based in Paris and an old friend of Brower's, met Barclay Inglis, a retired Scottish businessman and ex-Director of the Milk Marketing Board. Matthews was looking for people to help set up the UK branch of FoE and Inglis subsequently set to work, rounding up a group of committed young activists within three months.

In the autumn of 1970, Brower arrived in London to help consolidate the embryonic British chapter. Inglis had arranged a meeting at the Travellers' Club which included two people who would play an important part in the early days of FoE: Graham Searle from the National Union of Students, and Jonathan Holliman, a campaigner from the International Youth Federation for Conservation. After dinner, Brower gave his famous 'Sermon', compressing the evolutionary history of the planet into six days of creation lasting 666 million years each:

> At 4 p.m. Saturday, the big reptiles came in. Five hours later, when the redwoods appeared, there were no more big reptiles. At three minutes before midnight, Man appeared. At one-fourth of a second before midnight, Christ arrived. At one fortieth of a second before midnight, the Industrial Revolution began. We are surrounded with people who think that what we have been doing for that one-fortieth of a second can go on indefinitely. They are considered normal but they are stark, raving mad.[82]

Moving into a tiny office above Brower's publisher in St James's King Street, the group first caught the media's eye with a direct action protest, dumping 1,500 non-returnable Schweppes bottles on the doorstep of the company's head office. As Robert Lamb recalls, 'Some members of the King Street crew had to deal with all this while nursing week-old hangovers sustained in the attempt to build up a critical mass of empty tonic water bottles to arrange on Schweppes' doorstep.'[83] Pete Wilkinson remembers how 'We had about a week to go and simply couldn't find enough of the damn things . . . We had to go out and buy loads of Schweppes drinks, which we promptly poured into plastic containers. Graham produced a lot of gin and we drank it with tonic to justify our purchase.'[84] Wilkinson went on to become one of the country's most active campaigners. His link with Bryn Jones, the Industrial Editor at the *Daily Mirror*, helped make whaling a national issue and generate national opposition to nuclear waste issues during the 1975 inquiry at Windscale, the nuclear plant which was resurrected as Sellafield. Being an ex-lorry driver, however, Wilkinson often felt slightly displaced among the 'high-powered types' during the early days of FoE: 'Whenever they listed people that worked for the organisation, they squeezed me in between Amory Lovins and Walt Patterson to show we had width.'[85] He later became a key figure at Greenpeace.

Inspiration for the Schweppes campaign and another old friend of Brower's, Amory Lovins, a postgraduate physics student at Oxford's Merton College, was a founding member of the UK FoE branch and facilitated trans-Atlantic communication. Lovins has since become one of the world's leading energy experts and was recently described by the *Wall Street Journal* as 'one of the people most likely to change the face of business during the coming decade'. With his wife Hunter, Lovins collaborated with Paul Hawken on developing the concepts of 'natural capitalism', the eco-technologies and economic systems heralded as 'the next Industrial Revolution'. At his Rocky Mountain Institute, Lovins and his team have developed new building technologies such as 'super-windows', which keep buildings warm in summer and cool in winter: 'Super-windows have enabled experimental superinsulated eighties and nineties buildings to maintain comfort with no heating or cooling equipment in outdoor temperatures that range from about minus 47 to 115 degrees fahrenheit.'[86] As we shall see, his work with hydrogen fuel cells and the Hypercar concept promises to revolutionise the auto-motive industry.

FoE has progressed through many different guises during the last thirty years, under the leadership of Andrew Lees, Jonathon Porritt and now Charles Secrett. Throughout that time, the group's cerebral approach has contrasted with the more macho, hyperbolic actions of Greenpeace. Less radical than David Brower might have envisaged, but playing an equally crucial role within the diversity of an increasingly unified environmental movement, FoE deals with the entire spectrum of issues raised by the global crisis. As Tony Juniper, Executive Director at Friends of the Earth, says, 'FoE now talks to not just the Department of Environment but the Treasury, the DTI, the Departments of Health and Agriculture, because all these people have their part to play.'[87]

While Juniper accepts that the movement is more unified – 'with people building networks like the Green Alliance, feeding information to politicians'[88] – he remains sceptical about the coalition that has emerged from WTO protests in Prague and Seattle:

> This coming together – of radical environmentalists, grass-roots protest people, development people, poverty people, the animal welfare lot, the unions, indigenous rights groups, the women's movement – has been represented as anti-capitalist and entirely anti-globalisation; but there are some good aspects to globalisation, like bio-diversity treaties, the spread of eco-technologies, climate change agreements and the

> global networks that are emerging. What we don't like is a set of trade rules which favour trans-national companies from the North, lower environmental standards and prioritise economic growth over sustainability and ethical questions. That's where there isn't consensus within environmental groups and there could be a problem.[89]

Juniper remains confident that public opinion is shifting towards the green agenda and is realistic about the role that FoE has to play in accelerating this process: 'We have to convince people that they can have a good quality of life while protecting the environment. Humanity can survive and still preserve our natural systems.'[90] While he sees 'a new wave of green debate' in the wake of the British farming crisis, he highlights the way in which the issues are hardly ever related back to the environment.

> The public are being shaken out of their complacency about buying cheap meat at the supermarket but reacting about the safety of food rather than the deeper questions about the sustainability of our agricultural system. BSE and 'foot and mouth' becomes a food issue. Oil price protests become a transport issue. But these are all actually environmental issues. The environmental movement is speaking a different language, looking at the causes not the symptoms.[91]

When I asked him how he maintained a level of optimism when confronted by the enormity of the issues that confront him professionally every day, Juniper told me that 'You can't do this sort of work if you don't believe you can make a difference. Society is shaped by what individuals do collectively. By adopting a "green" approach to life, you will make a difference. Things are changing, but they need to change faster.'[92]

Unity in Diversity

Basic ecological principles suggest that divisions within the environmental movement should reflect the diversity of a living system and are ultimately subsumed by the whole. This pursuit of an ecological framework, within a social movement and a political party, has had some inevitable drawbacks, not least the maintenance of a non-hierarchical structure and the reluctance to appoint a leader. The environmental movement continues to attract individuals from across the political spectrum and is now integrating them within an ever-expanding network of people who are 'neither left nor right', but 'in front'.[93]

In their 1984 study, Fritjof Capra and Charlene Spretnak identify four areas from which 'green' politicians have tended to emerge: the 'visionary/holistic Greens', whose primary concern is to move beyond the old mechanistic paradigm, to integrate spiritual evolution within their politics and create 'a new society based on ways of thinking and being that reflect the interconnected nature of all phenomena' – they are often accused of being too ideological, naive, or even moralistic; the 'Eco-Greens', who concentrate on toxic hazards and the deployment of eco-technologies – they are usually from a conservative or liberal background and are considered by radicals to be taking too soft an approach; the 'peace-movement Greens', including the many CND activists and anti-nuclear campaigners who have since been aligned with the environmental movement; and the radical left, which includes all those Marxist/communist groups who made the transition from Red to Green.[94]

Throughout the 1970s, and well into the 1980s, the integration of Red and Green often alienated the movement from the public. Capra and Spretnak were first inspired to write their book after seeing how the European Greens had been misrepresented by the US media, described as recently as 1983 by *Time* magazine as 'romantic and dangerously simplistic' and by the *New York Times* as 'a jumbled alliance of ecologists, romantic far-leftists, Communists and enemies of nuclear weapons'.[95] This sort of reporting, combined with James Watt's comparison to Nazis and Bolsheviks, created a distorted impression of the Green agenda across Europe and the US.

Despite internal political divisions, the general trend was towards a united social movement, leading to some incongruous alliances. As early as 1974, it was noted how 'It is not easy to accept that the London Oxford Street

Action Committee, the Dwarves, the Street Farmers [pressure groups], and groups firmly embedded in the hippy world are part and parcel of a movement which includes bodies like the Civic Trust, the CPRE, and the National Trust.'[96] Derek Wall also observes how 'groups such as the Conservation Society and journals like *The Ecologist* were linking radical calls for transformation with conservative sentiments and had network ties to both established pressure groups and the "hippy world"'.[97]

The original formation of the Green Party mirrored the way in which green politics transcended previous ideological barriers, having been started by two ex-Conservative Party activists from the Midlands and 'attracting former activists from the Dwarves and other counter-culturalists, including teepee-dwellers from west Wales'.[98] Although the CND 'showed little sympathy for green politics',[99] peace movement activists saw themselves as increasingly aligned with a movement opposed to the technocratic and patriarchal control of the military-industrial complex. As one writer observed in 1988, the bottom line is that 'we are all harmed by the ecological crisis and therefore we all have a common interest in uniting together within people of all classes and all political allegiances to counter this mutually shared threat'.[100]

As various elements converged in the 1980s, so the scale and number of issues multiplied. Previously isolated protests were now seen as systemically inter-related, connecting global warming with deforestation with loss of bio-diversity with human rights issues with the power of multinational corporations. Campaigners who had previously been disillusioned with just whale-hunting, seal-bashing or the arms race were now disillusioned with the whole political process and the entire economic machine. Inevitably, the media seized upon issues like ozone depletion, climate change and the destruction of the rainforests, commissioning a spate of sensationalised, apocalyptic documentaries which many believe undermined the efforts being made by the movement, giving the public the impression that it was too late to save ourselves from imminent ecological meltdown and thereby promoting a sense of complacency. Of course, mainstream politicians were quick to jump on the bandwagon, with Prime Minister Margaret Thatcher famously declaring that 'We're all Greens now,' in a speech given at the Royal Society. Although the last years of the decade were seen to signal 'a period of green euphoria', this was almost inevitably followed by 'a time of green fatigue'. Far from being a positive step, the advent of 'green consumerism' was seen as a failure to address the root causes, yet another way of transferring the problem to a different area.

The empty rhetoric and lack of political vision reached a crescendo at the 1992 United Nations Conference on Environment and Development (UNCED), or Earth Summit, in the Brazilian city of Rio de Janeiro. More than 140 national delegations, and some 100 heads of state, converged on the event with over 3,000 support staff. Alongside the official event, some 20,000 members of NGOs from around the world met in a separate venue, the Global Forum. Twenty years previously, at the 1972 UN Conference on the Environment in Stockholm, the NGOs had seized the media spotlight and forced reluctant governments into agreements which went way beyond what they had imagined. In a bid to prevent this being repeated, Rio city council spent $14 million on extra security for the NGO event, known as Eco 92, and relegated it to a downtown site, miles from the enormous Riocentro conference complex where the politicians would meet. As Robert Lamb recalls, 'Green organisations were none too happy about this apartheid, though Rio's taxi drivers made fortunes from hauling delegates to and fro.'[101] In addition,

> A brand-new $150 million highway, nicknamed the Red Route, was constructed from the airport to the city centre and conference areas, ingeniously avoiding the slums and waste tips that encircled much of the city. Visiting dignitaries were spared the distastefully visible consequences of Brazil's crushing $123 billion foreign debt, the rural poverty that had filled Rio and other cities with desperate environmental refugees.[102]

The media hype that surrounded the Earth Summit almost guaranteed that it would prove a disappointment. Optimism was partly fuelled by the 1988 World Commission on Environment and Development report, 'Our Common Future', which called for a 'new economic world order' based upon a redistribution between North and South. The head of the commission, Norwegian Prime Minister Gro Harlem Brundtland, had proposed that a total re-evaluation of global resources would be the only way to balance economic development between an industrial, affluent North and a predominantly poor, agricultural South. However, as the Rio conference progressed, political leaders from around the world displayed their limited grasp of the issues, an inability to agree over virtually anything and a total inertia when confronting corporate excesses. At times, the whole event seemed to dissolve into chaos. Tony Juniper recalls how 'The Dalai Lama was rubbing shoulders with Roger Moore and a hundred other celebrities, while a weird army of skimpily clad young women and gun-toting security guards ran around trying to organise everyone. If they have cocktail parties in hell then Rio was some kind of earthly manifestation.'[103] Meanwhile the media were trying to cope with the complexity of issues and, as another member of FoE observed, 'journalists looked for soundbites and the coverage collapsed into cliches'.[104]

After the fiasco had died down, it became clear that Rio had proved little more than a gesture. As Juniper says, 'The whole thing was really a gimmick to satisfy public opinion and unfortunately it was all very effective.'[105] Ten years on, he highlights the fact that some positive results did emerge, including two biodiversity conventions, a commission on sustainable development and Agenda 21, a set of guidelines for local government.[106] However, the ultimate transparency of the event was illustrated by the WTO moving from Rio to the Uruguay round of GATT (General Agreement on Tariffs and Trade) talks and negotiating a completely opposite set of agreements. For people around the world, the Rio summit proved that the prevailing political and economic system would never produce the required change due to an inherent inconsistency between the mainstream economic agenda and the health of the planet. Ultimately, this was nothing but fuel to the activist fire.

The Eco-wars

Over the last decade, several factors have converged to create an increasingly unified movement, drawing existing activist groups into an expanding global network. In Britain, The Criminal Justice Act (CJA), designed to suppress undesirable elements like the 'rave scene' and 'New Age Travellers', only succeeded in bringing together previously disparate groups – ravers and travellers, united with cross-country Ramblers. The BSE crisis, and the opposition to GM, placed the Women's Institute next to eco-anarchists in demands for agricultural reform and restraints on bio-technology. Around the world, the Internet, one of the technological tools for economic globalisation, is successfully being used to subvert it, creating a global activist network which has already succeeded in bringing one WTO summit to a grinding halt.

Nowhere were the ironies surrounding unlikely new alliances more pronounced than in the so-called Eco-wars of the 1990s, the road protest campaigns which centred on sites like Twyford Down, Solsbury Hill and the Third Battle of Newbury (the first two being key battles during the English Civil War of 1643–44). Animal rights activists linked arms with fox-hunters to defend Twyford Down from bulldozers. Writing about the Solsbury Hill protest, John Vidal noticed how

> The Honourable Rupert Legge, son of the Earl of Dartmouth, novelist, landowner and a man with Etonian tendencies, sits by his son's tent. It's pitched in what, until last week, had been a modest suburban garden overlooking Bath but now resembles Beirut or Woodstock. There's a 15-foot high pile of bulldozed trees, rubble everywhere and dreadlocked men are playing drums and flute around a fire. The titled one is appalled, but only by the destruction.[107]

The Winchester section of the M3, which carved its way through Twyford Down, led another commentator to observe that 'When not only professional campaigners, but the headmaster of an ancient public school and a university professor resort to civil disobedience to disrupt a public enquiry in order to prevent it from being held at all, something has evidently gone wrong.'[108]

All three roads threatened historic, cultural sites. The Dongas, the ancient tracks which crossed Twyford Down, was adopted as a name for one of the neo-tribal groups which emerged from the protest. Solsbury Hill, immortalised in song by Peter Gabriel, is linked to the city of Bath, 'as it was on its slopes that the exiled King Bladud lived, and from where he followed his pigs to the hot springs that cured his leprosy'.[109] Newbury by-pass threatened three Sites of Special Scientific Interest (SSSIs), twelve archaeological sites, rare heathland, ancient woodland, bogs and wildflower meadows.[110] It is easy to see why the resistance stretched across social boundaries.

The road protests not only aligned upper-class and middle-class Britain with green anarchists, but provided a stage for the modern interpretation of an old activist tactic – non-violent direct action, or NVDA. One of the mobilising forces for the dissemination of extreme eco-tage tactics was the UK network of Earth First!, the radical US group inspired by Edward Abbey's novel. Despite some trepidation about 'this dangerous movement called Earth First!', one of the local Newbury campaigners, Dr

Sue Millington, found them to be 'some of the most wonderful people', who are 'living out their principles. Something that is very rare in our culture.'[111] When security guards physically and sexually assaulted protesters at a camp established by the Dongas and Earth First! activists in December 1992, the passion of the movement was ignited even further. Mobile phones and the Internet enabled activists to co-ordinate actions with greater efficiency and in larger numbers. One camp extended over 6 acres of woodland, connecting sixty tree-houses and 400 trees with 4 miles of suspended walkways. Over a two-year period, forty-six protest camps, housing some 500 people, sprang up along the proposed route for the Newbury by-pass. Establishing themselves as official squats meant that bailiffs were required legally to evict them. Up and down the country, construction workers were confronted with people tied to the top of trees, hand-cuffed to huge balls of concrete. Millions of pounds were added to road-building budgets to pay for ever greater numbers of security guards who, with the police, were given the task of extricating the protesters.

This took a considerable amount of time and effort. When work began at Newbury, two protesters, suspended from scaffold poles set in concrete, prevented 400 security guards from going to work. The government were embarrassed as public opinion veered against them. The media duly responded, turning Daniel Hooper, a young activist tunneller known as Swampy, into a national icon.

Opposition to road-building grew from an historical objection to the car itself. An Edwardian campaign poster hailed: 'Men of England. Your birthright is being taken from you by Reckless Motorists. Reckless Motorists drive over and kill your children. Reckless Motorists drive over and kill both men and women. Reckless Motorists kill your dogs. Motorists fill your houses with dust. Motorists spoil your clothes with dust.'[112]

By 1914, the British road system already served 400,000 vehicles and, by the 1920s, witnessed 6,000 fatalities a year.[113] It is ironic that conservation groups like the Council for the Protection of Rural England (CPRE), which was formed in 1926, should have first supported the trunk road network, seeing it as a means of protecting quiet rural areas from heavy traffic. This attitude sanctioned the continued expansion of the road network, leading to the birth of the motorway when the M1 was opened in 1960. Although sections of every motorway built since have been opposed, the effective use of mass NVDA had not been realised. Derek Wall cites the Stroud tree protest of 1989 as an 'early portent' of what was to come. Activists climbed into oak trees which were to be felled for the approach road to a new Tesco supermarket. Since Stroud was 'almost unique in being a local government Green party stronghold',[114] and thus raised the media profile, the action proved a success. Since then, thousands more have taken to the trees.

The road protests promoted a renewed sense of solidarity within the movement but there was also inevitable friction. Extreme green anarchists, some associated with Earth First!, were accused of compromising the non-violent ethic, or setting fire to bulldozers and portacabins, despite the group's decision that property damage was unacceptable. Some of the more extreme activist tactics, like 'tree-spiking' or 'ethical shop-lifting', have often been condemned by moderates and mainstream groups. This has sometimes created a rift between Earth First! and more established groups like FoE. Jake Bowers and Jason Torrance, two Earth First! veterans, recall how the group had been plagued from the beginning by 'people more interested in "me first", or "tea-by-the-campfire first" rather than putting the Earth first', while many seasoned activists, 'penniless after years of voluntary activism, went to work for mainstream pressure groups'.[115] For committed activists like Bowers and Torrance, the aim was

> to remind people that the Earth was not dying but being murdered, and that the murderers had names and addresses. If somebody was trying to rape and murder your mum, you wouldn't, we reasoned, write a letter to your MP about the issue – you'd physically intervene.[116]

Although life in the road protest camps was often physically and mentally challenging, living through harsh winter conditions, the psychological pressure of conflict and outbreaks of scabies, many recall deep emotional bonding and a sense of spiritual freedom, 'creating a magical sort of place where people of different aspirations could be'. One of the EF! activists remembers how he was affected by the Dongas and their neo-Paganism: 'They liked doing this Mother Earth kind of stuff, and it did seem to have a real power for all. I had an agnostic view of the world, but this spirituality that went around the camp did have a magical effect, it just did have a real magic.'[117] Hugh Warwick highlights the fact that a whole sub-culture emerged from the road protests, producing 'music, poetry, art and a way of life'. The Dongas proved to be much more than 'just a bunch of reactionaries looking for an opportunity to irritate road-builders. Much to the perturbation of the State, they have moved from instinctive to investigative campaigners. They have sparked off a veritable revolution in road protest.'[118] More often than not, this neo-tribal network has been misrepresented by the media, frequently reduced to criminal status.

In reality, communities around the country have been inspired by the integrity and passion which groups like the Dongas have conveyed through NVDA.

The forces that converged at Twyford and Newbury reflected a deeper malaise than just opposition to roads. One activist magazine claimed that 'cars are just one piece of the jigsaw' and that the protests were 'about the political and economic forces which drive "car culture"'.[119] The government insisted that 'roads are good for the economy', but protesters saw 'more goods travelling on longer journeys, more petrol being burnt, more customers at out-of-town supermarkets.' The policy was aimed at 'increasing "consumption", because that is an indicator of "economic growth". The greedy, short-term exploitation of dwindling resources regardless of the immediate or long-term costs.'[120]

While the road protests were part of a brewing resentment for the forces of capitalism itself, they were also propelled by a growing mistrust of the democratic process. Newbury resident Sue Millington believed that:

> When the State lets you down, the only way you can achieve change is by breaking unjust laws. Clearly the government has no intention to protect the environment or to honour its international commitments. In the same way as the Sufragettes had to break laws to get a vote, as Gandhi had to confront authority to have his voice heard, as Martin Luther King had to act to obtain Civil Rights for the blacks, and as women at Greenham Common had to break laws to highlight the absurdity of nuclear weapons, those involved with the Third Battle of Newbury were preparing to confront the full apparatus of the State and risk their own safety and liberty in the process.[121]

Events at Newbury revealed the extent to which government policy had enraged and alienated a broad spectrum of the population. The 'acid house' explosion, and the subsequent rave scene, united the nation's youth in a new sub-culture, the pervasive scale of which had not been seen since the sixties. Like the advent of LSD, the strength of this new counter-culture was enhanced by the widespread use of a new drug – MDMA, or Ecstasy. Although it falls into a slightly different chemical category, Ecstasy, like LSD, had a profound sociological impact, promoting an expansive, albeit misleading, sense of spiritual well-being, dissolving inhibitions and encouraging a sense of empathy which crossed conditioned social boundaries. A decline in football hooliganism in the early 1990s has been attributed to the widespread use of the drug – people who previously downed ten pints and went out looking for a fight, were now taking pills and hugging each other.[122]

After the second 'Summer of Love' in 1989, the rave scene escalated dramatically. Something that had been restricted to London clubs now swept through the country. Tens of thousands converged at outdoor events, prompting John Major's government to introduce sweeping legislation in an attempt to control it. The 1994 Criminal Justice Act (CJA) made it illegal for people to gather in large groups which have not been officially sanctioned, provided the police with new powers of eviction and effectively criminalised a whole section of society. It was the most controversial and opposed piece of legislation since Thatcher's Poll Tax and was instrumental in turning ever larger numbers of people against the State. In the first three months at Newbury, the CJA was used to make over 700 arrests for the new crime of aggravated trespass.[123]

Disillusioned with the repressive nature of a supposedly democratic society, ravers, Ramblers and travellers were all able to express their anger by joining the road protests. A new generation of activist was born, exploiting the so-called DIY culture which new technologies allowed: camcorders to record police brutality, photocopied leaflets, mobile phones and the Net to spread the word. For writer Roland Vernon, the CJA, and the events that unfurled at Newbury, were signs of a new civil war which was permeating the whole of British society:

> This war is being waged between members of the same nation state; it is a civil war, and one which is escalating despite the growing cost: severe injuries, miscarried babies, slaughtered animals, children deprived of education, huge policing expenditure and an ugly disease of hatred that has become tantamount to social ideology in certain areas. It is a war which need not and should not exist, and one which the established Church neglects at its peril, not just because of its duty to repair social degradation, but because the very issue is rooted in the spiritual vacuum into which our society has propelled itself.[124]

By criminalising the nomadic community of 'New Age Travellers', 'at one time an institutionalized and valued element of British society', Vernon believes we have turned our back on 'our lost "natural" selves'.[125] At Tinkers Bubble, the small self-sufficient community near where Vernon lives, he finds people who 'give us great hope for the future of our species':

> one cannot but be impressed by the conscientious effort shown by the temporary residents to live alongside nature with positive humility: propagating as well as consuming, recycling, patiently accommodating seasonal rigours, struggling to dissociate themselves from the temptation to accumulate unnecessary belongings, passionately adhering to codes of hygiene in the most inhospitable conditions.[126]

The road protests, the Dongas, and communities like Tinkers Bubble, have enabled much of middle-class Britain to overcome political prejudice about a previously vilified section of society. While their message may be tainted by a violent, extremist few, many of those who are criminalised and victimised within our society are now being seen as those that we should respect and admire for their conviction, their ecological wisdom and their courage to fight for a sustainable world. The road-building continues, but so do the protests. Far from being seen as a defeat, the Third Battle of Newbury consolidated an expanding activist network which has since turned its attention to the planetary excesses of corporate globalisation.

Convergence

Over the last decade, the push for free trade, and the concept of a global market-place, has become the holy grail for political leaders in the developed world. Tony Blair welcomes it as 'irresistible and inevitable'. Through institutions and agreements like NAFTA (North American Free Trade Agreement), GATT, the WTO, the EU and the IMF (International Monetary Fund), the G8 leaders are busy trying to introduce controversial legislation like the MAI, the Multinational Agreement on Investments.

The proponents of globalisation insist that the economic rewards will be shared by all. Those who oppose it have proved that the only real beneficiaries of an unrestricted international flow in capital, goods and labour, are huge multinational corporations based in Europe and the US. Globalisation effectively opens the doors even wider for corporate irresponsibility, increasing environmental destruction and social inequality, shifting pollution to new areas, exploiting cheap 'sweat-shop' labour and making peasant farmers in the South subservient to technologies pioneered and controlled by the North. Rather than closing the divide, globalisation accentuates it. Rather than alleviating poverty and injustice, it encourages it. The policies have been condemned by political leaders throughout the developing world and exposed by grass-roots activists everywhere, demanding not just their revision but the abolition of the entire institutional framework represented by the World Bank, the IMF and the WTO. In *Time* magazine, Walter Kirn observes how 'The irony of all this is stark, and possibly galling to the technocrats: the Web was supposed to be globalism's great tool, not a forum for its enemies. The Web was supposed to weld together markets into one enormous worldwide trading floor, not organize thousands into picket lines.'[127]

In *No Logo*, the new Bible for anti-corporate activism, Naomi Klein identifies the various strands of protest that have been converging in Britain to oppose globalisation:

> To fight the Criminal Justice Act, the club scene forged new alliances with more politicized subcultures that were also alarmed by these new police powers. Ravers got together with squatters facing eviction, with the so-called New Age travellers facing crackdowns on their nomadic lifestyle, and with radical eco-warriors fighting the paving over of Britain's woodland areas by building tree houses and digging tunnels in the bulldozers' paths. A common theme began to emerge among those struggling countercultures: the right to uncolonised space – for homes, for trees, for gathering, for dancing. What sprang out of these cultural collisions among deejays, anti-corporate activists, political and New Age artists and radical ecologists may well be the most vibrant and fastest-growing political movement since Paris '68: Reclaim the Streets (RTS).[128]

An amorphous, non-hierarchical network, RTS disseminated another form of NVDA, the impromptu street party:

> We are basically about taking back public space from the enclosed private arena. At its simplest it is an attack on cars as a principal agent of enclosure. It's about reclaiming the streets as public inclusive

> space from the private exclusive use of the car. But we believe in this as a broader principle, taking back those things that have been enclosed within capitalist circulation and returning them to collective use.[129]

As this RTS leaflet implies, the street party has evolved beyond opposition to 'car culture' as a way to express a basic mistrust of capitalism itself. For RTS activists, this form of NVDA has become more than just a peaceful form of protest. It's an entire philosophy and a way of life:

> Direct action enables people to develop a new sense of self-confidence and an awareness of their individual and collective power. Direct action is founded on the idea that people can develop the ability for self-rule only though practice, and proposes that all persons directly decide the important issues facing them. Direct action is not just a tactic, it is individuals asserting their ability to control their own lives and to participate in social life without the mediation or control by bureaucrats or professional politicians. Direct action encompasses a whole range of activities, from organising co-ops to engaging in resistance to authority. Direct action places moral commitment above positive law. Direct action is not a last resort when other methods have failed, but the preferred way of doing things.[130]

Derek Wall observes that the tactics employed by RTS – of closing a busy section of road and having a party – were first used in the early 1970s. Activists from groups like the Dwarves and the Planet Earth Survival Team (PEST) attempted to block Oxford Street in 1971, then Piccadilly Circus two years later. Since Oxford Street was later given restricted access, the action was deemed to have been a partial success. However, like Twyford and Newbury, the potential impact of these events was not realised until the mid-1990s. The first two street parties, at Camden and the Angel, Islington, were held in relatively easy locations, largely pedestrianised and known to attract weekend shoppers who might sympathise with the event. This gave the organisers sufficient confidence to try something more ambitious. In July 1996, 7,000 people converged on a stretch of the M40 in west London, sealing off the road with scaffold tripods set in concrete and booting up the sound systems. Activists, hidden under the costumes of huge carnival figures, dug up the tarmac with pneumatic drills and symbolically planted trees. According to Wall, less than ten people knew what the location would be and 'thousands of participants were redirected from a meeting point at Liverpool Street Station. The police presence was too small to prevent the street party, which mobilised more individuals in illicit activity than has any other anti-road direct action protest event.'[131]

Similar RTS actions have been replicated around the world, from Sydney to San Francisco, Helsinki to Tel Aviv. As in Britain, these have often been the product of a collaboration with the Critical Mass movement, the convergence of anything up to several thousand cyclists on the last Friday of the month, riding through urban areas and thus clearing the streets. This gives protesters the time to block off an area, bring in the sound systems – which are waiting in the wings – and, almost instantly, to start having a party. As Klein notes, the events have attracted mixed reactions from the police, the press and the protesters themselves. In Sydney, the police merely asked for the sound to be turned down as 4,000 people danced into the night. The police in Utrecht actually assisted in starting the sound system generator. In London, a Trafalgar Square party drew 20,000 people and was later described as 'the best illegal rave or dance music party in history'.[132]

Unfortunately, the events also attracted those determined to incite violence and cause criminal damage, sabotaging the whole ethic and undermining the impact. In London, the Futures Exchange was evacuated after one group smashed all the glass in the lobby. Others went on to deface a statue of Churchill and the Cenotaph. At Berkeley in California, Klein observes how protesters threw a foam mattress onto a fire – 'creating toxic fumes at an environmental protest – brilliant!'[133] In Prague, a police car drove into the crowd at full speed, was surrounded and overturned. Many of these events turned into riots, resulting in numerous arrests. The press usually portrayed all those attending as nothing short of hedonistic and subversive terrorists, overlooking the fact that many of those taking part were white-collar professionals, disillusioned with the very institutions for which they work.

However, at protests against G8 meetings in Gothenburg and Genoa during 2001, a more sinister truth emerged, exposing severe police brutality and collaboration between the so-called 'Black Block' anarchists and the security forces. Neo-fascists, dressed in black balaclavas and gas masks, were seen emerging from police vans before provoking violence and vandalism. Rather than attacking the violent element, the police turned their attention to the peaceful protesters who were demonstrating for legitimate reasons. Mark Covell, a 33-year-old British journalist, suffered a punctured lung from broken ribs and lost ten teeth. Richard Moth and Nicola Doherty, two care workers from London, were beaten with truncheons as they crouched inside their sleeping bags. Once they were in custody, the situation deteriorated further: 'Prisoners, including those with broken limbs, were spread-eagled against a wall for up to two hours while abuse was hurled at them. Prisoners were spat on, urinated on and not allowed to go to the toilet. One of Nicola's fellow protesters called Daphne, a German girl, had her nose broken when they forced her to stand outside. The police smashed a baton in her face while she had her hands tied behind her head.'[134] Meanwhile, Tony Blair and other G8 leaders conducted talks within a high security zone – which cost £78 million to install – choosing their snacks from 170 types of cheese, 54 varieties of bread and 7,000 bottles of wine.[135]

When the divergence between public opinion and the policies pushed by world leaders has become so pronounced, the whole question of living in a democracy is called into question. 'Ask what sort of "democratic" system needs these kind of measures to protect itself from 200,000 of its own people,' observed Paul Kingsnorth, 'and you already have your answer.'[136] Tony Blair blamed the protesters for hijacking 'democracy', and 'not being interested in dialogue'. The fact that Blair and the other G8 leaders have consistently failed to initiate any meaningful 'dialogue' with anti-globalisation groups is purely seen as acknowledgement that the free market agenda does not stand up to scutiny. 'Quite what the leaders of the G8 have to teach us about democracy is anyone's guess,' continued Kingsnorth. 'Blair was elected by just 25% of his people, while Bush wasn't elected at all.'[137]

A survey conducted by *The Ecologist* magazine during the summer of 2001, and published in the *Guardian* newspaper, revealed the true extent of the disparity between public opinion and UK government policy. Only 7 per cent felt that bio-technology should receive more funding than the organic sector, a staggering 72 per cent disbelieved the government when it assures the public that something is safe and 73 per cent would like to replace major government decisions with national referendums. As Zac Goldsmith concluded, 'This is not the picture of a public satisfied with the manner in which their taxes are being spent and their futures dictated, but rather a public with a healthy scepticism towards politicians, corporations and even the current definition of "progress".'[138]

Now the assumption that globalised free trade will alleviate world poverty is being questioned by an expanding number of people. Caroline Lucas, one of the first Green British members of the European Parliament, warns that

> If the EU continues to put its corporate-led, deregulated, neo-liberal agenda above social justice and sustainable development, the result

> will be further marginalisation and exclusion. People will only engage with an EU that is relevant to their everyday lives, and which they feel is democratic and accountable. The dominance of economic globalisation on the EU's agenda ensures that the EU is moving in precisely the opposite direction.[139]

Rather than listening to the voice of the protesters, G8 leaders seem hell-bent on accelerating their free trade agenda. The consequence will be more violent protests, while Carlo Giuliani, the young man killed by the police in Genoa, will be just the first in a long line of martyrs to the cause. As one young demonstrator said after Genoa, 'It is a war and in a war people die.'[140]

Naomi Klein's book, *No Logo*, is a detailed study of the way in which, since the 1980s, multinational corporations, especially major brands like Nike, The Gap, Disney and McDonald's, have made the progression from purely selling their products to marketing an image. Company logos, like the Nike 'swoosh', have spawned an almost cult-like allegiance amongst fashion-conscious youth. As the book shows, this approach has 'proved enormously profitable, and its success has companies competing in a race towards weightlessness: whoever owns the least, has the fewest employees on the payroll and produces the most powerful images, as opposed to products, wins the race'.[141]

The dark side to this is not just that teenagers are being murdered for an expensive pair of running shoes. In their race for weightless efficiency, an increasingly globalised economy has enabled corporations like Nike and Disney to exploit cheap labour and lax regulations in developing countries. Sneakers which sell for $120 are made by Indonesian workers, many of them children as young as twelve, earning less than $2 a day. Klein presents some of the most revealing discrepancies that globalisation promotes:

> All 50,000 workers at the Yue Yen Nike factory in China would have to work for nineteen years to earn what Nike spends on advertising in one year. Wal-Mart's annual sales are worth 120 times more than Haiti's entire annual budget; Disney CEO Michael Eisner earns $9,783 an hour while a Haitian worker earns 28 cents an hour; it would take a Haitian worker 16.8 years to earn Eisner's hourly income; the $181 million in stock options Eisner exercised in 1996 is enough to take care of his 19,000 Haitian workers and their families for fourteen years.[142]

The global reach of these brands is seen to be homogenising the world population into one extended market, replacing cultural diversity with the rampant consumer lifestyle of the Euro-American. This means little to those with an unbending faith in the 'trickle-down' benefits of capitalism. The fact that traditional diets throughout the world are being replaced by the fast-food culture of McDonald's – causing obesity in children, adding to pollution, accelerating deforestation and soil erosion through meat-intensive farming, destroying local markets and traditional local agriculture – is seen as 'progress', a triumph for the universal prosperity promised by economic liberalisation. However, as we are now seeing, the resistance to globalisation, and the cultural imperialism that comes with it, is as pervasive as Starbucks and the Golden Arches themselves.

The Greenwash

Why, when there is such overwhelming scientific evidence that we are trashing the planet, do so many of us seem unable to accept the reality? Why, as we watch intensive British farming bounce from one crisis to another, and climate change bring more devastating weather to every part of the globe, do most people remain indifferent?

There is no doubt that the human psyche produces various psychological defences when confronted with catastrophe and potential trauma. These responses are often justified by spurious information circulated by politicians, industry and big business, desperate either to convince the public that everything is under control, or perpetuate an antiquated economic agenda. Al Gore highlights internal memos circulated within the White House during the Bush administration, outlining the position that they should take to diminish the threat of global warming. Government officials were expressly told not to support action against climate change and that 'a better approach is to raise the many uncertainties'.[143] During the British 'foot and mouth' crisis, independent studies revealed the many inconsistencies surrounding government policy, which was based on unsubstantiated scientific evidence regarding the danger of the disease and was ultimately aimed at defending a relatively insignificant export market. Since BSE cost the country £607 million in 1996 alone, the logic of defending an intensive meat industry at all costs is clearly flawed. This is a system that makes the British taxpayer spend some £5 billion a year encouraging farmers to pursue the intensive, non-sustainable practices which lead to catastrophes like BSE in the first place, while a mere £9 million goes towards organic production. A recent study by Professor Jules Petty proved that every hectare of British farmland costs the taxpayer an average of £208 a year.[144]

The world's most powerful corporations constantly commission scientists, writers and journalists to publish material which contradicts the green agenda, exposing the way in which apocalyptic predictions have proved inaccurate, or deliberately confusing the issue by producing conflicting sets of data. As Helena Norberg-Hodge says 'Much of the information we are getting from mainstream sources is very suspect.'[145] Oil companies undermine efforts to reach a consensus on global warming, while pharmaceutical giants try to rubbish claims for alternative medicine: it transpired that recent studies to discredit St John's Wort, a herbal anti-depressant, had been funded by the manufacturers of Prozac. In environmental circles, this practice has become known as the 'greenwash' in the UK, or 'brownlash' in the US. Although it may be true that environmental groups have often resorted to scare-mongering tactics, it is usually an exasperated attempt to grab public attention. Forecasts about something like global warming, an unbelievably complex issue involving an endless list of variable factors, will always be subject to intense debate and open to margins of error. However, the evidence that confronts us now has been compiled by over a thousand independent scientists, none of whom feature on the pay-roll of multinational corporations.

One of the most famous British proponents of the 'greenwash' is the writer Richard D. North. Ironically, North started his career as the archetypal vegan hippie with green values. (On his website, he makes the bizarre confession that he was 'the first person to wear a poncho in Surbiton'.)[146] In the mid-1980s, he became the first environment correspondent for *The Independent* newspaper. Then something happened. Rather than writing about the destruction of rainforests and expanding holes in the ozone layer, he started to attack absolutely any aspect of the green agenda that he could find. 'What's so good about the wilderness?' he asked, claiming that 'the good bits of rainforest are the bits where somebody has obligingly logged and put in a road'.[147] *The Ecologist* thinks that the positive thing about the sheer absurdity of North's polemics is that they are 'always good for a laugh'. He loves nuclear power, landfills and road-building. 'Don't worry about pollution,' he says. 'It's all been sorted.' As for environmentalists, they are 'parasites getting an easy living off the back of people who are out there trying to make the world better'.[148]

So what prompted North's change of heart? He claims to have overcome his 'ignorant dislike of industry' and embraced all the western, material values which he had previously so despised. In fact, it later emerged that the research for his 'greenwash' book, *Life on a Modern Planet*, was funded by ICI. After local activist Ken Saro-Wiwa was murdered, Shell funded a trip to Nigeria's Ogoniland so that North could file pieces to the media which reflected well on the company. As *The Ecologist* observes, North often sounds 'as if he is venting his spleen on the elements of his former self that he sees in today's Swampies', concluding with his words to a group of journalists in 1998: 'Providing you are either amusing or terrifying – in any case providing you are shocking in some way – you are going to get paid.'[149]

North's extreme anti-environmentalism probably makes him less sinister than those who claim to be supporting green principles. On the other side of the Atlantic, Peter Huber, a senior fellow at the Manhattan Institute, recently published *Hard Green: Saving the Environment from the Environmentalists*. Huber seriously proposes that fossil fuels and nuclear energy are 'the greenest fuels' since they 'extract the most energy from the least land'.[150] Resource depletion is no problem because 'we will grow, find or invent others to replace them'.[151] He supports the use of chemical fertilisers, pesticides, packaging and preservatives because they 'permit us to capture more food from the sun, more efficiently, using less land'.[152] In an attempt to justify American energy use and consumption patterns, he maintains that reforestation in the country 'removes about as much carbon dioxide from the air as we emit by burning fossil fuels'.[153] This is simply not true, as thousands of independent studies have proved. Numerous studies have shown that organic agriculture can be as productive as energy-intensive techniques. And why rely on fossil fuels and nuclear energy when we have renewable energy systems and the technology available to create a hydrogen-based economy with zero-emissions?

As Paul and Anne Ehrlich point out, 'brownlash' agents almost invariably receive handsome financial returns for spreading misleading propaganda. Patrick Michaels, a climatologist at the University of Virginia and senior fellow at the Cato Institute, downplays global warming while receiving six-figure consulting fees from the energy corporations.[154] Fred Singer, another climate change cynic and Director of the Science and Environment Policy Project, has been a paid consultant for ARCO, Exxon, Shell, Sun Oil and Unocal.[155] He also believes that CFCs were phased out of production on the basis of 'insubstantial science'.[156] The Ehrlichs also draw attention to the 'greenscamming' tactics of US organisations which purport to be caring for the planet – the Alliance for Environment and Resources, the Global Climate Coalition, the National Wilderness Institute, the National Wetland Institute. Despite their names, these groups are actually working for their own economic interests rather than the environmental issues which they claim to defend, aligning themselves with the 'wise-use' movement rather than efforts to promote 'sustainability', regarded as the kiss-of-death for economic growth.[157]

In their detailed study of the way in which 'anti-environmental rhetoric threatens our future', the Ehrlichs pinpoint several 'brownlash' writers presenting questionable scientific data. The book that receives the most criticism is *A Moment on Earth* by Gregg Easterbrook, a journalist contributing to *Atlantic Monthly* and *Newsweek*. The back cover of the book claims that 'Planet earth is alive and well' and that 'pollution is almost over in the Western world'. *USA Today* called it 'this year's important Ecological Book'. *Business Week* thought it offered 'a refreshing, evenhanded appraisal of the state of the planet'. However, according to the Ehrlichs, 'the book contains so many serious errors that it has spawned a virtual cottage industry among scientists trying to correct them'. Jack Schultz, an entymologist from Pennsylvania State University, said the book 'contains some of the most egregious cases of misunderstood, misstated, misinterpreted, and plainly incorrect "science" writing I've ever encountered.'[158] Thomas Lovejoy, an ecologist at the Smithsonian Institute, 'was stunningly disappointed by the book's rambling prose and profusion of inconsistency and error'.[159]

For conspiracy theorists, the 'greenwash' is just one more aspect of a sinister plot to mislead the public and ensure that the global economy continues to be controlled by a powerful elite. Most of us now accept that the world is far from being run by politicians. Money equals power, and corporations are in the driving seat. Political decisions are made by business leaders and, however altruistic a politician may appear while running for office, the environmental agenda is soon quashed by the economic one when he or she assumes power. Despite Al Gore's environmental manifesto, published in 1992, he achieved virtually nothing during the Clinton era, while the last US election proved that the leader of the free world is now chosen according to his television persona.

Unfortunately, 'greenwash/brownlash' literature has become so pervasive that politicians, the media and the public find it difficult to sift through the distortions and uncover the real facts. However, every day an expanding network of independent scientists, environmental pressure groups and grassroots activists are documenting the destruction of the planet. Many are volunteers, working without income. They have no vested interests and no hidden agenda. They are committed to what they are doing by the passion they feel for the planet, and for the gift of Life itself.

4

A Green and Pleasant Land

Modern man talks of a battle with Nature,
forgetting that, if he won the battle,
he would find himself on the losing side.

E. F. SCHUMACHER[1]

What Happened to Our Food?

The consumption of food is one of the most direct interactions that occurs between Man and Nature. The basic energy for our physical existence is provided by the land around us, breaking down in our digestive systems to form the cellular structure of our bodies.

Given this basic understanding, that the food we eat forms the essence of the physical body, it may seem strange that the link between diet and health has only been officially recognised during the last century. Indigenous tribal cultures have developed sophisticated knowledge about the medicinal use of plants and herbs, but it has taken thousands of years within the evolution of 'civilised' man to identify any scientific correlation between the composition of food and its nutritional value. With hindsight, there seems to have been a similar lapse of reason over the dangers of tobacco – common sense suggests that inhaling clouds of smoke must have an effect on the lungs but it is only in recent years that conclusive research which proves the connection between tobacco and cancer has been made public. There is evidence to show that the tobacco companies were well aware of the dangers in the 1920s. This still did not prevent them advertising cigarettes as being positively beneficial to health, and CEOs of American cigarette companies recently swearing under oath that they did not believe such a link existed. The tobacco industry may be an extreme case but it illustrates the degree to which the corporate mentality is prepared to maximise profits at the expense of human life.

Tobacco is one of the most obviously carcinogenic compounds that corporations legally inflict upon addicted consumers but it is increasingly evident that we are all at risk from many of the food products which line the shelves of our supermarkets; pesticide residues in vegetables, sometimes exceeding the Maximum Residue Limit (MRL) by as much as forty-five times;[2] fungicides, like the highly toxic methyl bromide, sprayed all over fruits; concentrations of everything from DDT to organophosphates and chlordane in animal fats; levels of PCBs and dioxins in fish at the top of the food chain, like tuna and shark, which are up to 25 million times greater than when they were first released into the atmosphere.[3] We brush our teeth with fluoride, a by-product of the aluminium industry which has been pumped into our drinking water for decades and is known to have no discernible benefit whatsoever; some US studies attribute 35,000 cancer deaths per year to the practice and it has been linked to kidney failure in bottle-fed infants, thereby causing 'cot death'. Our children live on drinks flavoured with artificial sweeteners and recognised carcinogens like aspartame, a chemical compound which was first developed to treat ulcers, contains three neuro-toxic substances – phenylaline, methyl alcohol and aspartic acid – and is known to create tumours and microscopic holes in the brains of rats and epileptic seizures in monkeys.[4] We fill our fridges with food wrapped in clingfilm, containing phthalate plastic compounds which are thought to be responsible for falling sperm counts.[5] Supermarket shelves are lined with thousands of food products but, upon closer inspection, we find that most of them contain little more than refined flour, sugar, saturated fat, salt and chemical flavourings – a recipe for poor nutrition, heart disease and cancer. Cases of Creutzfeldt-Jakob Disease (CJD), the human variant of BSE, continue to rise, while some speculate that it 'could in time prove to be the most insidious and lethal contagion since the Black Death'.[6]

Perhaps the most horrifying of all is the widespread influence of synthetic chemicals that mimic hormones like oestrogen and disrupt the reproductive system. *Our Stolen Future*, the *Silent Spring* of the nineties, documents reports of whole bird populations born with twisted beaks, of dolphins and alligators with disfigured reproductive organs, of young girls born without wombs.[7] Over the last hundred years, the petro-chemical industry has synthesised some 10 million new chemical compounds, of which 150,000 have found their way into commercial production, and a tiny percentage of which have been thoroughly or reliably tested.[8] According to studies by the EU, the average European is exposed to at least 300 different chemicals every day, while the US National Academy of Sciences estimates that 37 million Americans suffer from environmental illness due to the proliferation of chemicals in the home and work-place.[9] In effect, corporate scientists invent new chemicals, think of reasons for using them and thereby create a market-place to unleash them upon the biosphere. As a consequence, we live in a carcinogenic environment and it is now estimated that one in three of us will die of cancer.

The main dumping ground for the chemical industry's innovations is agriculture. Modern farming has become inextricably linked with the agro-chemical industry, making it extremely hard for a farmer to make the switch to organic practices. The hold that these corporations have over the agri-business has reached a watershed with bio-technology. Farmers across the world, from the mono-cultures of the American Mid-West to rural Indian villages, are confronted with companies like Cargill and Monsanto, locking themselves into a contractual obligation to buy, not only the corporation's seeds, but also the chemicals which the seeds are genetically modified to be dependent upon. Despite the fact that the UN's Food Programme asserts that the world already produces one and a half times as much food as the global population requires, and that a quarter of the world's population eats half the world's food, the defenders of bio-technology continue to insist that genetic modification is necessary to feed the world.[10] When one considers that 25 per cent of the food that annually enters the American market-place ends up in the trash – enough to feed 100 million people in Africa – one begins to see where the disparity lies.[11]

Genetic engineering may indicate just how wide a rift has developed between our species and the natural world. Can we really defend the ethics of a science which breeds animals genetically disposed to develop cancer? Do we really need genetically engineered featherless chicken breasts? More and more of us now realise that intensive farming practices have been inflicting similar crimes upon domesticated animals for many years. How many of us really want to eat chickens which are so pumped full of hormones that they reach full size in a few weeks, their undeveloped legs buckling and breaking beneath them because of the excessive weight? Is it morally defensible to clip chicken's beaks and let cows milk themselves to death, suffering from chronic mastitis and distended udders? How many of us really want bacon from pigs bred in pens which prevent them from turning round, or lying down, and from which they have never seen the light of day?

Our separation from Nature has let us drift so far from the reality of what sustains us that we continue to support the methods of intensive modern meat production. But whatever happened to common sense? Who, in their right mind, would feed animals the ground-up remains of their own species? Why, in spite of BSE, do we continue feeding farmed salmon with ground-up chicken bones? How have we separated ourselves from the natural world to such a degree that children all over the developed world think that milk comes from a factory? How have we allowed the land to become so depleted and the production of our food to become so abominated, so contaminated and so removed from our daily lives? How much longer are we prepared to sit back and let multinational corporations destroy biodiversity, local communities and the soil on which our future depends? How much longer are we prepared to feed poison to our children?

The Agri-business

In 1842, an English farmer called John Lawes combined sulphuric acid with phosphate rock to produce the world's first artificial fertiliser, a concentrated superphosphate which could be applied to the soil. Not long after, Lawes founded the first chemical fertiliser company and was exporting his products to affluent farmers in Europe and the US.[12]

Adding nitrogen to the soil proved more challenging and it was not until 1909 that Fritz Haber, a German-Jewish chemist who created poison gas during the First World War, first extracted the element from the air through ammonia synthesis. Like Thomas Midgeley's suggestion of adding lead to petrol, or inventing CFCs, Lawes and Haber were blissfully unaware of how significant an impact their discoveries would have upon the planet, from disturbing global nitrogen and phosphorus cycles to the disruption of natural hydrology. By 1990, the world was using 150 million tons of artificial fertilisers every year.[13] We now live in a world where chemicals which have only existed for decades have become so pervasive that they can be traced in soil, water sources and living tissues all over the planet – from the ice shelf of Antarctica and the flesh of penguins, through to the upper reaches of the atmosphere. On the fiftieth anniversary of the Soil Association, of which he is the Royal Patron, Prince Charles highlighted the fact that British water companies would require £1 billion of capital investment to eradicate pesticides from our drinking water, while 'the monitoring and removal of pesticides from contaminated water supplies is already costing us £121 million every year'.[14]

The modern agri-business took shape after the Second World War. The industries which had produced the nitrates for explosives used similar processes to manufacture fertilisers, while the factories which had been making tanks now turned their attention to agricultural machinery, designing huge tractors and combine harvesters. The advent of chemical fertilisers and pesticides produced radical changes in our approach to agriculture. Thousands of years of traditional knowledge, encompassing methods for conserving nutrients in the soil and combating pests though diversification, were rapidly replaced by short-term chemical applications. The impact was phenomenal. Vast areas were opened up for mono-culture production, allowing farmers to concentrate on crops such as maize, which responded well to chemicals, at the expense of others. This in turn led to a more restricted diet and two thirds of global agricultural production is now devoted to just three crops: rice, wheat and maize. At the same time, the gulf between rich and poor farmers dramatically increased as those with access to agro-chemicals produced bumper yields, leading to vast grain surpluses in richer countries.

The application of chemicals has proved almost impossible to regulate. It has been estimated that over half the fertilisers applied to agricultural land end up in downstream water sources, leading to the eutrophication of lakes and rivers due to an excessive amount of nutrients. Perhaps most significantly, farming has become entirely dependent on the oil industry, which produces the chemical fixes required to stay in business. The petrochemical industry not only supplies the fertilisers and pesticides which the agri-business has become addicted to, but also the oil for the machinery which these energy-intensive methods of production require. In addition to soil, water and sunlight, our food is now made from oil.

When German U-boats had threatened to cut food supplies from overseas, Britain's ability to feed itself was severely jeopardised. At the time, much of the agricultural land was devoted to grass or barley for animal fodder and Britain only produced 30 per cent of its own food.[15] Post-war policy-makers responded by shifting the emphasis towards home-produced crops and introduced a concept which has plagued British farming ever since – the state subsidy. Like the introduction of chemicals, subsidies further encouraged intensified farming. Since the government was willing to pay a fixed price for crops, mixed farming was no longer practised as a way of insuring against market instability or freak weather patterns. Instead, farmers were pushed to specialise, aiming for bigger yields and bigger profits.

Armed with an expanding arsenal of products from the chemical industry, the drive for intensification had a dramatic effect on the countryside. As Andrew O'Hagan says, in his polemic called *The End of British Farming*, 'we turned the landscape into a prairie, trounced our own eco-system, and with public money too, and turned some of the biggest farms in Europe into giant, fertiliser-gobbling, pesticide-spraying, manufactured-seed-using monocultures geared only for massive profits and the accrual of EU subsidies.'[16] To maximise the use of land, and make way for larger machinery, ponds were filled in, meadows ploughed over and hedgerows ripped out. Since 1947, some 97 per cent of our wildflower meadows have been destroyed and 60 per cent of our lowland fens have been drained and ploughed.[17] This loss of habitat, combined with the chemical disruption of the food chain, has had a devastating impact on plant and animal life; wildflowers like lamb's succory and thorow-wax have become extinct while the corn buttercup, prolific until the 1960s, has been reduced to twenty-five sites;[18] many bird populations have dropped by half while the number of tree-sparrows has fallen by nearly 90 per cent.[19] As Aldous Huxley remarked after reading *Silent Spring*, 'We are losing half the subject-matter of English poetry.'

These issues were exacerbated by the Common Agricultural Policy (CAP) which was enforced after Britain's entry to the Common Market in 1973. Although the CAP was the policy which lay at the foundation of the EC, it has been consistently regarded as the most fundamentally flawed bit of legislation that the member countries ever introduced.

Designed to promote self-sufficiency in food production, guarantee a fair standard of living for farmers and stabilise markets by securing food supplies at a reasonable price for the consumer, the CAP has usually achieved the precise opposite of what was intended. By encouraging high levels of production, the policy has de-stabilised food prices by dumping EU surpluses onto the world market; the knock-on effect of these trade policies has been to destroy whole economies in the developing world, especially Africa, while the EU taxpayer carries the can by subsidising both the production and the sale of the food that is exported. A study by the Organisation for Economic Co-operation and Development (OECD) has shown that, for every pound given to farmers, consumers paid up to £1.80 in higher food prices and taxes.[20] The system of quotas and subsidies has benefited richer, larger farmers at the expense of those that it was supposed to protect, the traditional peasant farmer working a smallholding – about 80 per cent of the financial support going to the largest 20 per cent of farms.[21] An emphasis on high-tech mechanised methods of farming has promoted unsustainable practices and had a devastating effect on the environment, while the bureaucratic web surrounding the system of subsidies has spawned one of the biggest growth industries in Europe – fraudulent abuse of the CAP: in 1994, some 4,264 cases of fraud were investigated, involving 1.2 billion Ecu, estimated to be a mere 10 per cent of the total.[22]

Despite constant efforts to reform the CAP, it has been riddled with absurdities ever since its inception. By 1987, EC food stores contained more than 1 million tons of butter, 3 million tons of barley and 5 million tons of wheat. Two years later, politicians congratulated themselves on introducing quotas which reduced the butter mountains and milk lakes, overlooking the fact that they had cost £6,000 million in two years. Within a year, there was a surplus of 185,000 tons of oil seed. The farmers that first received subsidies to rip out hedgerows were then given subsidies to put them back, while those that had not disturbed them in the first place received nothing.[23] After handing out incentives to plant fruit trees, the EU tried to curtail production by offering thousands of pounds per hectare to those prepared to destroy orchards which were only three years old and had not even started producing a crop.[24]

By 1988, the Ministry for Agriculture, Fisheries and Food (MAFF) was doling out £1.5 billion in price support plus £150 million for 'special areas' while simultaneously trying to cut production and deal with vast surpluses. In effect, the government pays farmers to produce too much, then pays them again to buy the surplus while continuing to hand out subsidies to stop them producing and maintain their incomes. It seems doubly ludicrous that, while governments and multinational corporations defend the need for agro-chemicals and biotechnology – so that the expanding world population can be fed – farmers are paid to destroy their own crops, or not to farm the land at all. As one economist remarked back in 1983, 'When you buy agricultural land now, you're essentially buying a licence to receive very large sums of public money.'

The CAP is inextricably linked with a global trend towards promoting the concept of free trade, enforced by the World Trade Organisation (WTO) and the General Agreement on Tariffs and Trade (GATT). First signed in 1947, the central aim of GATT was to liberalise world trade, based on the principle of 'comparative advantage', whereby commodities should be produced by those with the cheapest methods of manufacture. However, like our entire economic system, GATT externalises all social and environmental factors, reducing the entire process to one of financial competition. In terms of food production, the concept of globalised free trade is especially flawed since agriculture cannot be treated purely as a business – it is essentially a way of life which produces food, rather than products that can be traded indefinitely. In addition, a world market for agricultural produce does not really exist since some 95 per cent of food is consumed close to where it is produced. That which does travel around the world purely adds to pollution and resource depletion through intensive transport use. Furthermore, there are intrinsic differences between systems of farming practised all over the world. Trying to establish a single global agreement over international food production is indicative of our search for simple solutions to complex problems, of a drive towards intensification rather than diversification.

The consequences of this are now hitting home. British farming is in crisis. UK farm income has dropped by 75 per cent in the last two years. 20,000 farmers have been forced off the land and suicide has become the leading cause of death, occurring at a rate which is three times the national average.

The spectre of 'foot and mouth' will be with us for many years to come as the truth behind the duplicitous handling of the crisis emerges. According to one source, Tony Blair signed an EU directive in 1998, in the wake of BSE, to abolish the British livestock industry and make way for mass GM arable farming.[25] One Welsh farmer told me that a MAFF official admitted they were aiming for a 40 per cent cull of the total livestock population and wanted 'no sheep left between Welshpool and Brecon'.[26] As I write, thousands of healthy sheep on the Brecon Beacons are being taken to slaughter while the politicians maintain that the crisis is over and impose restrictions on the British media. Up and down the country, there are reports of hauliers and timber merchants being approached in connection with transport plans and timber stocks for dealing with the crisis, months before the first case was even reported. According to one French vet, the virus was detected in one Welsh flock in early January, while infected sheep were exported to France a month before the first official case was made public on 20 February.[27] When you combine this information with reports of a phial containing the virus 'going missing' from Porten Down biological weapons factory two months earlier, the evidence for some hidden agenda looks increasingly likely. Even more sinister rumours have been circulating in the farming community around where I live, with stories about the virus being sprayed from helicopters, farmers being locked up for the night after refusing to have their livestock killed and returning to find dead animals stacked up in their barns.

Even if one discounts these stories, the government handling of the crisis has been suspicious from the start. An outbreak in Denmark in 1982 was brought under control in fifteen hours and affected twenty-two animals.[28] In 1998, a huge epidemic in Albania was controlled in twelve weeks.[29] Why, when we know that vaccination works, was MAFF so intent on incinerating thousands of animals on huge medieval pyres? Was this just another ploy to ensure the spread of the virus, making it airborne and releasing it into the jet-stream? We are told that our meat would lose its disease-free status abroad, while all the time we continue to import infected meat from countries like Argentina. Since MAFF claims that the export industry is worth £592 million – while other estimates put the figure closer to half that – it seems totally illogical to pursue a path which jeopardises the £64 billion generated by British tourism. Was this just another example of an antiquated civil service sticking to obsolete procedures? As Jonathan Freedland observed, 'even the "no entry" signs MAFF produced were printed in retro, postwar type: emblems of a dumb obedience to the past script and a failure to think anew'.

And what about this mysterious test tube that seemed to vaporise from Porten Down? For a start, the fact that Porten Down is storing the virus at all, alongside samples of other potential biological weapons like ebola and anthrax, is a clear violation of the Biological Warfare Treaty which was ratified in 1972. Interestingly enough, rather than consulting a competent experts' commission when the virus 'broke out', the government turned to just one man, Martin Hugh-Jones, a biological weapons expert with a specialised knowledge of anthrax. Hugh-Jones emigrated to the US in 1978 and is now Professor of Epidemiology at Louisiana State University. He also happens to be the World Health Organisation's (WHO's) co-ordinator on Anthrax Research and Control and Director of the WHO Collaborating Centre for Remote Sensing and Geographic Information Systems for Public Health. Why did a biological warfare expert, who has emigrated to the US, become MAFF's chief advisor during the 'foot and mouth' crisis? As one commentator has observed, 'this man evidently works for both American and British intelligence agencies'.[30]

The evidence seems to suggest that the apparent incompetence over handling this crisis was designed to obscure the government's real agenda. Whatever the case, the nation deserves to know the truth about this sorry, sinister saga. 'We need a serious, probing public enquiry to lay bare what really happened,' says Freedland. 'For a kind of collective madness descended on these islands – and we were all infected.' Should it transpire that this was a deliberate plan to destroy the British livestock industry, it will go down in history as one of the greatest evils ever perpetrated by a modern government on its own soil and to its own people. Even if we never learn the truth, hundreds of thousands of healthy, innocent animals have been quite literally sacrificed to 'economic interests'. The Welsh hill farmers near where I live – most of whom earn less than £4,000 a year, the majority of which is subsidy – have been sacrificed along with them. A whole way of life, which has always been seen as quintessentially British, has been traded in for Tony Blair's vision for the future of British farming, a vision which sees no value in sustainable rural communities and traditional rural life. All that has been left behind in parts of the British countryside, in the aftermath of this mass murder killing spree, are rotting carcasses, smouldering pyres, broken lives and thousands of very angry people.

To add insult to injury, the man that Blair has chosen to head the programme in rural recovery is Lord Haskins, Chairman of Northern Foods and an active exponent of bio-technology. As George Monbiot notes, putting this man in charge of rural recovery 'is like putting Lord Tebbit in charge of race relations'.[31] Haskins is known to be hostile to organic farming, dismissing it as being 'for the birds', and has made no secret about his plans to eliminate small farms in favour of the giant agro-industrialists which supply the ingredients for his packaged, processed products. 'Lord Haskins presents himself as the champion of the poor', says Monbiot, 'but he and the supermarkets he sells to are impoverishing people at both ends of the production chain, while enriching themselves.'[32]

By treating agriculture as just another type of business, the separation between the land and the people has become even more pronounced. The majority of farmers have been forced to turn their back on traditional techniques and intuitive knowledge, locked into a pact with multinational corporations which provide the energy-intensive inputs that their livelihoods have become dependent upon. As Graham Harvey observes in another recent polemic about the state of British farming, this has produced 'the perfect technocracy: Whitehall and industry working as one to reshape the countryside. A symbiosis of public service and private capital, with the taxpayer picking up the bill while being excluded from the decision making. The chemical industry provides the technology to get the people off the land. In return the government delivers a form of subsidy that is guaranteed to lift returns to farm suppliers, particularly fertiliser and agro-chemical suppliers.'[33] As a result, 'our taxes go to subsidise hard-headed businessmen; exploiters of resources rather than guardians of the landscape', while modern farmers are 'more likely to be wearing Armani suits than overalls, and the closest they get to the fields is driving over them in the Range Rover'.[34]

To regard the land as just another resource, and farming as another type of business, is simplistic in the extreme. Those few inches of topsoil, which world food production relies upon, is the basis of civilisation itself. The health and preservation of the soil cannot be left to short-term fixes imposed by politicians and bureaucrats from centralised urban offices. It requires the intimate knowledge and understanding which can only develop between a community and the land in which they live. The future, not only for British farming but for global food production as a whole, depends on that relationship. The soil is an intensely complex, evolving living system. It does not behave like a machine and quite simply will not survive if we treat it as one.

Bio-technology: Why?

The supporters of bio-technology often insist that genetic engineering is nothing but the latest development in Man's long history of manipulating the natural world to his benefit, the logical progression from hybridisation and selective breeding. Domesticated animals, ornamental flowers and the staple crops of the modern global food system have all come a long way from the wild animals and plants from which they originated.

There is, however, one fundamental difference about genetic engineering. By transferring genes from one species to another, say from a scorpion into a tomato to try to make it resistant to freezing temperatures, we are doing something which is quite simply impossible within the processes of natural evolution. The chances of a scorpion mating with a tomato are less than slight and successful mutations which do occur in Nature happen over considerable periods of time.

The bio-tech industry has not only taken a quantum leap in tampering with the evolutionary process, but is literally doing it overnight. We have absolutely no idea what the consequences could be and, once the new organism has been created, the process is totally irreversible. The assumption that the desired characteristic of a certain organism, for example the scorpion's ability to cope with dramatic fluctuations in temperature, will be all that is replicated within the tomato, is not only staggeringly simplistic but representative of our continued search for simple solutions within inherently complex processes. There is every reason to suppose that, by transferring genes from one species to another, we will also be transferring all sorts of undesirable traits, which may include diseases or viruses which medical science is incapable of dealing with. We are quite simply playing with fire and, like DDT, asbestos and thalidomide, the consequences could be far more dramatic than any of us currently supposes.

Various worst-case scenarios have been suggested, ranging from the creation of a superbug which could decimate vast portions of the food supply, to all manner of twisted genetic mutations entering our food chain. Jeremy Rifkin, one of the most vocal opponents of the bio-tech industry, spells it out:

> Imagine the wholesale transfer of genes between totally unrelated species and across all biological boundaries – plant, animal and

> human – creating thousands of novel life forms in a brief moment of evolutionary time. Then, with clonal propagation, mass-producing countless replicas of these new creations, releasing them into the biosphere to propagate, mutate, proliferate and migrate, colonising land, water and air. This is, in fact, the great scientific and commercial experiment underway as we turn the corner into the Bio-tech Century.[35]

One of the main objections raised about this technology is an ethical one, that we are usurping the creative role of Nature and 'playing God', that we are entering a domain which should, to some degree, remain 'out of bounds'. For George Wald, a Harvard Professor and Nobel Laureate, we are witnessing the 'largest ethical problem that science has ever had to face'.[36] However, the geneticists who defend this type of research see no such cause for alarm. As Rifkin says,

> they see no ethical problem whatsoever in transferring one, five, or even a hundred genes from one species into the hereditary blueprint of another species. For they truly believe that they are only transferring chemicals coded in the gene and not anything unique to a specific animal. By this kind of reasoning, all of life becomes desacralised. All of life becomes reduced to a chemical level and becomes available for manipulation.[37]

This attitude is endemic within reductionist science, which has become so focused on the building blocks of life that it is blinded to the mysteries of life itself. As the biologist Rupert Sheldrake observes, even though we are told that genes are supposed to determine the form that an organism takes, 'no mechanistic explanation of the development of even a simple plant or animal has so far been achieved, but the belief that such an explanation is possible in principle remains a fundamental article of the mechanistic faith.'[38] Reductionist methods may tell us what does what within a living organism, but it is a long way from explaining why certain strands of DNA develop into the millions of uniquely different life forms that surround us. Why do two identical strands of DNA produce such entirely different organisms as a scorpion and a tomato? Similarly, reductionists like Francis Crick have reduced the human identity to 'nothing but a pack of neurons'. However, as Susan Blackmore points out, 'this does not address the "hard" problem of consciousness: what is the nature of experience? Why should there be experience associated with all these neural goings-on?'[39] What is consciousness? Why does it exist and where does it come from? By ignoring such questions, reductionist science completely fails to accept its limitations, while arrogantly congratulating itself on de-constructing living cells. In the process, it cannot see the wood for the trees.

The most insidious aspect of the industry that has mushroomed around genetics is the level to which it is controlled by a handful of transnational corporations. With almost evangelical zeal, media machines are bombarding us with information about how they are going to feed the world and eradicate all manner of diseases. Many of these arguments are fundamentally flawed. For example, Zeneca/Syngenta, who have pioneered 'golden rice', claim that it will cure 2.4 billion rice consumers in the developing world of vitamin A deficiency. However, independent studies by nutritionists have shown that the majority of them will not absorb the pro-vitamin A in the rice due to an absence of fat in their diet.[40] Most of those dying of starvation in the developing world are victims of famine caused by climatic changes and non-traditional, unsustainable agricultural systems which have led to high degrees of erosion and salinisation in the soil. UN figures show that global food supplies are more than adequate without the need for GM, producing one and a half times the amount required to feed the expanding population.[41] While EU farmers are busy ploughing surplus crops back into the ground and, given current trends, almost the entire American population is projected to be officially suffering from obesity within thirty years, it seems fairly iniquitous to continue preaching this message. Similarly, since recent studies suggest that up to 90 per cent of modern cancers can be attributed to dietary and environmental factors, it is hard to see how genetic engineering is going to make much contribution there.[42] Given that the vast increase in various cancers, as well as the surge of modern diseases like Alzheimers, is being related to the synthetic chemicals developed and pedalled by these same corporations, it is even more sinister that they should now claim to be curing them. Although governments and the medical establishment have pinned the blame for the cancer epidemic on cigarettes and high fat diet – on it being your fault for smoking and eating badly – there is much to suggest that these campaigns overlook the part played by environmental factors, most notably the accumulation of chemicals in the food chain.[43]

One can see why conspiracy theorists are having a field day, suggesting that corporations are creating problems which never existed so that they can then implement the solutions which they already have waiting in the wings. In a sense, that is exactly what is already happening with GM crops, which are being specifically designed to be dependent upon chemicals which are already patented by the same company. Monsanto's genetically modified soya, which has already found its way into many of the processed foods sold in this country, is sold in conjunction with their leading herbicide, RoundUp. In the words of David Ehrenfeld, a biology professor at Rutgers University in the US, 'the whole point of genetic engineering is to increase the sales of chemicals and bio-engineered products to dependent farmers'.[44] Jane Rissler, from the Union of Concerned Scientists, believes that 'Crops genetically engineered to resist herbicides, insects, and virus diseases, like chemical pesticides, will be sold to farmers as single, simple-to-use products to control pests and sustain continuous monoculture. They are being developed to fit immediately and easily into conventional agriculture's industrialised monoculture.'[45] Salil Shetty of Action Aid maintains that 'Rather than reducing world hunger, genetic engineering is likely to exacerbate it. Farmers will be caught in a vicious circle, increasingly dependent on a small number of giant multi-nationals for their survival.'[46]

This inherent dependency on the multinational's products has produced the most blatant attempt at corporate control to date – the 'terminator gene', adding the most sinister twist yet conceived by the industry. By treating the GM seed with an antibiotic like tetracyclene, the plant cannot produce fertile seeds, further insuring that farmers meet their contractual obligation to buy new patented seeds each year. Like the 'oncomouse' – mice genetically engineered to develop cancer – the ethics of 'terminator' technology are especially questionable, designing premature death into the life that is being created. Clearly, there is absolutely no benefit to the farmer, only to the multinational's balance sheet. AstraZeneca also developed what is being called 'verminator' technology, making the germination and subsequent growth of their seeds entirely dependent on repeated applications of their own chemicals. Edward Hammond, from the Rural Advancement Foundation International (RAFI) sums it up: 'Essentially, they're talking about the manufacture of junkie plants that are physically dependent on a patented chemical cocktail.'[47]

Typically, those likely to suffer the most will be in the Third World. Peasant farmers throughout the world have been saving seeds from one year to the next for at least 12,000 years. Some 1.4 billion of them still do.[48] However, for many this logical traditional practice has now been made illegal, due to legislation concocted by multinationals and implemented through the free trade agreements imposed by institutions like the WTO. Bio-tech giants, who have merged with major seed producers, keep tabs on farmers using their seeds and make sure that contracts are honoured. Without any prior warning, Canadian farmers who had failed to do so received letters from Monsanto imposing fines of $35,000.[49] In addition, the corporation is given the right to access the land for the next three years and test the crops, as well as imposing a clause which makes it illegal for the farmers to disclose the details of the letter. Thousands of peasant farmers in India have risen up in opposition to the contracts they have signed, burning seeds and attacking the offices of corporations like Cargill, which now controls 80 per cent of the world's grain distribution. Just four companies – Syngenta (formerly AstraZeneca and Novartis), DuPont, Monsanto and Aventis – account for two-thirds of the global pesticide market, a quarter of the global seed trade and virtually all the transgenic seed in circulation. Monsanto owns all the world's genetically engineered cotton.[50]

Another way in which bio-tech corporations exploit the Third World is through 'bio-prospecting', more accurately known now as 'bio-piracy'. Corporate scientists have been busy travelling the world, gathering samples of genetic material from people, plants and animals, hoping that they might develop miracle drugs worth billions of dollars. The pharmaceutical giant Merck has patented samples from nine countries, ranging from soil bacteria from heather on Mount Kilimanjaro to a soil fungus from Namibia.[51] This practice only became legal in 1985, when the US Patent Trademark Office (PTO) repealed an earlier ruling made in 1971, when Ananda Chakrabarty, an Indian microbiologist working for General Electric, was prevented from patenting a bacteria which could digest oil. In 1987 the PTO extended the new law to include all forms of life, opening up the door for projects like the Human Genome Diversity Project (HGDP) which has taken blood, tissue and hair samples from hundreds of tribal people around the world.[52]

The ultimate injustice of bio-piracy is that, having stolen the material from a Third World source in the first place, corporations then try to sell it back to them in a new guise as a patented product. A good example is the neem tree, esteemed in India for thousands of years because of its extraordinary qualities. The twigs contain high levels of a natural antiseptic and are used to brush the teeth. The leaves have been an important part in traditional ayurvedic medicine and also make a highly effective and natural insecticide. US and Japanese companies took out over a dozen patents on the various properties of the neem tree, with a view to marketing their products in India.[53] As a consequence, the price of neem seed in India has escalated, distorting the local market. However, as events in recent years have shown, Indian farmers and activists are far from being hoodwinked by multinational corporations, mounting such fierce resistance to Kentucky Fried Chicken that the company was forced to abandon its operations in the country. The neem patent was finally prevented and opposition to globalisation is huge, inspired by such charismatic leaders as Vandana Shiva, who believes that 'Patents on life are so immoral, and so unjust, and so against Nature and people, that it really only needs awareness in larger numbers for the whole thing to come to a stop.'[54]

The global resistance to bio-technology is spreading all the time. In the UK it has been especially pronounced, possibly because the public is still reeling from the implications of the BSE fiasco. Environmental groups like Greenpeace have campaigned hard to raise public awareness and their Director, Lord Melchett, was arrested after leading a high-profile action to destroy a trial site planted with GM maize near his own farm in Norfolk. Monsanto themselves have been surprised by the level of opposition and, after their share prices took a plunge, went away to reconsider. In his editorial for *The Ecologist* magazine, Zac Goldsmith congratulated Monsanto, 'who have single-handedly managed to unite a divided social and ecological movement'.[55]

The whole concept of genetic manipulation clearly incites tremendous indignation in people who have never previously been concerned about the environment. Food is an emotive issue. It touches people at the core of their being, precisely because it is their most direct physical contact with the environment. In the long run, the bastardisation of our food supply may well prove to be the critical issue which galvanises public opinion to such a degree that politicians will have no option but to listen. In 1999, one lady in her 80s was so incensed by GM maize being planted next to an organic farm near Totnes, that she walked 3 miles to attend the first demonstration of her life.[56] This sort of commitment, to what so many of us believe to be inherently and fundamentally wrong, may ultimately close the door to the giants of the bio-tech industry. As George Monbiot observes, 'If one million peasant farmers, most of them illiterate, can take to the streets of Bangalore in southern India in protest at the implications of trade-related intellectual property rights, as negotiated in the Uruguay Round of the General Agreement on Tariffs and Trade, I don't see why people in Britain can't get involved in debates about bio-technology.'[57]

Genetic engineering incites tremendous passion on both sides of the table. Executives within the bio-tech corporations may genuinely believe that they are going to feed the world. However, the messianic fervour with which they defend their cause usually prevents them from engaging in any progressive debate. The environmental journalist Hugh Warwick refers to the experience of Dr Ricarda Steinbrecher, a geneticist who turned her back on the industry and now works for the Women's Environmental Network (WEN). During a round-table discussion, she found that Monsanto executives 'were not prepared to shift from their original position by even a fraction of an inch' and that they 'show an astounding disregard for the democratic process'.[58] In a speech directed at Robert Shapiro, the CEO of Monsanto, Peter Melchett made the following accusations: 'You behave not as a company offering life and hope, but as bullies trying to force your products on us. You sue those who oppose you, and try and injunct them and anyone they've been in contact with – suppressing dissent, not encouraging debate. When you do debate, as in your recent UK press ads, you get your facts wrong.'[59] He went on to point out that 'Agricultural GM techniques have been the subject of an immense amount of hype, portraying them as "the future" and even essential to our survival as a species. In reality they represent more of the past. A past in which over-confident technologists, out of touch with the values and aspirations of ordinary people, have tried to impose "solutions" on society.'[60]

The under-hand tactics employed by the bio-tech industry have extended to blatant attempts at sabotaging the organic movement. Despite appeals from both politicians and the public, Scimac are adamant about pursuing GM crop trials at a site down the road from the Henry Doubleday centre in Warwickshire, Europe's largest organic research station. 'This is the forces of darkness deliberately trying to wreck organic agriculture by growing GM crops next to a centre of organic excellence,' said Patrick Holden, Director of the Soil Association. 'There are sinister motives at work here. Once the GM industry can contaminate organic seed there is no going back. They know that and they see this trial as a way of doing it.'[61] Bees are known to travel up to at least 3 miles from the hive, and pollen carried by the wind can clearly travel even further. Ironically, while the country was indoctrinated about the virulent spread of airborne foot and mouth, the political defenders of bio-technology continued to insist that GM pollen obediently stayed where it was told.

There is evidence to suggest that the projections made about bio-technology will prove equally inflated and even more disastrous than the chemical excesses of the so-called Green Revolution. Although bumper yields were consistent at the start, the intensive and unregulated use of chemicals in Third World countries has had devastating effects on the soil and the local hydrology, not to mention the number of pesticide-related deaths within farming communities and those who have eaten produce with excessive residues. Indian farmers used to grow 200,000 varieties of rice which, over thousands of years, developed in symbiosis with the local soil and climate and were largely resistant to pests and disease. This has now been reduced to less than fifteen.[62] Contrary to the industry's original claims that global food production would not survive without the introduction of pesticides, it is now estimated that pests have destroyed two or three times as many crops since chemicals were first introduced.

The brilliant Indian scientist and activist Vandana Shiva observes that 'the expansion of monocultures has more to do with politics and power than with enriching and enhancing systems of biological production. This is as true of the Green Revolution as it is of the gene revolution or the new technologies.'[63] There are numerous examples, from all around the world, that productivity actually increases when chemical dependence is reduced or abandoned altogether. In Indonesia, yields have risen by 15% since pesticide use was cut in half.[64] Hundreds of farmers, from Mexico and Brazil to Kenya and India, have turned to organic methods, reduced their external costs and increased their production.[65] In 1998, research from the University of Wisconsin revealed that seventeen out of twenty-one samples of GM soya actually produced lower yields than conventional varieties.[66]

Like so many of the innovations developed by the scientific community, there is absolutely no proof that we *need* this technology. It is just another example of 'technological determinism'. By letting it happen, we are blindly putting our faith in a science which threatens the very basis of life itself. 'Somehow, in the chaos of technological change', says David Ehrenfeld,

> we have lost the distinction between a person and a corporation, inexplicably valuing profit at any cost over human needs. In doing so we have forsaken our farmers, the spiritual descendants of those early Hebrew and Greek farmers and pastoralists who first gave us our understanding of social justice, democracy, and the existence of a power greater than our own. No amount of lip-service to the goal of feeding the world's hungry or to the glory of a new technology, and no amount of increases in the world's grain production, can hide this terrible truth.[67]

Aside from politicians and the bio-tech industry itself, the only people who actively support genetic engineering are the scientists who are paid to develop it, offering hollow promises of the benefits that it will bring and consistently over-looking the multiple, systemic dangers of creating self-replicating life-forms over which we have absolutely no control.

Supermarkets and the Global Food System

The resistance which the environmental movement has generated towards agri-business and bio-technology extends into every corner of the modern global food system, not least the purveyors of the produce which it supplies. Since 1995, average farm incomes have dropped by 60 per cent, thousands of farmers have been driven into bankruptcy, while Tesco's pre-tax profits have grown from £551 million to £842 million.[68] A savoy cabbage, which costs the farmer 13 pence to produce, is sold to the supermarket for 11 pence, then the supermarket sells it on to the consumer for 46 pence.[69] At the same time, the supermarket chains activate their PR machines, claiming that they are supporting British agriculture and small producers.

Supermarkets are responsible not only for squeezing small businesses out of the market-place, thus destroying local communities, but also for encouraging a variety of ecologically damaging practices. Heavily processed foods, which form the bulk of the modern diet and provide most of the revenue for supermarkets, are energy intensive in their production, distribution and packaging. Products with a high fat content, like cheese, absorb particularly concentrated amounts of toxic residue from the transparent plastic in which they are wrapped. By insisting on standardised products, supermarkets promote the use of chemicals. Fruit and vegetables must conform to certain specifications and show no signs of damage or variation. Nature does not observe such rules so farmers are forced to apply chemicals if their produce is not to be refused – a single blemish can lead to the rejection of an entire consignment. Similarly, by offering out-of-season produce, people all over the world are denied the basic food that they need. Vast areas of agricultural land in Kenya, which used to supply the local people with their staple diet, are now devoted to growing green beans and carnations so that consumers in Europe can purchase them throughout the year. By relaxing world trade barriers, institutions like the WTO purely accentuate the problem so that, while countries like Mali, Niger and Senegal were suffering famines during the 1980s, they continued to produce record harvests of cotton for export to industrialised countries in the north.[70]

One of the most ecologically damaging, and most frequently over-looked consequences of our global food system, is what has come to be termed 'food miles'. Since our economic system externalises all the social and environmental costs of intensive energy use, like the effects of airborne pollution on human health and the contribution of carbon dioxide to global climate change, the cost of transport is artificially low. As a consequence, it is considered 'economic' to send food all around the world, leading to the ludicrous situation where lamb, fruit and dairy products from New Zealand are 'cheaper' than those produced on farms a few miles down the road from the local supermarket.

A study by the SAFE alliance (Sustainable Agriculture Food and Environment) followed vegetables from a field outside Evesham to a co-operative in Herefordshire, then to a packhouse in Dyfed in Wales, on to two separate distribution depots, one just south of Manchester, and then back to a supermarket in Evesham. One supermarket chain has been known to haul salmon from Scotland to Cornwall to be smoked, then back to supermarkets in Scotland. This is clearly absurd and shows just how much our economic thought is in need of reform. The absurdity is perpetuated by supermarkets using a system of just-in-time (JIT) deliveries, which sends orders straight from the supermarket till to the nearest depot and leads to lorries making deliveries whenever goods are needed, travelling huge distances while only partly loaded. The supermarket lorries which are pounding up and down our motorways are often less than half full. Government policy compounds the problem, shifting increasing amounts of freight onto the road network rather than the railways. Over 80 per cent of freight in Britain is currently contributing to road congestion, noise pollution and greenhouse emissions by travelling in trucks rather than trains.

The other issue which has incited opposition to supermarkets is urban planning. Not only are most stores situated on the outskirts of urban areas, thus encouraging car use and depriving traditional small businesses in our town centres of much-needed commerce – as well as all the positive benefits that they bring to our sense of community – but they are part of a planning process which is riddled with corruption. Campaigns like The Land is Ours (TLIO), based in Oxford and led by the charismatic activist George Monbiot, have been at the forefront of highlighting these issues. In *Captive State* – his most recent book and a scathing attack on the way in which British culture is being taken over by corporate interests – Monbiot draws attention to myriad cases, throughout the country, in which supermarket chains have bought their way into urban areas. Through exploiting a process called 'off-site planning gain', which, as Monbiot says, 'you and I would recognize as bribery', developers can offer as much money as they see fit to a local authority, in exchange for planning permission.[71] His book contains a detailed account of the way in which Safeway were not only given access to a site in the Welsh market town of Brecon, but also allowed to build a new 'by-pass', in addition to the one that already exists, which mysteriously came to an abrupt halt outside the superstore car park. In Stornoway, in the Scottish Hebrides, Safeway offered to pay £375,000 for a sports facility if the local council prevented the Co-op from building a competing store.[72] As Monbiot points out, the system almost appears to be designed to encourage this sort of corruption: 'You don't like my high-rise multiplex hypermarket ziggurat? Here's a million quid – what do you think of it now?'[73]

In 1996, TLIO led a high-profile action in the London borough of Wandsworth, taking over 13 acres of derelict land, owned by the brewing giant Guinness and scheduled for the ninth major superstore within one and a half miles. One Saturday morning, a small army of activists poured into the site and started building an eco-village, complete with vegetable beds, geodesic domes and renewable energy systems. The activists drew attention to the fact that the land had been derelict for seven years and should be used for what the local community so desperately needed: green space for children to play in and low-impact affordable housing. They were evicted from the site, and the sustainable regeneration of urban wasteland, which city centres so desperately need, continues to be systematically ignored. 'Where we need affordable, inclusive housing, we get luxury, exclusive estates,' says Monbiot. 'Where we need open spaces, we get more and more empty office blocks; where we need local trade, we get superstores.'[74]

And the problem is not limited to urban areas. The law makes it almost impossible to build sustainable communities which actually improve the local environment rather than destroying it. Members of Tinkers Bubble, a small self-sufficient community in Somerset, have been constantly harassed by local planners and probably only held on to their land because of their profile in the media. As Monbiot observes, 'You can throw up a barn for 1,000 pigs with very little trouble, but try living in a hole in the ground in the middle of the woods, and you'll find all the hounds of hell unleashed upon you.'[75]

Most sinister of all is the extent to which government, the bio-tech industry and the global food system is being homogenised into one monolithic web of corporate intrigue. This is most pronounced in the US, where Linda Fisher, Marcia Hale, Josh King, along with numerous other government advisors and FDA officials, have taken up positions as directors of Monsanto.[76] Perhaps the most controversial example in Britain, which Monbiot presents in revealing detail, is Lord Sainsbury of Turville. Before making huge donations to New Labour, and taking his position as Minister of Science,

Lord Sainsbury was not only Chairman of the J. Sainsbury supermarket chain, but also the principal backer of the bio-tech company Diatech. The *Observer* subsequently revealed that Diatech paid for the renovation of Lord Sainsbury's country home. Among many other GM crop-related projects that he has funded, Lord Sainsbury paid for the John Innes Centre, a genetic-engineering research institute in Norwich. He has had meetings with Monsanto to discuss GM crops and has repeatedly defended the technology in public. At the same time, however, he claims that he has 'not taken part in any government decisions or discussions relating to GM food policy'[77] and that he is unaware that he has any commercial interest in bio-tech firms.[78]

Like virtually every area confronted by the environmental movement, government policies from around the world continue to expand a global food and farming system which is in direct opposition to that which is considered sustainable, ethical and ecologically sound. Rather than promoting small-scale diversified farming, which serves local markets, bolsters local trade and binds local communities, science and industry work with government to encourage globalisation and high-tech intensification. Instead of encouraging the transition to organic farming, which could feed the nation with healthy nutritious food, governments bow to corporate pressure, subsidsing the bio-tech industry, research into GM crops and the energy-intensive inputs of the agri-business. This trend is unlikely to change until there is sufficient pressure to restructure our economic system, thereby undermining the power of multinational corporations and rescuing our democratic system from their manipulation.

The Organic Movement

Before the advent of the agri-business, set in motion by the Agriculture Act of 1947, there were half a million farms in Britain, the majority of which were small mixed farms of less than 50 acres.[79] Almost 1.5 million families made part or all of their income from the land, maintaining a rich biodiversity and preserving the environment at no extra cost to the taxpayer. Contrary to claims made by both government and the bio-tech industry, it has been estmated that British farming could support the entire population using as little as one fifth of the land which is currently under cultivation. However, rather than growing food to feed the population, government policy is devoted to competing on the world market with countries whose agricultural base is infinitely larger than our own. Despite numerous studies which prove that sustainable farming practices can produce high yields of safe nutritious food, preserving soil fertility and protecting the environment, government incentives for organic agriculture remain negligible, dissuading many farmers from making the transition.

One of the first to predict that industrialised farming would create problems was the rural commentator H.J. Massingham, who saw the peasant farmer as 'the base of the pyramid which we call civilisation'. In *The Wisdom of the Fields*, published in 1945, he refers to a couple in Somerset who grew enough food to feed a small village from 4 acres of steeply sloping land; they produced 120 pounds of strawberries in a year, kept 130 chickens, six ewes and a lamb, a breeding sow with a litter of eight and and 30 hives of bees. Another couple cited by Massingham 'grew wheat, barley, oats, kale, mangolds and turnips; milked 11 cows, taking 35 gallons a day and carting the manure to the fields; and fattened 60 hoggets (yearling sheep) on the roots, stubbles and pastures. In six years the yields from the farm had doubled, as had the fertility of its soils.'[80]

The modern organic movement is usually aligned with the Soil Association, founded in 1946 by a group of individuals concerned about the implications of the emerging agri-business. Soil erosion, the loss of nutritional value in chemically produced food, the welfare of intensively reared animals and the impact of large mechanised farming on the countryside, were all factors which they recognised. Like so many pioneers in the environmental movement, the driving force behind the Soil Association was a woman – Lady Eve Balfour, niece of the former Conservative Prime Minister A.J. Balfour. From the age of twelve, Lady Eve knew that she wanted to be a farmer, becoming one of the first women to study agriculture at Reading University, enrolling in 1915 when she was just seventeen years old. Three years later she was running a small farm in Monmouthshire for the War Agricultural Committee, in charge of a team of land girls, ploughing the land with horses and milking cows by hand. With her older sister Mary, she bought New Bells Farm in Suffolk in 1919 which, together with the neighbouring Walnut Tree Farm, would become the birthplace of the Soil Association and the 200 acre site for the organic farming research known as the Haughley Experiment.

Lady Eve was clearly a formidable and energetic woman. In addition to running the farm, she was an expert at breaking horses, played the flute and then the saxophone in a jazz band and wrote a series of detective novels in the 1920s. However, it was not until 1938 that she had absorbed the various influences which would lead her to write *The Living Soil*, her seminal study of soil, diet and health, which was first published in 1943. In addition to Lord Lymington's *Famine in England*, which raised questions about the sustainability of industrialised farming, she assimilated the work of men like Sir Albert Howard, Weston Price and Sir Robert McCarrison.

Howard was a British scientist who had spent years in India and developed a composting method which he called the Indore Process, producing fodder that enabled animals to resist diseases like 'foot and mouth', even in contact with infected livestock. He proposed that the health of soil, plant, animal and human were part of one interconnected chain and that any defect in any level of the chain would manifest itself as disease. Howard would have seen the cancer epidemic in the western world as the product of unhealthy agricultural systems. Price was a dentist who had travelled extensively around the world, studying sound tooth and bone formation and relating it to a whole food diet. McCarrison's study of the Hunza tribe on the north-west frontier in what is now northern Pakistan was one of the first studies to prove a correlation between farming methods, the nutritional quality of the food produced and the health and stamina of those who ate it. The extraordinary longevity and overall health of the Hunza was attributed to their wholefood diet, produced from a humus-rich soil maintained by composting.

The crucial importance of humus, and the microbial biological processes which were accelerated by composting, became central to Lady Eve's book, connecting soil with nutrition and health: 'My subject is food, which concerns everyone; it is health, which concerns everyone; it is the soil, which concerns everyone – though they may not realize it . . . [this book] is the history of certain researches linking these three vital subjects.'[81] Like *Silent Spring* twenty years later, the book was an extraordinary success, entering its eighth edition within five years. This prompted a landmark meeting between those involved in the research, from which the Soil Association was officially founded.

Lady Eve also initiated the Haughley Experiment, dividing the farm into three sections to conduct the first comparative study between organic and conventional farming. However, her passion for research was opposed by Howard, who believed that the limited funding available should be used to develop a demonstration farm which would become a living testament to the benefits of organic techniques. The early years of the association were plagued by this indecision and the constant economic strain led to the experiment being abandoned after twelve years. However, by 1952 the organisation had attracted 3,000 members from forty-two countries and was spreading awareness through a variety of publications and educational campaigns.

The Living Soil was published at a crucial time for the future of British farming and was praised by agricultural commentators like Sir George Stapledon. The issues raised in the book were even debated in the House of Commons and the so-called 'Battle for the Soil' raged during the autumn of 1943. Perhaps the most unlikely praise for the book came from Donald P. Hopkins, the most vocal opponent of the organic movement who had defended the use of artificial fertilisers throughout the 1940s. Hopkins welcomed *The Living Soil* as 'the best book produced by this particular school of thought' and suggested that it 'should be in every library of works upon soil fertility'. However, he could not accept that reliance upon organic compost was all that was needed and continued to support the additional application of chemicals.

Although Lady Eve's book had struck a chord with politicians and the public, the Agriculture Act of 1947 officially sanctioned the new direction for British farming, paving the way for the highly mechanised, intensive methods which have prevailed to this day and which are now in desperate need of reform. Inevitably, the financial injection to the economy which the agro-chemical industry promised played a significant role in this decision, emphasising the reliance upon external inputs and highlighting a fundamental ignorance about the nature of biotic processes. Lady Eve predicted where this would lead and the final chapter of the book draws attention to the crucial link between the land and the people, suggesting that the health of the soil and the health of society were part of the same equation.

The controversy which surrounds the organic debate is even more heated today, with big business and politicians insisting that chemicals are required to maintain productive yields. However, the social and environmental costs of this approach far outweigh the benefits. Studies show that organic farming techniques require half the amount of energy, while the use of compost can save up to 80 per cent of the energy consumed by using chemical fertilisers.[82] Organic farmers use none of the 600 or so pesticides permitted by the EU and if the member states converted to organic methods this would reduce the 314,000 tons of accumulative toxic materials entering the environment every year.[83] The level of nitrates leaching into water sources from organic farms has been found to be half that of conventional fields, [84] while German studies have proved that organic techniques generate greater profits per hectare than those dependent upon external inputs. Although milk yields have been found to be 15 per cent lower on organic dairy farms, another German study found that the total yield during the productive life of cows is the same.[85] A fifteen-year study in the US has shown that organic yields are only a fraction lower than those produced by what we ironically refer to as 'conventional' methods.[86]

In addition to the basic facts which these studies have revealed, public opinion throughout Europe is vastly in favour of organic produce. In recent years, the organic sector has become the fastest growing part of the British economy, with the demand for produce far out-stripping the supply. Demand exceeds supply by 230 per cent and is growing by 40 per cent each year.[87] Although organic box schemes have sprung up all over the country, trying to cater to this demand, some 70–80 per cent of organic produce is still imported from abroad, adding to greenhouse emissions through intensive transport use. Buying an organic vegetable which has been grown abroad may have a greater impact on the planet than buying non-organic local produce and it has been estimated that a mango landing at Heathrow airport has already consumed 800 times the calorific energy provided by the fruit itself.[88]

In the light of the above, one wonders why there is such inertia about making the transition to organic methods? Why is only 0.5 per cent of UK land devoted to organic agriculture, compared with 4 per cent in Germany and 8 per cent in Austria? Why, when there is such widespread public resistance to genetically modified crops, did the British government pour £52 million into the bio-tech industry during 1998 and only £1.7 million into organic research?[89] (The following year, funding for bio-technology research jumped to £600 million.)[90] Why are so many farmers still prepared to handle known carcinogens and pour highly toxic chemicals all over the land?

The answer, of course, is money. Multinational corporations are now so intimately curled up in bed with government that public opinion has little bearing on the decisions that are being made. AstraZeneca, one of the giants of the bio-tech industry, which has since merged with Novartis to form Syngenta, had representatives on all the government grant-making bodies dealing with biological research. Lord Sainsbury sees a future where

'The most progressive farms will be those on which herbicides are applied by robots under the management of satellites.' As one writer recently remarked, 'People with a mindset like this obviously have difficulty in understanding the importance of biodiversity, conservation of soil, or the value of vital rural communities.'

Meanwhile our countryside is systematically being turned into a toxic disaster zone and the organic sector remains hopelessly under-funded. As Graham Harvey says, why bother making the transition to organic farming, 'when all you have to do is sow the crops that carry the most subsidy, spray whenever the crop consultant recommends it, then collect both a fat subsidy and a high price for selling onto a buoyant commodity market?'[91] Meanwhile, the BSE and 'foot and mouth' style disasters continue. How long do we have to wait before common sense prevails? High-input, energy-intensive, highly subsidised and chemically dependent monocultures are just not viable, either ecologically or economically. Rather than destroying the environment, diversified organic farming techniques have consistently been shown to produce comparative yields of nutritious, chemical-free food while positively contributing to the land.

The Vegetarian Movement

People in the West eat an average of 71 kilograms of meat a year, compared with an average of 2 kilograms per person in Asia. Much of the agricultural land in developing countries like Brazil and Thailand is devoted to growing fodder crops to support this meat-intensive diet, while some studies suggest that 1 acre of land devoted to the meat industry could feed ten times as many vegetarians.

In light of these statistics, it is easy to see why vegetarianism has assumed a political dimension, transcending issues of health and animal welfare, as well as its previous association with the stereotyped sandal-wearing hippie subsisting on lentils. There is no doubt that there would be considerably less strain on the global system if the western world stopped eating so much meat. Not only would this help to re-correct the balance between North and South, alleviating hunger and famine throughout the world, but it would cut the global greenhouse effect by lowering methane emissions and save billions in medical expenses related to a meat and dairy based diet. In recent years, militant groups like the Animal Liberation Front (ALF) have pushed the parameters of the vegetarian movement to include direct actions against fox-hunting, vivisection and the fur trade.

One of the most complex debates prompted by vegetarianism is whether or not our body is really designed to cope with eating meat. Some say that the human digestive system most closely resembles that of a fructivore and that it evolved while our ancestors were eating nuts and berries. Others undermine this by highlighting the health and vitality of tribes like the Masai in East Africa, or Inuit in the Arctic regions, who subsist on a diet which is almost entirely dependent on meat and animal products. Some studies suggest that stomach and colon cancers can be attributed to the accumulative effects of undigested meat, or that animal fats are the fundamental cause of many modern diseases, while meat-eaters insist that a vegetarian diet lacks the basic levels of protein which the body requires. Others claim that we all eat too much, that our energy reserves would be infinitely greater if we ate only raw fruit and vegetables, stopped eating processed foods and reduced our excess body fat to zero.

The practice of vegetarianism has a long history, first advocated in the western world by ancient Greek writers like Plutarch and Pythagoras, whose objections to eating meat were later resurrected in translations by the Roman poet Ovid.[92] In the East, the tradition is older than recorded history itself, forming a basic principle of the *sattvic* diet espoused in the ancient teachings of yoga. Although the principles of yoga were not formally written down until Patanjali's *sutras* appeared about 1,500 years ago, it is thought that the basic concepts had existed for thousands of years and that vegetarianism was practised by the *rishis*, the holy men of India's ancient Vedic culture. Although vegetarianism is undoubtedly a crucial part of the Jain religion, which sees a living spirit in every form of organic life, there is some doubt about its association with Buddhism. Tibetan Buddhist culture is dependent upon animal products and there has been speculation that the Buddha himself died from pork poisoning. Modern exponents of a vegetarian diet include Gandhi, Tolstoy and the Romantic poet Shelley, while notable opponents include the philosopher Spinoza, who believed that it was 'based upon an empty superstition and womanish tenderness, rather than upon sound reason'.[93]

According to the historian Keith Thomas, the idea 'that man was originally vegetarian is ancient and worldwide', and 'may reflect the actual practice of our remote ancestors, for apes are largely vegetarian, and it was probably only with the rise of a hunting economy that the change to meat-eating occurred'.[94] However, the fact that some species of monkey are known to practise cannibalism, eating their own off-spring, seems to prove that there are always exceptions to the rule.

The consumption of meat was probably most excessive during the Middle Ages. In 1452, a feast in Oxford involved some 900 dishes served over two days, the majority of which were meat based. A big banquet of the time might have included cranes, herons and swans, along with pigs, rabbits, partridges, curlews and quails. Despite the overall anthropocentrism of the Christian tradition, there are verses in Genesis and the Acts of the Apostles which prohibit the eating of blood, while Roger Crab, the seventeenth-century mystic, 'held it sinful to eat flesh, both because it strengthened human lusts and because it was produced by "bloody butchers" who "destroyed their fellow creatures"'.[95] In the late eighteenth century, Shelley proposed that vegetarianism struck 'at the root of all evil', while William Lambe believed that there would be an end to war if man stopped eating meat.[96] As the division between man and beast was slowly being eroded, so was the moral defence for killing and eating animals. However, most of the population were able to justify their continued consumption of meat: 'Upon serious reflection', said Lord Chesterfield, 'I became convinced of its legality, from the general order of Nature, who has instituted the universal preying upon the weaker as one of her first principles.'[97]

Seen within the wider context of the natural world, the killing and eating of other organisms appears perfectly legitimate. Like Erasmus Darwin, it is easy to look upon Nature as 'one great slaughter-house',[98] as wildlife documentaries on television so often prove. It is only with the evolution of human ethics that we find the moral ground with which to attack the carnivore. As one poet has humourously suggested,

> God doesn't care
> What you had for lunch.
> He created tofu and sausage
> With the same thought.[99]

However, the modern implications of a meat-intensive diet have taken the issues which surround vegetarianism to a new level. Objecting to eating other animals purely because they are sentient life-forms is one thing. Objecting to the modern meat industry because it inflicts hideous crimes upon animals, destroys local ecosystems, encourages the use of chemicals and hormones, adds to global climate change, exacerbates world poverty and leads to such catastrophic outcomes as 'foot and mouth' or the BSE crisis is clearly another.

Alternative Agriculture Systems

In addition to the organic methods proposed by Lady Eve Balfour and the Soil Association, there are a number of other alternative agriculture systems which have shown just how productive farming can be without the use of chemicals. These include bio-dynamics, permaculture, agro-forestry, bio-intensive farming and Masanobu Fukuoka's 'do-nothing' system of organic farming.

Bio-dynamic farming was developed in the 1920s by Rudolf Steiner, the visionary Austrian philosopher and founder of anthroposophy. Steiner drew from extensive esoteric knowledge, vigorously opposed the introduction of chemicals to the food chain and combined sophisticated methods for boosting nutrients in the soil with a schedule for sowing and harvesting crops according to phases of the moon. Although it has been dismissed by many for not being grounded in proven science, the vitality of produce grown on bio-dynamic farms speaks for itself.

Bio-dynamic techniques have been adopted by farmers all over the world. Wine producers in Burgundy have found that production is greatly enhanced by basing such decisions as when to harvest the grapes, or prune the vines, on lunar activity. It is thought that the gravitational pull of the moon has an effect on the manner in which sediments form in the wine when it is bottled and many believe that biological cycles of growth and decay are similarly related. Advocates of Steiner's techniques also believe that his methods help living organisms to combat disease and harmful radiation, referring to biodynamic farms which seemed to survive the fall-out from Chernobyl while neighbouring farms using conventional methods did not. With prophetic insight about what has since transpired in the BSE crisis,

Steiner declared in the 1920s that 'If you feed a ruminant on animal matter, it will go mad.'[100]

Permaculture is much more than an approach to agriculture. It is a design system for ecological lifestyles, based upon detailed observation of natural processes. The basic premise is to use minimum inputs to achieve maximum returns, to work with Nature, rather than against it, developing low-maintenance but highly productive systems. Rather than relying on energy-intensive and expensive external inputs, permaculture seeks to harness the inherent energy of Nature, allowing natural processes to do the work. Human interference is kept to a minimum, using techniques of selective planting to encourage biodiversity and promote mutually beneficial relationships.

Permaculture was first developed in Australia in the 1970s, by Bill Mollison. Drawing from traditional knowledge around the world, especially agro-forestry systems – where a great diversity of crops are grown together in different layers – Mollison's aim was to develop a complete agricultural ecosystem, an edible landscape which would encourage self-reliance. The permaculture system has been extended to incorporate every aspect of human lifestyles, from the implementation of alternative energy systems to architectural design. It is perhaps the most comprehensive model for sustainability that the environmental movement has produced and has been successfully introduced to every type of climatic system on a variety of scales, from Nepalese villages high in the Himalayas to suburban back gardens in Europe. Crystal Waters, in Australia's Queensland, is a complete community modelled on permaculture principles. Mollison's ideas have also proved extremely effective at rehabilitating arid and eroded soils, transforming desert ecosystems into productive gardens.[101]

While Mollison was developing permaculture in Australia, Robert Hart was drawing from agro-forestry techniques to build his forest garden on the border of Shropshire and Wales. He was especially influenced by the work of Toyohiko Kagawa, the Japanese founder of three-dimensional forest farming which was in turn inspired by J. Russell Smith's classic book *Tree Crops – A Permanent Agriculture*. After studying at Princeton University, Kagawa returned to Japan and encouraged upland farmers to plant fodder-bearing trees, such as quick-maturing walnuts, which could be used to feed their livestock. This helped to prevent erosion and conserve nutrients in the soil as well as making them and their animals independent of external inputs. Similarly, through strategic planting, Hart was able to create several layers of vegetation in his Shropshire garden, with fruit-bearing trees co-existing above berry and nut-bearing shrubs, perennial herbs and vegetables.

Once the system is in place, the maintenance is minimal, mainly consisting of harvesting the produce and making sure that the various elements remain in balance. As Hart points out,

> it is self-perpetuating, because almost all the plants are perennial or active self-seeders . . . self-fertilising, because deep-rooting trees, bushes and herbs draw upon minerals in the subsoil and make them available to their neighbours . . . self-watering, because deep-rooting plants tap the spring-veins in the subsoil . . . self-mulching and self-weed-suppressing, because rapidly spreading herbs soon cover all the ground and thus create a permanent 'living mulch' . . . self-pollinating, because the trees are carefully selected to be mutually compatible or self-fertile . . . self-healing, because the scheme includes a number of aromatic herbs which deter pests and disease-germs and because any complex comprising a wide spectrum of different plants does not allow the build-up of epidemics such as affects mono-cultures.[102]

Hart believed that when replicated in a small town garden, this system would allow a large family to be self-sufficient in fruit and vegetables for seven months a year. Since it does not require the labour-intensive maintenance of annual vegetables, it could easily co-exist with busy urban lifestyles. Similarly, vast areas of derelict urban wasteland could be turned over to forest farms which would feed the local community. The huge potential for urban agriculture is well illustrated by projects like Ashram Acres in Birmingham, where a small Asian community has created a thriving business growing specialist herbs and vegetables. The forest garden in an urban setting would also serve the dual purpose of absorbing carbon dioxide from the atmosphere, as well as providing green space for communities and all the physical and spiritual benefits which contact with the living soil provides.

The forest garden concept has been well established in various parts of the globe and there are numerous examples of the high productivity that can be achieved. Rather than felling the existing trees, the Chagga settlers on the slopes of Mount Kilimanjaro planted bananas, fruit trees and vegetables in their shade.[103] Now the individual plots, which average 0.68 hectares in size and contain some seventeen stories of vegetation, provide the entire subsistence for a family of ten people.[104] The south Indian state of Kerala, the most densely populated area in the country, contains some 3.5 million forest gardens. One plot of just 0.12 hectares has been known to contain twenty-three coconut palms, twelve cloves, fifty-six bananas and forty-nine pineapples, with thirty pepper vines trained up the trees. Associated industries in the area include the production of rubber, matches, cashews, furniture, pandanus mats, baskets, bullock-carts and catamarans, along with the processing of palm oil, cocoa and coir fibres from coconuts. Many families meet their own energy requirements through biomass systems fed by human, animal and vegetable waste, while the forest gardens provide full-time occupations for families which average seven members.

Another approach which is well suited to small-scale cultivation is bio-intensive farming, pioneered by Alan Chadwick, an English horticulturalist. Chadwick was heavily influenced by Steiner and intensive methods of vegetable cultivation used by the French. In the 1960s, he applied his knowledge to a 4 acre student garden at the University of California's Santa Cruz campus, giving birth to the bio-intensive method which has been popularised around the world by John Jeavons' book *How to Grow More Vegetables (Than You Ever Thought Possible on Less Land Than You Can Imagine)*.

Bio-intensive farming combines four basic gardening principles: deep-bed cultivation to encourage root growth; growing crops specifically for compost – or dynamic accumulators like comfrey; closely spaced planting to optimise micro-climates; and companion planting to combat pests and disease. Like permaculture and forest gardening, Nature does most of the work after the initial soil preparation, and the results are truly staggering: up to 88 per cent reduction in water consumption, a 99 per cent reduction in energy use, up to 400 per cent increase in calorific production per unit and a 100 per cent increase in both soil fertility and income. A modern meat-intensive diet, as practised by most of the western world, requires at least 45,000 square feet of land to feed a single person, compared with about 10,000 square feet for a vegetarian. Bio-intensive methods can provide the entire diet for a vegetarian on as little as 2,000 square feet, including the composting crops required to maintain the system indefinitely.[105]

Since the amount of arable land available to feed the world is currently estimated at 9,000 square feet per person, and is decreasing all the time due to a combination of rising population, desertification, soil erosion, salinisation and urbanisation, the potential for these methods is clearly enormous. What makes these systems even more attractive is their ability not only to maintain the fertility of the soil but actually to build it up as much as sixty times faster than Nature. Since some studies estimate that there is only enough topsoil left to last another fifty to a hundred years, the need for such a system is paramount.[106] As Donald Worster says, 'We can no more manufacture soil with a tank of chemicals than we can invent a rain forest or produce a single bird.'[107] The fact that bio-intensive techniques are now being practised in 107 countries is an indication of just how successful they are.

Another inspiration for bio-intensive mini-farms was the organic system developed by Masanobu Fukuoka in Japan. By concentrating on the precise sequence in which the various stages of cultivation are carried out, Fukuoka created what must be the most energy-efficient form of agriculture being practised in the world today. On a quarter of an acre, his farm produces 22 bushels of rice and 22 bushels of winter grains, enough to feed up to ten people and requiring a few days' work for one or two people to hand-sow and harvest the crop. Like Robert Hart's forest garden, labour-intensive methods of weed control and compost application are all achieved automatically through a sophisticated knowledge of what to do when and what to plant with what, hence the 'do-nothing' tag. The Fukuoka system has spread widely though Japan and is now practised on nearly a million acres in China.

It is beyond doubt that the global implementation of these alternative agricultural systems could feed the expanding population without the need for chemicals or bio-technology. In addition, the alarming prospect of topsoil depletion, through erosion and loss of fertility, could be avoided indefinitely. However, there would be no profit to assuage the greed of corporate interests. So, while multinational giants like Monsanto, Syngenta and Cargill are allowed to control the fate of the world's food supply, our supermarkets will be filled with abominated food, our bodies will continue to do battle with toxic residues, and the world's topsoil, one of our most fundamental resources, will continue to wash out to sea.

From Diggers to Dongas: The Alternative Society

Ever since industrial societies first emerged, minority groups have not only questioned their sustainability but actively sought to create alternatives. From Gerard Winstanley's seventeenth-century Diggers, through to William Morris, the 'utopian socialists' and the eco-tribe of Dongas that emerged during the 1990s, men and women throughout Britain have challenged the assumptions we make about the industrial economic system. As we have seen, most of these maverick movements have failed to fulfil their utopian dreams and been swallowed by the very system which they sought to oppose.

However, now that the linear, hierarchical system has reached breaking point, a nucleus of cyclical networks has started to emerge, creating an interconnected web of planetary communities which are the seeds of an Ecological Age. These experiments stretch from the north of Scotland to the south of India, from California to the Australian outback. They have proved that humanity can live both sustainably and comfortably, that an Ecological Age does not necessarily mean shunning the 'non-negotiable demands of modern life'[108] – electricity, cars and televisions – but that we need to re-evaluate both their methods of production and our relationship to them.

As Simon Fairlie points out, the fact that the number of households without a car is increasing faster than the number of households with one, suggests that 'equitable private car ownership sounds not only ecologically devastating but physically impossible'.[109] Rather than aspiring to the non-sustainable, unachievable goal of equipping each member of the global population with a car, a computer and a television, should we not be looking at ways in which whole communities can share and benefit from these technologies? Contrary to the battle-cry about the personal freedom and independence which these technologies provide, we now find that they accentuate a sense of self-alienation, de-humanise our interaction with the world and destroy local communities. Millions of people sit in traffic for hours every day, on their own in a little metal box, incubating road rage and discharging greenhouse emissions. Streets where children used to play have become corridors for pollution and angst. Television and computers have reduced us to sitting in segregated spaces, staring at screens like hypnotised zombies, so removed from Nature that we have become anaesthetised to the wholesale destruction of life that surrounds us.

One experiment on the north-east coast of Scotland has proved to be a pioneering light within this planetary effort to create an ecological community. One snowy day in November 1962, Peter and Eileen Caddy moved their 30 foot caravan trailer into the Findhorn Bay Caravan Park, accompanied by their three sons and a friend called Dorothy Maclean.

They lived in this caravan for the next seven years, gradually creating a productive garden in the barren desolation that surrounded them. The stories that surround this garden are almost legendary; fox-gloves 8 feet tall and cabbages weighing several pounds, all growing in the middle of sand dunes but bursting with vitality. The extraordinary success of the early Findhorn garden – the germinating seed of an international community which has transformed the lives of thousands – is attributed to the psychic communication, or channelling, which manifested through Dorothy and Eileen. By contacting the *devas*, or Nature spirits associated with each plant, they were able to advise Peter exactly what nutrient the soil required to encourage productive yields, how to deter disease and pests without chemicals and how to combine species which encouraged systemic, synergistic benefits. Within two years they were growing sixty-five different types of vegetable, twenty-one fruits and forty-two herbs, creating a complex, self-regulating system which produced astonishing yields.

The Findhorn story struck a chord with people all over the planet and, over the last forty years, a flourishing community has established itself around the original site of the garden. Students come from around the globe to take courses in permaculture, ecological building practices and the opening of intuitive, shamanistic or psychic faculties which catalysed the cross-species communication first developed by Dorothy and Eileen. Contrary to the cynical derision usually levelled at those associated with the New Age, the community has given birth to numerous practical and progressive answers to ecological problems, ranging from appropriate building technologies and renewable energy systems to ways of recycling waste heat from grills in fast-food restaurants. Far from being naive, idealistic solutions, these are examples of the hands-on, cutting-edge developments that we so urgently need to adopt.

Through the dissemination of an ecological world-view, as presented by its courses and its publications, the community sees itself as part of a larger global network. According to Carol Riddell, 'The Findhorn Community generates energy at a particular vibratory frequency . . . we are part of a network of energy transformation on the planet which is spreading wider and wider and steadily increasing in power.' Another British example of this expanding network is the Centre for Alternative Technology (CAT) in Wales, which has evolved around a 40 acre disused quarry in the last twenty-five years. The centre has developed wind turbines, photo-voltaics, biomass systems and ecological building practices which now attract some 90,000 visitors every year. An extensive course programme covers everything from straw-bale building to woodland management, solar housing and water conservation.

In India, the utopian community of Auroville has emerged from a chequered political background to become a living example of the way in which ecological communities can regenerate both the soil and society itself. Auroville was first conceived by The Mother, a visionary French psychic and consort of Aurobindo Ghose, a political revolutionary turned mystic who became the first man seriously to challenge British colonial rule in India.

Situated on the outskirts of Pondicherry, an old French colony in south-east India, The Mother saw Auroville as 'a universal town where men and women of all countries are able to live in peace and progressive harmony above all creeds, all politics and all nationalities'. Inaugurated on 28 February 1968, the community is ultimately intended to form a city of 50,000 people. At present, there are just over 1,000 permanent members from thirty different countries, living in small communities spread over 2,500 acres, incorporating thirteen Tamil villages with a local population of about 40,000. The aim is to integrate the local inhabitants with the rest of the community. The Mother's collaboration with French architect Roger Anger produced a futuristic model for the layout of Auroville, with International, Cultural, Residential and Industrial zones radiating from the Matri Mandir, the Temple of the Mother and the focal point of the community, forming one vast sweeping spiral surrounded by a green belt of thick vegetation.

When the first settlers moved out to Auroville in 1968, they were confronted by a dying habitat. There was little shade, provided by a few lone banyans, and hardly any water. Two hundred years of deforestation, bad land management and over-grazing had turned a jungle into an open expanse of red laterite soil, scarred by gullies and ravines created by years of monsoon rains. According to local records and temple inscriptions, tigers and elephants had once roamed the area, which had an ecosystem unique to the Coromandel coast. The process of deforestation was accelerated by the British, allocating plots of land to anybody who would clear-cut and cultivate them for a year and, in the early fifties, the last area of forest on the plateau was cleared to make way for a mono-culture cashew plantation.

To replenish the soil and conserve water, the Aurovillians dug thousands of kilometres of *bunds*, raised earth banks to hold rain water and control the run-off. This encouraged percolation which re-charged the underground aquifers. An intensive tree-planting programme began in the late seventies, introducing hundreds of species of timber, fencing shrubs, firewood and fruit trees. As the trees grew and the micro-climates formed, many species of birds returned, reflecting the balance of a semi-desert ecosystem changing into a forest. Birds and animals have helped the forests propagate and it is estimated that there are now over 2 million trees on Auroville land.

In addition to healthcare and education projects, which have helped to integrate the local villagers, Auroville has made progress with renewable energy sources and appropriate building technologies; over 1,200 photovoltaic panels are in use, about thirty windmills help to pump water and specially designed bio-gas systems process organic waste to produce methane and fertilisers. Construction work utilises compressed earth blocks, made on site from local earth in a manual press. Since no kiln is required, this non-polluting process does not deplete the surrounding forests.

As Aurovillians are quick to point out, the community is a bold and ambitious experiment, still very much in its infancy. The experiment has certainly had its share of problems but the regeneration of the land is testament to its intrinsic value.

A much smaller but equally important experiment has been underway in Somerset, England, since 1994. After living as a rural worker in France, Simon Fairlie returned to this country to do the same, making the logical assumption that he could live on a piece of land that he owned. However, an archaic planning policy not only made this impossible but revealed its own failure to adopt the guidelines produced by Agenda 21, the list of ecological principles for local government which had been drawn up at the 1992 Earth Summit in Rio. In 1996, Fairlie explained how 'In the two years since we moved onto our land, we have been through almost the entire gamut of planning procedure: committee decision, enforcement order, stop notice, Article 4 application, Section 106 agreement, appeal, call in by the Secretary of State and statutory review in the High Court. All this for seven tents.'[110]

Fairlie applauds the strict regulations of the 1932 Town and Country Planning Act, without which we would have lost much more of the British countryside in the last fifty years. However, he also highlights the fact that, by failing to embrace the notion of low-impact housing development – 'which either enhances or does not significantly diminish environmental quality'[111] and complies with Agenda 21 – the law fails to address the problems of the time. As Fairlie argues, 'If one is faced with eviction, on environmental grounds, from a small tent on one's own small-holding, a stone's throw away from a new and empty thirty foot high concrete block barn erected with the blessing of the planning system, and from a cottage occupied by a man who commutes to the nearby town, one's initial reaction may, like mine, be that the regulations are daft.'[112] An attempt to create a self-sufficient, low-impact community like Tinkers Bubble becomes illegal, while building regulations insist on the use of highly toxic, energy-intensive materials made from non-renewable resources. This is in direct opposition to Agenda 21, which calls for a reduction in energy use, pollution, waste and the use of raw materials.

During the Industrial Age, the distinction between rural and urban areas has become increasingly blurred, torn between the demands of intensive farming and urban developers. Fairlie observes that these two factors have turned the British countryside into 'a cross between a factory and a drive-in museum'.[113] At the same time, new technologies and materials have combined with increased mobility to transform our approach to building, bringing slate from Spain, timber from Indonesia and aluminium from bauxite mined in Asia. Local materials have been abandoned in favour of cheaper imported alternatives. The style of rural buildings has changed as well, says Fairlie, since 'Craftsmen with modern materials have no choice but to build straight and true; they have traded the limitations of geology and geography for the tyranny of mechanical accuracy.'[114] The result is what Clough Williams-Ellis, the inspiration behind the surreal Welsh village of Portmeirion, likened in 1928 to an octopus spreading its tentacles through the country: 'Having made our towns with such careless incompetence, those who have the means to be choosers are calmly declining to live in them and are now proceeding with the same recklessness to disperse ourselves over the countryside, destroying and dishonouring it with our shoddy but all-too-permanent encampments.'[115] In the process, 'British society entered into a Faustian pact: the right to build anywhere was to be sacrificed for the right to drive anywhere.'

A system that allows supermarket chains to build enormous retail outlets – which are designed to last less than fifteen years and are constructed from toxic, ecologically damaging, energy-intensive materials – while standing in the way of grass-roots communities which conform to the guidelines agreed in Agenda 21, is clearly in need of revision. As the Tinkers Bubble experiment has shown, this type of low-impact development not only conforms to Agenda 21 but can provide affordable housing in a way which regenerates local communities and ecosystems. As an example, Fairlie points to Tir Penrhos Isaf, a permaculture project pursued by Chris Dixon in Snowdonia National Park where a complex ecosystem has evolved, with aquaculture ponds and an edible landscape of plants, shrubs and trees co-existing with livestock. After initial objections, local planners have seen the systemic benefits provided by the project and there are plans to replicate it elsewhere.

From its humble beginnings, Tinkers Bubble has inspired a national debate about rural planning policy. The Liberal Democrat MP Paddy Ashdown, who lives nearby, has expressed his support for the community: 'I have been fascinated by the Tinkers Bubble experiment. It is "in my backyard". It has generated considerable and powerful feelings, including in my own village. But my judgement is, that after two or three years of this experiment, the outcome has been to add, not diminish the quality of life in our village as we have had to cope with different lifestyles and different ways of looking at our world.'[116]

As Agenda 21 states, 'A change in consumption patterns, particularly in industrialized countries, towards those which can be attained by all within the bounds of the ecologically possible has to be a central component in the drive for sustainable development.'[117] Although some would say that 'sustainable development' is a contradiction in terms, and has become little more than a political buzz word, this statement does raise the fundamental issue addressed by alternative communities. By treating consumption as growth and, thereby, as an indicator of economic prosperity, we externalise the factors which we so urgently need to address. In the same way that building more roads encourages more traffic, we have to recognise that building more houses encourages more households. We have a stable population in this country but the government projects that we need 5 million new houses over the next twenty years. This demand is partly fuelled by the fragmentation of families and the number of people with two or more homes. However, rather than just building new roads and homes because we think we need them, why are we not building sustainable, ecological communities which conform to Agenda 21?

5

Techno-addicts

You never change things by fighting the existing reality.
To change something, build a new model
that makes the existing model obsolete.

BUCKMINSTER FULLER

The Luddite Legacy

Seven hundred years after Robin Hood roamed Nottingham, England, the region became the epicentre for one of the most famous confrontations between the British people and the State. In reaction to new technologies, mainly within the textile industry, huge numbers of workers went on the rampage, breaking into factories and destroying the machines that were putting them out of work.

Far from being the motley band of trouble-makers that history has portrayed them as, the Luddites were a highly organised and well-disciplined force. Over a two year period, 1811–12, they were responsible for £100,000 worth of damage – a considerable sum at the time.[1] They were seen as such a threat to industrial progress that the death penalty was introduced for the destruction of machinery. Some years later, Charlotte Brontë referred to the Luddite uprising in her novel *Shirley*:

> Certain inventions in machinery were introduced into the staple manufactures of the north, which, greatly reducing the number of hands necessary to be employed, threw thousands out of work, and left them without legitimate means of sustaining life. A bad harvest intervened. Distress reached its climax . . . Misery generates hate: these sufferers hated the machines which they believed took their bread from them: they hated the buildings which contained those machines; they hated the manufacturers who owned those buildings.[2]

The Luddite uprising was the result of one particular innovation, the powerhouse of the Industrial Revolution itself – James Watt's steam engine. The scientist Norbert Weiner refers to the 'technical determinants' dictated by technologies and how the steam engine inevitably leads to 'large and ever larger scales because it can power so many separate machines at once, to ever increasing production because it must pay back its high investment and operating costs, and to centralization and specialization because factors of efficiency and economy supersede those of craftsmanship or aesthetic expression'.[3] By 1833, it was estimated that the steam engine was doing the work of 2.5 million people, from a manufacturing work-force of about 3 million, and that more than 100,000 steam-powered textile looms were in operation.[4]

In a few short years, the British economy had been transformed from the organic to the mechanical, from a system that revolved around local land, local labour and local markets, to one that was based on fossil fuels, fuming factories and foreign trade. While Thomas Carlyle boasted that 'We war with Nature and, by our resistless engines, come off always victorious, and loaded with spoils,'[5] others chronicled the consequences of this industrial explosion. In *Hard Times*, Dickens described Manchester as a 'town of red brick, or of brick that would have been red if the smoke and ashes had allowed it . . . a town of machinery and tall chimneys, out of which interminable serpents of smoke trailed themselves for ever and ever, and never got uncoiled', while Engels described the river in the town as 'a long string of the most disgusting, blackish-green, slime pools . . . from the depths of which bubbles of miasmatic gas constantly arise and give forth a stench unendurable.'[6]

The Luddites failed to halt the triumph of 'progress' and by 1844 there were 340,000 workers in the cotton factories alone. However, like the Diggers, their legacy survives, and the scale of their resistance posed a serious threat to those in power, finally quashed by the mobilisation of some 15,000 troops in what is still regarded as the most massive repression that the British government has ever launched on its own people.

Nowadays, the term Luddite is usually applied disparagingly, suggesting that any resistance towards technology is a failure to move with the times. In reality, the Luddites themselves did not oppose technology *per se*, merely the application of machinery they saw as 'hateful to commonality', which would have a disruptive influence on their communities and way of life. The modern mantra that 'technology is not the problem, it's the way that we use it', does not stand up to scrutiny. The belief that technology is politically neutral is immediately disproved if we take a look at television, the perfect medium for mass manipulation of the media by a governing elite, or nuclear energy, which cannot be controlled by the public and by definition requires a centralised power base to try to keep it safe. 'The idea of technology being a neutral, discreet thing and whoever is in charge can use it this way or that way, that's really missing the point,' says John Zerzan, an activist author based in the anarchist stronghold of Eugene, Oregon, and famous for having sold his own blood plasma to finance his writing. 'It's inseparable from the system, it's the incarnation of the system and it's always been that way. You can't take a totally alienating technology and use it for anything except more alienation, more destructive impact on every level from the psyche to the rest of the biosphere.'[7]

Jerry Mander, one of the most penetrating analysts of the social impact that modern technology is having, believes that the juggernaut is thundering along without question, leading us into a 'worldwide, interlocked, monolithic, technical-political web of unprecedented negative implications'.[8] In 1990, the psychologist Chellis Glendinning published an article entitled 'Notes toward a Neo-Luddite Manifesto', in which she clarifies the position of those seeking to make technology accountable:

> Neo-Luddites are twentieth-century citizens who question the predominant modern world-view, which preaches that unbridled technology represents progress. Neo-Luddites have the courage to gaze at the full catastrophe of our century. Like the early Luddites, we too are seeking to protect the livelihoods, communities and families we love. Stopping the destruction requires not just regulating or eliminating individual items like pesticides or military weapons. It requires new ways of thinking about humanity and of relating to life. It requires a new world-view.[9]

Perhaps the most prophetic insight into the dangers of unrestricted technological innovation comes at the end of Mary Shelley's *Frankenstein*, when the monster turns to the scientist and says: 'You are my creator, but I am your master.' Today we see the genetic engineer usurping Nature's position as the universal, creative force, tampering with the very matrix of life itself. We have yet to see who will end up being in control of this process, Man or Nature, but we don't have to look far to hazard a guess. It would be difficult for even the most hardened technophiliac to convince anyone that we have maintained control over nuclear waste, DDT, PCBs, CFCs, carbon dioxide emissions and acid rain, not to mention numerous other chemicals and heavy metal pollutants which we continue to release into virtually every water source on the planet. Waiting in the wings are those who want to use nanotechnology to move into the 'post-biological age', proposing to restructure matter at a sub-atomic level in the belief that we will one day manufacture any resource we want, as and when we need it – wood, water and oil, off the shelf and made to order. Mander thinks that these people 'don't even pretend to care about the natural world. They think it's silly and out of date.'[10] Bill Joy warns that, compared with weapons of mass-destruction, 'robots, engineered organisms and nanobots share a dangerous amplifying factor: they can self-replicate. A bomb is blown up only once, but one altered gene can become many, and quickly get out of control.'[11]

The spell of the western ego has become so ingrained in our psyches that we continue to think that we are both the creators and the masters of our ingenuity. But are we? Computers may appear to have made it easier for us to control various aspects of our lives, from running our finances to buying our groceries, but they have also made it that much easier for us to be controlled by multinational corporations and the globalised economy. The history of Man's relationship to Nature must surely make it evident that all sense of human control is limited. As the historian Clive Ponting has shown, every major civilisation in history, from the Mayans and the Sumerians to the Egyptians and the Romans, has over-extended their resource base and thereby precipitated their demise through a combination of environmental factors like deforestation, soil erosion and the salinisation of water sources. The evidence shows that, when the pack of cards starts to fall, it falls very quickly. Why, one wonders, should Western 'civilisation', and its policy of globalised, technocratic expansion, prove to be the exception?

TV and Techno-addiction

The impact of mankind on the planet has clearly been accelerated by the implementation of various technologies. Deforestation began with primitive Man's discovery of fire and basic tools. Around the seventh century BC, cultivation of the land was facilitated by the invention of the plough, regarded by Lynn White Jr as the 'knife' which 'attacked the land' and marked Man's transition from being 'part of nature' to becoming 'the exploiter of nature'.[12] The Industrial Revolution was dependent on the steam engine, and the internal combustion engine redefined mobility in the twentieth century. Every issue confronted by the environmental movement is, in one way or another, related to the technologies which human innovation has produced and our industrial economic system has deployed – from global warming, ozone depletion and depleted fish stocks, through to radioactive waste, intensive farming and genetic modification, technology is inherently involved in what appears to be one seamless web of scientific progress and ecological destruction. In the last century, the number of lives lost to the by-products of technological 'advances', from radiation and asbestos, to pesticides and leaded petrol, runs well into the millions.[13]

Most of us believe that the negative implications of these technologies are more than made up for by the positive ones; few of us would now be prepared to live without washing machines, fridges, cars or televisions, while our entire economic system is now dependent on computers. Whether these technologies are viewed as good or bad, they are justified by the relentless march of human ingenuity: 'You can't stop progress.' It is taken for granted that our lives have been immeasurably improved by technology, and anyone suggesting otherwise is immediately branded a Luddite, or accused of romanticising some Dark Age, characterised by poverty, ill-health and hard labour. However, this black and white division is simplistic in the extreme and the faith that we have instilled in the religion of high technology is now being undermined. Clearly, some technologies can have a beneficial effect on the planet, like renewable energy systems and zero-emissions transport. However, the direction taken by most scientific research is now governed by corporate funding within our universities and institutions; science can no longer be viewed as some rarefied domain, exempt from human values, morals and ethics, as many would like us to believe. The effects of a technology are not always determined by 'the way in which we use it', since many of them are thrust upon us by those that maintain control over it.

Perhaps the most obvious example of this is television. Given current viewing figures in the US, where the average adult clocks up five hours per day, watching television has become the activity which the population does more than any other, except sleeping, working or going to school. In his study of the impact of technology, Jerry Mander concocts an imaginary report made by a team of anthropological aliens:

> We are scanning the Americans now. Night after night they sit still in dark rooms, not talking to each other, barely moving except to eat. Many of them sit in separate rooms, but even those sitting in groups rarely speak to each other. They are staring at a light! The light flickers on and off many times per second. The humans' eyes are not moving, and since we know that there is an association between eye movement and thought, we have measured their brain waves. Their brain waves are in 'alpha', a non-cognitive, passive-receptive mode. The humans are receivers. As for the light, it comes in the form of images, sent from only a few sources, thousands of miles from where the humans are gathering

them in. The images are of places and events that are not, for the most part, related to the people's lives. Once placed in their heads, the images seem to take on permanence. We have noticed that these people use these images in their conversations with other people, and that they begin to dress and act in a manner that imitates the images. They also choose their national leaders from among the images. In summary, this place seems to be engaged in some weird kind of mental training akin to brainwashing.'[14]

Aside from the wry humour that Mander imbues in this report, the most frightening aspect of it is the fact that we now know it to be true. Scientists have shown that television triggers the alpha brain state, whereby information is directly digested by the mind, without participation by the viewer. Therefore, in contrast to reading a book, which stimulates the theta state in the brain, television suppresses our intellect – we absorb information without thinking about it. By encouraging the alpha state, television can be equated with drug addiction, providing the perfect escape from the psychological pressures of modern life. Studies have also shown that, through an alternating cycle of impulse and suppression, accentuated by modern fast-cut edits, television has a subversive psychological impact which can lead to hyperactivity and even violence. By staring at sex or violence on the screen, our emotional reaction is suppressed. Therefore, when we re-engage with physical reality, the natural response for the repressed emotion is to seek expression.

The really scary implications of this are obvious, especially since 75 per cent of US commercial network television is paid for by the 100 largest corporations in the country. Since there are 450,000 corporations in America, and some 250 million people, this leads to an extremely biased media, or an 'effective censorship'.[15] Combined with an average of 22,000 commercials seen per year, in which the American public are bombarded with images persuading them to buy and consume even more than they do already, television becomes a technological tool with an extraordinary power to manipulate public opinion. This medium is then used by the same corporations to prepare the viewing public for the next innovation that they want them to buy. Technologies are pre-sold, promising a new era of health, leisure and happiness through scientific innovation. As Mander says, television becomes 'a training instrument for new consciousness' and 'the organizing tool for those who control society'.[16]

Over fifty years ago, with the advent of radio, Huxley noticed how the intrusive nature of public broadcasting bombarded the population with useless information and the endless run of soap operas created an emotional dependency which distracted the participant from their own lives: 'It penetrates the mind, filling it with a babel of distractions – news items, mutually irrelevant bits of information, blasts of corybantic or sentimental music, continually repeated doses of drama which bring no catharsis, but merely create a craving for daily or even hourly emotional enemas.' He also noted the power for manipulating the consumer and creating a population subservient to the Almighty Dollar: 'broadcasting stations support themselves by selling time to advertisers, the noise is carried from the ears, through the realms of phantasy, knowledge and feeling to the ego's central core of wish and desire', with the express intention of preventing 'the will from ever achieving silence' since 'the condition of an expanding and technologically progressive system of mass-production is universal craving'. Ultimately, he saw this process of self-perpetuating desire as 'the greatest obstacle between the human soul and its divine Ground'.[17]

Perhaps the most amazing thing about all this is that we continue to buy the whole package. However, if we stand back and cultivate a level of objective detachment, we see that technology has consistently failed to deliver what it promised. Rather than creating 'Better Things for Better Living Through Chemistry', the 'scientific miracle' of the pesticide revolution created a carcinogenic world. Rather than providing a limitless supply of virtually free energy, nuclear power plants have proved to be nothing but a liability; an article in *The Economist* has noted how 'not one, anywhere in the world, makes commercial sense'. The automobile may have increased independent mobility, but at considerable cost to the planet and our own peace of mind. All of us are familiar with the psychological stress of sitting in traffic while running late for an important engagement. Ivan Illich observes that, if you add the time required to earn the money which pays for labour-saving gadgets to the time taken to learn to use and repair them, then modern technology actually deprives us of time.[18] E. F. Schumacher famously declared that 'The amount of genuine leisure available in a society is generally in inverse proportion to the amount of labour-saving machinery it employs.'[19]

As many have observed, so-called primitive societies had infinitely more leisure time than we do today, enabling them to pursue spiritual matters, develop a sophisticated knowledge of astronomy and build monuments of extraordinary precision and complexity. Today, most of us in the western world are so pre-occupied with paying the bills, securing promotion at work, or putting our children through school, that we don't have the time even to think about what we are doing. We automatically assume that it could not be any other way. Through television, consumerism and the high-speed lifestyle, the system actually encourages us not to attempt such a subversive activity as to sit down and ask fundamental questions about what is important to us.

Eco-psychologists like Chellis Glendinning have proposed that the Euro-American personality is actually addicted to technology itself and that this is now being replicated by people throughout the developing world. The tool that helps to achieve this is, of course, television. Others have even suggested that 'retail therapy', that compulsive urge to go shopping – which in Britain has become the second most favoured 'leisure' activity – is the modern expression of our primal urge to go out gathering food. Glendinning observes how our society is riddled with inconsistent behaviour towards technology, suggesting that recognised symptom of modern addiction – denial. Governments deny any link between technological development and global warming, while simultaneously calling for technological development to counter it.[20] The medical establishment refuses to accept the existence of environmental illness, despite conclusive evidence to the contrary. Corporations continue to deny that their products are toxic when countless studies prove that they are. Many of us in the developed world continue to support environmental causes, campaign against corporate profligacy and dutifully go to the bottle bank, while simultaneously purchasing beyond our means and maintaining extravagant patterns of consumption. Then we beat ourselves up for not being environmentally responsible consumers. Until there is a fundamental change in human behaviour, a shift in values at a basic psychological level, it is hard to see this paradox being resolved.

Within the context of human evolution, the addiction to technology is a relatively recent phenomenon, another indication of the split between Man and Nature that the mechanistic paradigm has ingrained in the western mind. The Industrial Age only started seven generations ago. Only 0.003 per cent of our evolutionary existence has been taken up with controlling the natural world through agriculture and the domestication of animals.[21] Vine Deloria argues that the impact of mass technology is 'outside the range of human experience',[22] and that 'through a mechanised culture, we have lost touch with our essential humanity'.[23] The visionary thinker Gregory Bateson believed that 'addictive behaviour is consistent with the western approach to life, which pits mind against body', concluding that 'it is doubtful whether a species having both an advanced technology and this strange polarized way of looking at its world can survive'.[24] Paul Shepherd, another eco-psychologist, cites the sixteenth-century fixation with the impurity of the body, compared with the efficiency and tidiness of the machine, suggesting that this created an obsessive-compulsive complex within the human psyche, fuelling 'a tapestry of chronic madness in the industrial present, countered by dreams of absolute control and infinite possession'.[25]

The bottom line seems to be that 'the grass is always greener'. There is something within us, which we might call the fully developed western ego, that is rarely satisfied with what it has in the present moment. This is what the Buddha called the bondage of desire, the ultimate cause of human suffering. Our seemingly inexhaustible thirst for consumption, which is accelerating rather than slowing down, is fuelled by our basic inability to be happy with what we already have. Lewis Lapham, an Editor at *Harpers* magazine, conducted a survey over several decades. 'No matter what their income', he reports, 'a depressing number of Americans believe that if they only had twice as much, they would inherit the estate of happiness promised them in the Declaration of Independence. The man who receives $15,000 a year is sure that he could relieve his sorrow if he had $30,000 a year; the man with $1 million a year knows that all would be well if he had $2 million a year . . . Nobody ever has enough.'[26]

That which never has enough, or fails to accept what it has, is the ego, the restless chattering mind which most of us identify with. Until there is some sort of transcendence of this egoic structure, a disidentification with the psychological desire to want something other than what is right here, right now, the human race seems destined to express its sense of alienation from Nature, and its consequent lack of self-worth, by buying things it doesn't really want and certainly doesn't need.

Speed

Computers have been embraced by people around the world, from Silicon Valley to the south Indian city of Bangalore. For many of us, life without one has become almost inconceivable. Everything from banks, businesses and financial markets, to schools, universities and an increasing amount of our shopping, is now dependent on the technology which transformed life in the late twentieth century. Even environmental groups have accepted the technology as being entirely benign, over-looking the fact that it accelerates globalisation, enhances corporate control and contributes to existing environmental problems. The World Wide Web may have facilitated an expanding network between pressure groups and grass-roots activists, promoting a de-centralised global movement, but Internet shopping continues to erode local business and add to energy use as courier companies speed up and down the country.

This may sound like the proverbial swings and roundabouts, but there are several other implications of computer technology which are rarely taken into account. According to Mander, high concentrations of trichloroethylene have seeped into Silicon Valley's drinking water and the Environmental Protection Agency (EPA) has identified eighty chemical spill sites associated with computer manufacture. Ted Smith, a local attorney, believes that 'Workers and the general population are being exposed to the most deadly chemicals that have ever been synthesized,' while there is evidence that occupational illness within the industry is three times the national average.[27]

Then there are numerous studies suggesting debilitating side effects from using computers, ranging from Chronic Fatigue Syndrome to migraines, miscarriages and even infant deaths. In Stockholm, the leading European city associated with dot com start-ups, there have been recent cases of 'burn-out' which have resulted in death among young people working regular 18 hour days. Long shifts at computer terminals have even been called 'the coal mining of the nineties'.[28] Naomi Klein's *No Logo* shows how corporations and their brands are infiltrating the educational system with television and computers as part of the 'convergence' we are seeing between different technologies. It is obvious why the industry is so keen to put a computer on every school desk. Traditional interaction between young children playing games is effectively being replaced by interaction with a computer screen. The technology is giving birth to a generation of amplified human beings whose physical reality has been absorbed into cyber-space.

The most insidious aspect of a computerised world is the Orwellian concept of Big Brother surveillance. One corporation in the US holds credit records for 120 million Americans.[29] Using the underhand approach of the 'reward card' system, a similar pattern is now emerging in Europe, accumulating information about where we shop, what we buy, what we own, where we work and live, what our income is and how well we pay our bills. It is estimated that the FBI and CIA now hold an average of seventeen files on each person in the US,[30] while every year the laws which grant government agencies access to these files are relaxed. In Britain, the police are pushing for legislation which will allow them to monitor any telephone call made by any member of the public. While some environmentalists celebrate the decentralisation that the Internet has provided, others argue that computers continue to centralise society into one homogeneous factory of consumers. While serving as a catalyst for a unified global activism, the computer has also accentuated the manipulative control of corporations and their ability to sell you something.

Mander believes that computers have given rise to one pervasive system of 'megatechnology', controlled by a technocratic elite:

> Our assumption of technology's beneficence, combined with our passivity to its advance, has permitted certain technological forms to expand their scale of impact, and to interlock and merge with one another. Together, they are forming something new, almost as if they were living cells; they are becoming a single technical-economic web encircling the planet, *megatechnology*. Among the key components of this invisible apparatus are computers, television, satellites, corporations and banks, space technology, genetics, and the alarming 'post-biological' machinery: nanotechnology and robotics.[31]

Lewis Mumford, the architectural critic and radical town planner, was one of the first to present a detailed critique of this phenomenon. Inspired by a group of social ecologists at the University of Chicago in the 1920s, Mumford was one of the first writers to integrate ecological principles within the structure of human organisations. Books like *The Culture of Cities* and *Technics and Civilisation* have become crucial texts in the development of a green political ideology and cited as an inspiration for counter-culture leaders like Barry Commoner and Murray Bookchin. Mumford believed that, ever since the late Neolithic period, two technological systems have existed in parallel: 'one authoritarian, the other democratic, the first system-centred, immensely powerful but inherently unstable, the other man-centred, relatively weak, but resourceful and durable'. In *The Myth of the Machine*, Mumford equates the modern alliance between government and science with the fusion of military authority and the ruling class in ancient Egypt, resulting in what he calls the 'megamachine'. Without a dramatic shift in consciousness, 'a move from mechanical to an organic ideology', he warned that the technological control maintained by the scientific elite and the American military-industrial complex would have catastrophic consequences. If we are to be saved from being exterminated by our own innovations, 'the God who saves us will not descend from the machine: he will rise up again in the human soul', then 'the gates of the technocratic prison will open automatically, despite their ancient rusty hinges, as soon as we choose to walk out'.[32]

The US military-industrial complex is the primary recipient and source of funding for Silicon Valley's cutting-edge research. Many aspects of computerisation, which have percolated down to the public domain, were first developed for the military. The high-speed agility associated with computer games is not far removed from modern computerised warfare and could almost be seen as a training ground. However, any form of training would seem to be made redundant by such policies as Mutually Assured Destruction (MAD). As Mander observes, 'In modern computerized warfare, human involvement becomes so proscribed at the most critical moments as to be effectively meaningless.'[33] The role of rational human decision-making has been replaced by a computer programme. There is clearly an enormous capacity for error, as displayed by the 'millennium bug' fiasco. The fact that such a basic concept as a change in date could have led to such widespread alarm, not to mention the unbelievable expense, has worrying implications for our faith in those that designed the technology. A group of programmers in Silicon Valley have raised serious doubts about the long-term safety of computerised warfare, since in 'all but the simplest computer programs, hidden design flaws can persist, sometimes for years, even though the system appears to work perfectly'.[34] Since the world is filled with nuclear warheads, controlled by computer programmes, there is evidently some cause for alarm.

The rising addiction to computers is symptomatic of a modern addiction to speed, described by Jay Griffiths as 'something of a holy cow to modern westernised culture'.[35] Our financial markets can trade £200 million in a minute while computers perform 307 gigaflops per second. We are addicted to faster food, faster cars, faster computers, faster cash. Whole communities are wiped out, ancient sites destroyed and Sites of Special Scientific Interest (SSSIs) laid low by the construction of new roads which take five minutes off a one-hour journey. We consume more and more, faster and faster, filling up landfills with all our unwanted waste. Fresh Kills, New York's dumping ground, receives 26 million pounds of waste per day and has become the highest mountain on the eastern coastal plain.[36] 'Bulimia is indeed a disease of today,' says Griffiths. 'Consumer society speedily scoffs food beyond need, speedily reaches for the laxatives, and speedily excretes.'[37]

This addiction to speed is as much of an illusion as the buzz produced by amphetamines or cocaine. While we are lured by the idea of squeezing more and more into our alloted time on the planet, living the high-speed lifestyle, life actually passes us by. The faster we hurl ourselves into the future, the less time we have actually to sit back and experience the present. Then, suddenly, it's all over. 'The danger of speed', says Griffiths, 'is in its black opposite, in the instant of expiring – the stock market crash, the racing crash, the computer crash, a culture speeding up to its expiry date, the darkness over the event horizon, the moment of death.'[38]

Ever since the Industrial Revolution, this desire for increasing speed has evolved in synch with our technology. The natural rhythms of the planet, the cycles of the sun and moon, of night and day, were replaced by the amplified rhythms of the machine, electricity and the wheel. As a result, our nervous systems accelerated as well, to the point where most of us now find it almost impossible to sit down, relax and 'do nothing'. Doing 'nothing' is usually regarded as a 'waste of time' but is the essence of meditation and the peaceful state of mind which such practices promote and so many of us strive for. Our social conditioning is so powerful that we feel an obligation to be 'doing something' all the time, constantly removing us from the inherent peace and happiness which is our natural state, always there behind the speedy machinations of the modern mind. The physicist Peter Russell describes the silent mind as 'our evolutionary inheritance' and 'the state of grace to which we long to return; from which we fell when language took over our consciousness'.[39] Much of the technology which we have embraced with open arms, be it cars, computers or televisions, purely accentuates this barrier. Our excessive consumption patterns, and the dissatisfaction we feel with what we already have, is fuelled by the indoctrinated belief that happiness is to be found in objects: 'Civilized human beings do not, on any level of their being, live in harmony with Tao, or the divine Nature of Things,' observed Huxley.

> They love to intensify their selfhood through gluttony, therefore eat the wrong food and too much of it; they inflict upon themselves chronic anxiety over money and, because they crave excitement, chronic over-stimulation; they suffer, during their working hours, from the chronic boredom and frustration imposed by the sort of jobs that have to be done in order to satisfy the artificially stimulated demand for the fruits of fully mechanized mass-production.[40]

David Brower set the criteria by which Mander believes all technology should be judged – that it should be assumed guilty until proven innocent.

In reality, the situation is the reverse. Corporations provide the best-case scenario for every innovation, setting out the myriad social benefits which their products will provide while conveniently over-looking any of the negative implications. By accepting their claims, and failing to engage in any meaningful public debate about the potential problems posed by a new technology, we become party to their promise. Finally, with the uproar over bio-technology, it seems that this might be changing. This is only one of many sci-fi style concepts which are being developed and one can rest assured that, despite considerable opposition to the technology, someone, somewhere, is already cloning human embryos. The day when we will be able to determine every characteristic of our offspring, from the colour of their eyes to their basic disposition, is just around the corner.

Eco-technology

Fritz Schumacher recognised that 'there are two sciences – the science of manipulation and the science of understanding'. This definition can be neatly applied to the scientific world, separating those who seek to manipulate Nature with techniques like genetic modification from those who understand natural processes and learn from them. This latter category of scientist has produced innovative eco-technologies which could revolutionise our relationship with the planet.

All around us, at every moment, Nature effortlessly produces substances, structures and organisms which modern science cannot begin to replicate. The scientist Janine Benyus observes how

> spiders make silk, strong as Kevlar but much tougher, from digested crickets and flies, without needing boiling sulphuric acid and high-temperature extruders. The abalone generates an inner shell twice as tough as our best ceramics, and diatoms make glass, both processes employing seawater with no furnaces. Trees turn sunlight, water and air into cellulose, a sugar stiffer and stronger than nylon, and bind it

> into wood, a natural composite with a higher bending strength and stiffness than concrete or steel.[41]

Millions of bio-chemical processes, most of which we hardly understand, maintain homeostasis, the balanced conditions that life requires, linking micro-organisms in the soil, photosynthesis in leaves and plankton in the oceans with world weather patterns and the composition of our atmosphere. Humans are like cells within one vast interconnected, infinitely complex living organism.

Our arrogance ensures that we continue to believe we can understand the entirety of this system while forming a relatively insignificant part. Despite being a created object, we assume subjective control, insisting that we can understand that which created us. Metaphysics would suggest that this is not only rather ambitious but logically impossible. Consciousness cannot understand the source from which it came and, however close astrophysicists come to deconstructing the moments after the Big Bang, they will never comprehend that which preceded it.

In recent years, the close observation of cyclical natural processes has fused with scientific innovation, giving birth to what has been hailed as a 'design revolution'. One example of this is the 'Living Machine' concept, developed by Dr John Todd, an American biologist. By passing contaminated effluent through a series of tanks, populated with a variety of bacteria, algae, plants and fish, Todd's 'Living Machines' not only provide clean drinking water, but also generate fertilisers and maintain a miniature ecosystem in perpetuity. No chemicals are required and some of the systems even double up as miniature fish farms. With a higher degree of biodiversity than the conventional filtration achieved by a reed bed, the Living Machine treats a much wider range of toxic effluents. Some of the plants, like bullrushes, even sequester heavy metals and secrete antibiotics which kill pathogens. The machines are capable of treating sewage from anything between one and 10,000 households, with one in Vermont handling 80,000 gallons per day. The systems are equally suited to heavy industry, transforming toxic pollution into a beneficial resource.

Part of the inspiration for Todd's design came from a farm in central Java, where soil fertility had been steadily increasing for hundreds of years:

> The farm was located on a hillside that was particularly vulnerable to soil erosion which was prevented by mimicking nature's most efficient erosion control strategy, namely, tree-covered slopes. It was not a wild

> forest, but a domestic one in which the biota were fruit, nut, fuel, and fodder trees useful to humans. Nevertheless, it had some of the structural integrity found in the wild. Without the trees on the hills it would have been very hard to sustain the land's fertility. The farm received its water from an aqueduct flowing across the slope halfway up. The water came from a farm higher up and arrived in a clean, relatively pure state. Upon entering the farm it was, within a short distance, intentionally polluted first by passing it directly under slatted livestock barns and then under the household latrine. Although it might appear shocking at first glance, the livestock and household sewage was then utilized in a very clever way. The solids were 'digested' by a few fish whose sole function was to provide primary waste treatment. The nutrient-laden sewage was then aerated and exposed to light by passing over a low waterfall. Secondary and tertiary treatment were agricultural. The sewage was used to irrigate and fertilize vegetable crops planted in raised beds. The nutrient-rich water flowed down the channels and dispersed laterally on the soil to feed the crop roots. It is important to note that the secondary sewage was not applied directly to the crops but to the soil. The water emerged from the raised bed crop garden with nutrients removed and at least in an equivalent condition to our tertiary treatment. It then flowed into a system that requires pure water, namely, a small hatchery for baby fish. Here in the hatchery pond the young fish began the enrichment cycle again by slightly fertilizing the water with their wastes. This triggered the growth of algae and microscopic animals that helped feed the young fish. This biota was also carried along with the current to add nutrients and feeds to the larger fish cultured in grow-out ponds below. These highly enriched grow-out ponds fertilized the rice paddies that were just downstream. The rapidly growing rice used up the nutrients and purified the water before releasing it again to a community pond in the basin below.[42]

Todd realised that this farm was something which is almost unheard of in western farming – 'a complete agricultural microcosm', in which 'trees, soils, vegetable crops, livestock, water and fish were all linked to create a whole symbiotic system in which no one element was allowed to dominate'. However, this intrinsic harmony would be destabilised by the introduction of just one external input: 'One single toxin, like a pesticide, will kill the fish and unravel the system.' The long-term sustainability of traditional agriculture is therefore in total contrast to the intensive, disruptive inputs of the modern agri-business. As Todd concluded, we are faced with a simple choice: 'we can create ecological agri-systems and let nature do the recycling, or we can manage a complex system chemically and ultimately destroy its underlying structure'.

This concept of 'closing loops', thereby eliminating 'waste', is one of the basic principles of the design revolution proposed by 'natural capitalism'.[43] Nature itself has no concept of 'waste'. Everything is reabsorbed within a cyclical system. Rotting leaves, animal excrement and dead organisms all decompose and ultimately create the humus from which other trees and crops will grow, soaking up carbon dioxide and providing the oxygen and nutrition that all living organisms require. Since the Industrial Age began synthesising new chemical compounds, thereby generating pollutants which had never previously existed, the human race has become the first species to generate more waste than can be recycled by the planet. By using, rather than abusing, the extraordinary resilience and regenerative powers of Nature, 'Living Machines' may ultimately become the technology which reverses this process.

Living Machines are an obvious example of 'closing loops' in a literal sense, but the same concept can be applied to all our industrial processes. As legislation is slowly introduced to penalise companies for excessive pollution, those that make the quantum jump to a closed system will benefit the most. 'Closing loops' is not about minimising pollution by fitting filters to the top of smokestacks, it is about eliminating waste from the entire industrial process. Companies like Xerox are aiming for 'zero to landfill' goals, developing photocopiers which exceed all global standards for energy efficiency, as well as E-paper, 'a flexible and cordless computer screen that looks like a sheet of paper, uses no memory for storing images or for viewing, and can be electronically written and rewritten at least a million times'.[44] With the Z-1 sports car, BMW have produced a recyclable thermoplastic skin which can be removed from the chassis in twenty minutes.[45] After suffering considerable humiliation about its packaging in the McLibel trial, McDonalds conducted tests with biodegradeable cartons made from potato starch and limestone.[46]

Perhaps the most progressive example cited by the authors of *Natural Capitalism* is the Interface carpet company from Atlanta. Having realised that some 5 billion pounds of Interface carpet was now residing in landfills, where it would remain for the next 20,000 years, the company realised that they were quite literally throwing money into the ground. Their carpets are now made from a polymeric compound called Solenium, which can be completely remanufactured into itself. In the process, the company has not only reduced their waste by 99.7 per cent, but created a renewable resource. In addition, rather than selling their product, Interface now leases their carpet to offices across the US, creating a 'service economy'. By leasing 'carpet tiles', the company is able to replace worn out sections without laying acres of brand new carpet. The customer's capital investment is turned into a lease expense and Interface is able to reduce the net flow of materials and embodied energy by 97 per cent, increasing the efficiency of the company by a factor of 31.[47]

A distinguishing feature of many eco-technologies is their astounding common sense simplicity, their efficiency and the multiple systemic benefits they provide. For example, a farmer from Kansas has devised a zero-energy way of drying grain in a silo, a process which uses 5 per cent of direct energy use on American farms:

> He simply bored a hole in the top of the structure, atop which a hollow shaft connects into the hollow blades of a windmill. As the prairie wind spins the blades, centrifugal force slings the air out the holes at the ends of them. The resulting vacuum pulls a slow, steady draft of air up through the grain from small, screened vents at the bottom of the silo. This gradually dries the grain – and evaporatively cools it, making any insects infesting it too sluggish to move and eat. This in turn means that no chemicals are needed to prevent mould or kill bugs. Ward's process not only saves chemical costs but also keeps organically grown grain uncontaminated so it can fetch a premium price.[48]

This sort of efficiency is characteristic of many traditional agricultural systems around the world and the alternative methods being pioneered today. Rather than burning their fields after harvest, some Californian rice growers have taken to flooding them, creating wetland areas for migrating ducks and birds. As a result, the decomposing rice stubble rebuilt the soil, the ducks aerated and fertilised the fields – thus reducing inputs – hunters paid to visit, productivity increased and incomes rose. In addition to growing rice, these farmers are now involved in straw production, managing wetlands and conserving a wildlife habitat.[49]

Unfortunately, the present structure of our economic system guarantees that most corporations, and the scientists they employ, are not interested in the systemic gains that this sort of thinking provides. Rather than learning from the inherent wisdom of Nature, then applying her basic principles to their work, they seem determined to try to make improvements. Rather than feeling a sense of humility when confronted by the diverse beauty of the natural world, there is an intellectual arrogance, an assumption that human ingenuity is in some way transcendent to it. This is an antiquated, old-fashioned way of looking at the world, an obsolete paradigm which subordinates life to the status of a machine and will one day be viewed as deluded collective amnesia. It has only been accepted for a fraction of our evolutionary history and is perpetuated by an elite minority, a scientific priesthood which has divorced itself from the rest of society and arrogantly assumes itself to be intellectually superior. When asked whether the public should be concerned about GM crops, Professor Janet Bainbridge, from the UK Advisory Committee on Novel Foods and Processes, replied that 'most people don't even know what a gene is. Sometimes my young son wants to cross the road when it's dangerous. Sometimes you just have to tell people what's good for them.'[50]

The extremes to which supposedly rational scientific thought is prepared to go are often so absurd as to be laughable. Recent suggestions of ways to counter global warming have included a plan to cover the world's oceans with polystyrene chips, reflecting sunlight back into space, or releasing thousands of tons of sulphur dioxide into the upper atmosphere, thereby cooling the earth's surface. The man behind this latter inspired idea, Dr Wallace Broecker, Professor of Geo-chemistry at Colombia University, admitted that this would not only increase acid rain but change the colour of the sky. However, he thought that this was an acceptable price to pay, 'compared to the impact on industry if we give up fossil fuels'.[51]

The prize for the most ludicrous idea of the last millennium, however, must go to Professor Alexander Abian, from Iowa State University. Abian decided that the moon was responsible for undersirable weather patterns across the planet, exerting a gravitational pull on the Earth and causing us to spin through space on an axis tilted to 23 degrees. Therefore, all that needs to be done is to fire nuclear rockets at the moon and get rid of it altogether. Abian also made provision for those romantics who might object to the disappearance of the moon: 'Once human beings learn the secrets to re-arranging the Universe, scientists will be able to pluck moons from other planets and bring them closer to earth – but not so close that they interfere with the weather.' Far from being a joke, Professor Abian was dismayed by the lack of enthusiasm for his plan, complaining that 'From the earliest traces of primate fossils, some 70 million years ago, no one – but no one – has ever raised a finger of defiance at the celestial organisation.'[52]

As Teddy Goldsmith observes, this sort of extreme faith in Man's right to interfere with cosmic law is quite staggering – 'God obviously did a bad job, and it is incumbent on our scientists to rearrange the universe according to their vastly superior design.' The most frightening thing about Abian's idea is that it was seriously considered by the Czechoslovakian Academy of Sciences.[53]

Intermediate Technology

The first economist to make a detailed study of the flaws within our modern economic system was Fritz Schumacher. His most famous book, *Small is Beautiful*, sits alongside other classics like *Silent Spring*, *Limits to Growth* and *Blueprint for Survival*, and is regarded by many within the movement as the text which first sparked their interest in environmental issues. His legacy survives, forming the ideological background to the Schumacher Society and Schumacher College, an international centre for ecological studies in Devon which draws teachers and students from around the world.

In the opening pages of his book, Schumacher exposed the illusion of infinite growth and introduced the notion of 'natural capital':

> The illusion of unlimited powers, nourished by astonishing scientific and technological achievements, has produced the concurrent illusion of having solved the problem of production. The latter illusion is based on the failure to distinguish between income and capital where this distinction matters most. Every economist and businessman is familiar with the distinction, and applies it conscientiously and with considerable subtlety to all economic affairs – except where it really matters: namely, the irreplaceable capital which man has not made, but simply found, and without which he can do nothing.[54]

Schumacher realised that an industrial system which, at the time, used 40 per cent of the world's primary resources to supply 6 per cent of the population, could hardly be regarded as efficient. Similarly, he saw that fossil fuels, the life-blood of our economy, are 'merely part of the "natural capital" which we steadfastly insist on treating as expendable'.[55] In a speech given in April 1961, he predicted that the energy crisis would hit Britain, 'not when the world's oil is exhausted, but when world oil supplies cease to expand'. When this happens – and the indications are that it already is – then 'what else could be the result but an intense struggle for oil supplies'.[56] Hence we have the Gulf War and a large military presence in eastern Europe, standing guard over trans-Siberian pipelines, while it becomes increasingly clear that the wars of the twenty-first century will be fought over two of our most vital resources – oil and water.

What set Schumacher's vision apart from that pursued by conventional economists was his holistic approach. Rather than seeing economic health and prosperity in isolation, he combined his insights with philosophical and spiritual enquiry, realising that human happiness was not entirely dependent on financial gain. He saw that the first question that conventional economics fails to address is 'What is enough?' Basic logic tells us that 'infinite growth' will never produce 'enough', because it is intrinsically seeking 'more'. Similarly, the modern notion of abundance and universal prosperity will always fail to deliver, because 'such prosperity, if attainable at all, is attainable only by cultivating such drives of human nature as greed and envy, which destroy intelligence, happiness, serenity and thereby peacefulness of man.'[57]

Schumacher believed that the only way to overcome this dilemma was to incorporate the ancient perennial wisdom, and the spiritual and moral truth which it conveys, within our economic system:

> But what is wisdom? Where can it be found? Here we come to the crux of the matter: it can be read about in numerous publications but it can be found only inside oneself. To be able to find it one has first to liberate oneself from such masters as greed and envy. The stillness following liberation – even if only momentary – produces the insights of wisdom which are obtainable in no other way. They enable us to see the hollowness and fundamental unsatisfactoriness of a life devoted to the pursuit of material ends, to the neglect of the spiritual. Such a life necessarily sets man against man and nation against nation, because man's needs are infinite and infinitude can be achieved only in the spiritual realm, never in the material.[58]

Schumacher's attempt to fuse spiritual truth with material comfort formed the foundation of what he called 'Buddhist economics', overcoming the mistaken assumption that the two are mutually incompatible:

> It is not wealth that stands in the way of liberation, but attachment to wealth; not the enjoyment of pleasureable things but the craving for them. The keynote of Buddhist economics, therefore, is simplicity and non-violence. From an economist's point of view, the marvel of the Buddhist way of life is the utter rationality of its pattern – amazingly small means leading to extraordinarily satisfactory results. For the modern economist, this is difficult to understand. He is used to measuring the 'standard of living' by the amount of annual consumption, assuming all the time that a man who consumes more is 'better off' than a man who consumes less. A Buddhist economist would consider this approach excessively irrational: since consumption is merely a means to human well-being, the aim should be to obtain the maximum of well-being with the minimum of consumption.[59]

The logical extension to this is that, in a world of finite resources, a human-scale, self-sufficient community is more likely to be at peace than a globalised economy dependent upon intensive energy use and free trade agreements. Therefore, since non-renewable resources, like fossil fuels, are unevenly distributed across the planet, 'it is clear that their exploitation at an ever-increasing rate is an act of violence against Nature which must also inevitably lead to violence between men'.[60]

The question of scale was central to Schumacher's vision for the future, predicting that the trend towards globalisation, centralisation and mass production would increasingly remove technology from the community level, raise unemployment and have a disastrous sociological impact. As Karl Marx noticed, 'the production of too many useful things results in too many useless people'.[61] Schumacher proposed that 'the technology of mass production is inherently violent, ecologically damaging, self-defeating in terms of non-renewable resources, and stultifying for the human person'.[62] In contrast, he suggested that 'the technology of production *by* the masses, making use of the best modern knowledge and experience, is conducive to decentralisation, compatible with the laws of ecology, gentle in its use of scarce resources, and designed to serve the human person instead of making him the servant of machines'.[63] He called this concept Intermediate Technology, although he saw that it could also be called 'self-help technology, or democratic or people's technology',[64] and acknowledged his debt to Gandhi's vision of *swadeshi*, a sort of 'think global, act local' philosophy which inspired thousands of Indian villagers to spin their own cotton rather than rely on imported cloth from Britain.

Schumacher founded the Intermediate Technology Development Group (ITDG) to further his goal of developing appropriate, human-scale technologies. Their achievements in the Third World go largely unrecognised, but their implementation of everything from mini-hydro-electric projects to windmill water pumps have brought electricity and clean water to thousands of villages. Rather than funding the application of these technologies, institutions like the World Bank continue to pour billions of dollars into vast hydro-electric schemes, like Narmada in India and the Three Gorges Dam in China, which have displaced millions of people, flooded thousands of acres of fertile, arable land and destroyed entire ecosystems. Those who have had their land and their homes taken from them receive little in the way of compensation and the electricity generated is used to feed heavy industry and urban centres, hundreds of miles from the site. The Tehri Dam, in the Indian Himalayas, is constructed over a seismic fault, where an earthquake killed thousands less than two decades ago. Millions of lives are at risk should the dam be damaged in the future. In contrast, small hydro-electric projects could have been built over hundreds of mountain streams, having minimal ecological impact and supplying power to thousands in local communities. Of course, this sort of policy would not provide contracts for huge western corporations.

By promoting this scale of development, Schumacher and his adherents are accused of 'standing in the way of progress', of advocating a return to a form of technology which is in some way out-dated and inferior. These critics assume that, just because we know how to dam three of the largest rivers in China, that we should just go ahead and do so. Who wants lots of piddly little dams when we can have the biggest one in the world? However, there are hundreds of human-scale technologies, which are so inherently beautiful in the simplicity and efficiency of their design, that they simply defy improvement. Jay Griffiths points to that 'green car', which 'runs on tap water and toasted tea cakes, and has an inbuilt gym. It is called a bicycle'.[65] John Whitelegg, director of an environmental transport consultancy, believes it to be 'far more sophisticated and useful than anything NASA has ever done'.[66] Over the last century, millions of people in the Third World have been given access to a form of zero-emissions transport, which keeps them fit and healthy. The American space programme could hardly be seen to have achieved anything vaguely comparable in addressing humanitarian needs. The systemic benefits of the bicycle have been somewhat distorted in parts of the developed world. Thousands of Californians drive their gas-guzzling SUVs through the congested highways of Los Angeles, sit on a bicycle machine in the gym – where they are able to imbibe an extra hour of television – then burn their way through another gallon of petrol going to the office.

By failing to develop a holistic approach to specialised fields like science and economics, our world-view is blinded to the repercussions for ourselves and the rest of the planet. We are so absorbed with abstract notions about the rate of growth, GDP and inflation, that we seem to forget that basic human values should be an integral part of the equation. As Schumacher said, we need 'a study of economics as if people mattered', because 'what is at stake is not economics but culture; not the standard of living but the quality of life'. The successful application of such a system will ultimately depend upon a shift in basic human needs, where subjective spiritual well-being is recognised to be of greater value than the material wealth displayed by the accumulation of objects.

Auto-addiction

The automobile has become the most pervasive symbol of humanity's techno-addiction. In his study of the global environment, John McNeill described it as 'a strong candidate for the title of most socially and environmentally consequential technology of the twentieth century'.[67] It is easy to see why this may be true. The car is responsible for combusting 8 million barrels of oil every day, contributing to nearly a quarter of total global greenhouse emissions and causing major increases in bronchial diseases like asthma and emphysema.[68] In America, it has been responsible for killing six times as many people as have died in combat during the last hundred years and injuring a further 250 million.[69]

We are inclined to think of the exhaust pipe as the source of a vehicle's negative impact on the planet and the biosphere, but the manufacturing process itself generates more pollution per car than ten years of average driving.[70] In Germany, during the last decade, 29 tons of waste were generated for every ton of car.[71] Each unit involves the assembly of some 15,000 parts by an industry which uses more resources than any other[72]

– 20 percent of the world's steel, 50 percent of the lead and 60 per cent of the rubber.[73] Since our economic systems fail to take account of this resource depletion, it now costs less per pound to make a car than a McDonald's burger[74] and, because of such concepts as 'built-in obsolescence' and the culture of the company car, another 40,000 new cars roll off the production lines every night. In America, there are more registered car owners than registered voters and it is now estimated that there are well over half a billion vehicles on the planet.[75]

However, cutting edge 'eco-technology' developments are about to transform not only the basic propulsion systems of the vehicles we drive, but the entire manufacturing process as well. Auto-motive design is gearing up for a revolution which will implement completely different technologies and by-pass many of the established manufacturing industries like oil and steel. Computer software companies may feel more at home in this emerging market than many contemporary car producers. A combination of ultra-light composite materials, low-drag design, integrated micro-electronics and hybrid-electric propulsion, incorporating the hydrogen fuel cell, is giving birth to an entirely new concept in clean, zero-emissions transport, which minimises the 'ecological footprint' it leaves on the planet.

One of the people at the forefront of this revolution is Amory Lovins, a founding member of Friends of the Earth (FoE) in the UK. His Rocky Mountain Institute (RMI) has pioneered much of the research on his Hypercar concept and Lovins predicts that the first zero-emissions vehicles will be commercially available within three years. To start with, Lovins and his team realised the intrinsic inefficiency of modern car design, inherited from the mass production methods pioneered by Henry Ford, which are reliant upon steel construction. The vehicle ends up being twenty times heavier than the driver and needing an engine about ten times larger than average driving requires.[76] From the potential energy within the fuel of a modern car, 80 per cent is wasted through heat in the engine and the exhaust, 95 per cent of the remaining 20 per cent moves the car, while only 5 per cent moves the driver. By using ultrastrong carbon, Kevlar and glass fibres, embedded in specially moulded plastics, the weight of an average car could be reduced by half without reducing safety, since these materials absorb five times more energy per pound than steel.[77] By reducing the overall weight, all sorts of other features become unnecessary, such as power steering. At the same time, the use of 'regenerative braking' would recover electricity during times of deceleration rather than losing it to heat as in mechanical systems.

Perhaps the most revolutionary part of the Hypercar concept is the actual drive system. The electric car has always been fundamentally flawed for two reasons – firstly, it does not overcome the problem of greenhouse emissions since it relies on power generated from fossil fuel sources. The pollution may become more localised, but there is still pollution. The second problem is the sheer weight of the batteries required to power the car at a satisfactory speed over reasonable distances, coupled with the lengthy time required to re-charge. In a hybrid-electric drive, the wheels are turned by electricity generated within the car from a separate fuel source, ideally hydrogen fuel cells, which Lovins describes as 'solid state, no-moving parts, no-combustion devices that silently, efficiently, and reliably turn hydrogen and air into electricity, water, and nothing else'.[78]

The fuel cell was actually invented as early as 1839 and is similar to the process of electrolysis, except conducted in reverse. Using a thin platinum-dusted plastic membrane, it combines oxygen and hydrogen to create pure hot water and electricity. It is an electro-chemical process which requires no combustion. People on submarines and space missions drink the fuel cell's by-product, water, while the mayors of Vancouver and Chicago have recently been photographed drinking liquid from the exhaust pipes of fuel-cell buses being tested in their cities.

The Hypercar is just one of several such projects being conducted in this area. In 1997, Daimler-Benz announced a $350 million venture to develop hydrogen fuel cell engines with the Canadian firm Ballard, aiming for an annual production of 100,000 such vehicles by 2005.[79] Toyota have since aimed to beat that goal, predicting hybrid-electric cars would fill a third of the world market by the same date. Since then they have introduced the hybrid-electric Prius sedan, General Motors have developed production hybrids and Volkswagen have talked about models which will achieve 235 miles per gallon from conventional fuel sources.[80]

Lovins believes that the Hypercar 'could ultimately spell the end of today's car, oil, steel, aluminium, electricity and coal industries – and herald the birth of successor industries which are more benign'.[81] The proposed production and marketing methods are as revolutionary as the design itself, conforming to the principles of 'natural capitalism' and incorporating many examples of 'advanced resource productivity'; the materials would flow in 'closed loops', eliminating waste and toxicity; all the parts would be recyclable and could be up-dated according to the customer's needs; the cars would be leased as part of a diversified 'mobility service', rather than sold as a product with 'built-in obsolescence', while the flow of energy and materials would not deplete non-renewable resources or add to global warming. In fact, when fuel cells become cost-effective, our vehicles could become our own clean, silent power stations on wheels, generating electricity while they are parked and feeding it back to the national grid. Over time, that could signal the end of the nuclear industry as well, ushering in a hydrogen-based economy and an era of clean, sustainable energy systems which will move us out of the Fossil Fuel Age forever.[82]

6

Conclusion: Towards an Ecological Age

When the forms of an old culture are dying, the new culture is created by a few people who are not afraid to be insecure.

RUDOLF BAHRO[1]

The New World-view

We are living through an unprecedented era in the history of our planet. As we have seen in the discussion throughout this book, the human population has grown at an exponential rate during the last hundred years and inflicted irreversible damage to the systems which support life. The scale and the speed at which this is occurring is gathering momentum every second, while science and technology continue to redefine life on Earth.

We have explored outer and inner space with the Hubble telescope and sub-atomic physics. Now we are using genetics to redesign Nature itself. The established scientific paradigm has produced major medical breakthroughs, and life expectancy for many human beings has increased. Few would argue that certain technologies appear to have made our lives more comfortable. However, these apparent gains have carried the seeds of their own destruction. The biosphere is riddled with carcinogens that never previously existed. Millions of people are dying from toxic environmental pollutants, and the long-term implications of global warming are catastrophic. We have given birth to myriad new ways in which to destroy ourselves, from thermo-nuclear meltdown to drug-resistant viruses. As cultural historian Richard Tarnas observes, 'the human species is facing its own mortality on the planet as never before'.[2]

At the same time, the prevailing world-view which has brought us to this point is slowly cracking apart, revealing its mistaken assumptions and inherent contradictions. Rather than opening us up to the transcendent, divine dimension of human existence, world religions reinforce the divisions between us and precipitate violent conflicts. Rather than distributing material wealth, our economic systems widen the gap between the rich and the poor. Speculators are driving financial markets to a state of systemic instability which promises to come down with an infinitely more spectacular crash than in the late 1920s. The health system is not actually producing health but extending life by attacking symptoms, while encouraging new strains of drug-resistant disease through the profligate introduction of antibiotics and prophylactic drugs. The education system is not really producing educated people, but imposing external information which is increasingly determined by governments and corporations.

Along with 'infinite growth' and 'progress', another illusion which the mechanistic world-view has instilled in western culture is a linear conception of time. Indigenous cultures that maintain an ecological world-view tend to have a cyclical notion of time. By constantly living in the past, or worrying about the future, most of us have forgotten how to live in the reality of the present. As a consequence, we assume that time is speeding up and find ourselves hurtling into a conceptual future at an ever-increasing rate. The economic system which western society has embraced and exported to the rest of the world guarantees that most people spend their lives working like maniacs, saving for a future which many are unable to enjoy because of the stress-related illness which they are left with. As philosopher Alan Watts used to say, we have ended up in a huge restaurant where we are all sitting around eating the menu rather than the food.

The etymology of words like religion, economics and education reveals just how far our world-view has drifted from rational, logical thought. Religion, from the Latin root *religio*, literally means 'to connect', rather than divide. Economics shares the same Greek root as ecology, *oikos*, meaning house, implying a co-operative system which is mutually beneficial to the household of the planet rather than a competitive system which bolsters the wealth of an elite minority. Education is derived from *educare*, a Latin word which literally translates as 'extracting' and suggests drawing out the latent skills and abilities of a child rather than imposing external knowledge.

These sorts of failure within our social, political and cultural paradigm have led to a new world-view which recognises the fundamental need for change. There have been numerous projections about this emerging world-view, many of which were ascribed to some sort of pre-millennial psychosis. The New Age movement certainly produced some of the more extreme visions of impending planetary transformation. We may not become 'invisible light-beings' at the end of the Mayan calendar, but there is abundant evidence that we are witnessing a shift within the prevailing western paradigm. Richard Tarnas, who wrote *The Passion of the Western Mind*, one of the most celebrated studies of the western mind ever published, believes that 'we are at the end of a long trajectory that is coming to some sort of dramatic climax right now', drawing attention to the 'tremendous resurgence of the feminine archetype' and the notion that the sense of 'separation of the individual mind is gradually being shattered'.[3] The physicist and writer Peter Russell believes that the number of computers connected to the Internet is nearing the same number as our own neural connections, giving birth to what he calls 'the global brain'.[4] Gary Zukav, one of the leading writers about the 'new physics', believes that our intuitive sense is rapidly evolving, giving birth to 'multi-sensory human beings'.[5] The economist Hazel Henderson talks of a transition to the dawning Solar Age, or an Age of Light, based on benign lightwave technologies like fibre optics, lasers and photo-voltaic cells, harnessing photons rather than fossil fuels.[6]

Even if we discount these visionary concepts, there is an undeniable feeling that religion has somehow failed us, as has the mainstream scientific world-view which replaced it over the last 300 years. We are within a period of crisis and opportunity, and it seems that the old paradigm has to break apart before a new one can break through. However, as most commentators in this area agree, it is no longer a question of making incremental improvements to an intrinsically flawed system. It is about making the quantum leap to a new vision, a new global consciousness which recognises the systemic inter-relation of all life, the need for a transition from hierarchies to networks, the limitations of materialism, the basic illusion of linear time and the notion of being separate egocentric individuals. By looking at new models, frameworks and disciplines, like Gaia, General Systems Theory, Deep Ecology, Natural Capitalism and Eco-psychology, we can assess the impact that the environmental movement is having on science, politics, economics and our own conception of self within this new world-view.

The New Science

The most influential scientific theory to have been aligned with the emerging world-view is James Lovelock's Gaia Theory, named after the Greek goddess of the Earth by the writer William Golding. Although similar concepts have been maintained by indigenous cultures around the globe, Lovelock has produced the first western scientific model to explain the planet and the biosphere as one integrated self-regulating organism. His research has shown that processes as fundamental and diverse as weather patterns, salinisation levels in the sea and the formation of clouds are inextricably linked to the function of micro-organisms like plankton and algae. Similarly, through computerised models like Daisy World, he has shown that the composition of the atmosphere and the temperature of the planet are maintained at remarkably constant levels by complex systemic processes.

When I visited him at his home in Devon, which doubles as a laboratory and research centre, Lovelock explained how his theory sprang from previous work with NASA, developing instruments for detecting life on other planets:

> When we analysed the composition of the atmospheres on Mars and Venus, we found that they were primarily made of carbon dioxide. This showed that the planets were in what chemists call the 'equilibrium state', whereby an atmosphere made of carbon dioxide indicates a lifeless state. When we looked at the atmosphere of the Earth, it was such a rich mixture, almost like the gas that goes into the intake manifold of your car, hydrocarbons mixed with oxygen, compared to Mars which is more like the exhaust gases that come out the other end. So it appears that life on Mars and Venus may have exhausted itself.[7]

In light of this discovery, Lovelock paints a fairly bleak picture for the future of global warming:

> The real problem facing everybody today is the combination of expanding greenhouse emissions and the loss of habitat which contains the systems responsible for regulating the planet. We are now in what I would term a state of 'positive feedback' in which, far from ameliorating the harm that we do, the system is actually increasing so that as it warms, the systems are wiped out and process speeds up. I think that we are going to find in the next ten years or so that global warming is taking place considerably faster than we had previously thought. In fact, I think that we already know that. And what do the Greens do about it? They start fussing about genetically modified foods and other issues, all of which may be important in their own small way but pale into insignificance when compared to extinction of all life on the planet. Talk about fiddling while Rome burns![8]

Although his work has been firmly aligned with the Green agenda, Lovelock has frequently dismayed, alienated, or even enraged members of the environmental movement with some of his radical views, most famously by expressing his support for nuclear power. He firmly maintains that the dangers of radioactivity have been grossly over-exaggerated and believes that future generations will curse the anti-nuclear movement for closing down the only viable alternative to fossil fuels. However, he has been known to make some fairly dramatic mistakes during his career, insisting at one stage that CFCs posed no discernible threat to the biosphere.

Unlike many modern scientists though, Lovelock is quite happy to admit to his mistakes, recognising the arrogance of our species and the limitations of the predominant world-view:

> The most important thing to remember with science is that it is provisional. It can never be certain about anything. Although Newton's world was modified by Einstein, Newtonian physics remains a perfectly good way to navigate yourself around the solar system, except in the orbit of Mercury, where relativity begins to rear its head. Now Einstein's notions are coming under threat, but the theory of relativity will continue to be of great importance. But there will always be something else if you like. Humans are full of hubris. They always think they've worked it all out. One of the human characteristics, which may go back to our being tribal carnivores, is that we need something to worship, it's in our nature to want that, and therefore that side of our character is something that science cannot help with, because of its complete provisionality. The fact that it can never be certain about anything means that it is not very satisfying to the man in the street. It's probably why there's been no great music written to science, no great works of art attached to expounding science, in the way they do religions. Our psyches need something to worship and respect, and one of my hopes was that our vision of the earth might fill a gap here, especially now that religions have taken a downturn, largely because they provided the information about cosmology and biology before science replaced them. It's not that religions have been discredited, just shown to be inadequate as sources of information. Science can't provide moral guidance. Having supplanted religion, it has left the world in a moral vacuum. However, being accountable to Gaia clearly has strong moral implications. One of the laws of Gaia is that any species that damages its environment makes it worse for its progeny. Therefore, if it continues to do so it will go extinct. The converse is also true. Any species that makes its environment better for its progeny has an advantage.[9]

When it was first published in 1979, Gaia was scathingly attacked by the mainstream scientific community, partly because of its close parallels to animistic beliefs – seeing the planet as somehow alive – but also because Lovelock's holistic approach is in direct contrast to the mechanistic approach of conventional modern science. Reductionist scientists like Richard Dawkins dismissed Gaia as being teleological, or implying some sense of purpose on the part of the biota. However, in the same way that physiologists have shown that the human body automatically adjusts its chemical composition in response to changes in the external environment, Lovelock's theory has conclusively proved that the planet has self-regulating mechanisms which maintain homeostasis, the balanced atmospheric conditions that life requires. The theory has gained more and more recognition over the last twenty years and is now generally accepted by the scientific establishment. Much to the dismay of his reductionist colleagues, the eminent biologist William Hamilton, mentor of Richard Dawkins and inspiration for the 'selfish gene' metaphor, finally accepted Lovelock's theory in 1998, thereby giving Gaia mainstream acceptance. However, many still think the term Gaia has too many overtly mystical overtones, preferring to call it Earth Systems Science, bio-geochemistry, or geo-physiology.

By elevating the theory to an almost cult-like religious status, the New Age movement only undermined Lovelock's efforts to gain scientific credibility and perpetuated the notion that Gaia was little more than airy-fairy neo-Paganism. At the same time, as Lovelock himself admits, Gaia goes some way to filling the spiritual void which has appeared within our society. Far from promoting a misanthropic vision of the universe, as some have mistakenly perceived it, Gaia gives mankind a sense of moral duty to preserve the natural world for future generations. At the same time, it erodes the anthropocentric world-view, stressing the fact that the universe is not human hearted and that all species are of equal importance. Gaian processes are always at work, trimming populations in relation to their habitats. As Lovelock is always at pains to point out, Gaia is neither fragile nor delicate, as the media so often conveys. Even if every atomic bomb on the planet was to be detonated, some micro-organisms would survive and precipitate a new stage in evolution.

Similarly, Gaia is not limited to events and processes which mankind regards as positive. Volcanoes, floods, hurricanes and earthquakes are just as much a part of the equation as the global mechanisms which support life. Our world-view needs to incorporate the 'bad stuff', recognising the role that it plays beside the 'good stuff' within a dualistic universe. As the black and white Taoist symbol of *yin* and *yang* conveys, every action and event carries the seed of its polaric opposite within it, represented by the black and white dots within the opposing colour. Everything is in a state of constant flux, an endless fluid process of impermanence. Phenomenality only functions within this duality and the universe runs on the dynamic interaction of these polarised energies. Black does not exist without white, nor the good without the bad. The only aspect of Gaia to make reflective judgements about this process is the individual human ego. As Hamlet said, 'There is no good or bad, only thinking makes it so.'

Gaia Theory is just one of several scientific approaches that recognise the need for a holistic world-view. In the 1940s, biologist Ludwig von Bertalanffy developed General Systems Theory and 'established systems thinking as a major scientific movement'.[10] Like the first ecologists and organismic biologists, Bertalanffy saw the inherent limitations of studying any individual organism or phenomenon in isolation from its larger environment. Ultimately, he saw that everything was connected to everything else, in a systemic manner, which was infinitely more complex than reductionist, mechanistic science acknowledged.

Before Lovelock had even dreamt of Gaia Theory, Bertalanffy had noticed that complex biological systems developed the capacity for self-regulation and self-organisation. His ideas have more recently been applied to human social organisations and business itself, allowing modern thinkers to develop the principles of 'industrial ecology', which endeavours to achieve systemic benefits by 'closing loops' in the production process, thereby eliminating waste and generating useful by-products. General Systems Theory also influenced Ilya Prigogine, the Nobel prize winning Russian scientist whose concept of 'dissipative structures' examined the way in which spontaneous self-organisation emerges from inherent instability. This in turn became a defining aspect of Chaos Theory, which seeks to understand the extraordinarily complex order that evolves in living systems.[11]

In the last decades, the reductionist approach has been increasingly exposed by scientists dissatisfied with the way in which the entire framework fails to account for fundamental processes within the living world. One of the most controversial of these 'new scientists' is the biologist Rupert Sheldrake, who developed the concept of morphic resonance to explain why identical strands of DNA, the building blocks of life, evolve into such a stunning diversity of unique living organisms. Sheldrake continues to confront the mechanistic paradigm with its failure to address countless other phenomena within the natural world: How do carrier pigeons navigate? Why do pets telepathically know when their owners are nearing the house? Why do we know when we are being stared at? How can consciousness affect the results of independently formulated empirical experiments?

The common thread that unites all these scientific approaches is a basic recognition of the interconnected nature of all life. This basic insight is now shared by scientific disciplines which range from ecology to quantum physics. As Descartes realised, the root at the base of the scientific tree, from which all these different schools develop, is ultimately metaphysical. Deep enquiry into the nature of the self proves that the observer cannot be separated from that which is observed. When we try to find the observer, we find that no such entity exists. There is just observing.

The new paradigm in science therefore shares the same vision as the ancient mystics, suggesting that there are no boundaries between the individual and the rest of the universe. As Alan Watts said, any effort made by the ego towards accepting this reality is like trying to pull yourself into the air by yanking at your shoelaces.

The New Politics

As an ecological world-view replaces an outmoded paradigm, a new political framework will also have to emerge. Once again, a brief glance at the true definition of democracy – 'a form of government in which the people govern themselves' – shows just how far we have drifted from the original concept. The last US election made a mockery of the democratic process and, like America, British politics has become firmly tucked up in bed with corporate interests and the wealthy elite. With characteristic insight, Gandhi exposed the distortions surrounding western 'civilisation', describing it as 'a very good idea'.

The environmental movement has produced three different schools which will facilitate this transition from the hierarchical social organisations of today to the systemic networks of tomorrow. Although ideological arguments have developed between proponents of Deep Ecology, Social Ecology and Eco-feminism, many observers believe that these schools of thought can be successfully woven together to create a new political framework which recognises the inherent value of all forms of life, the way in which our social and economic institutions have destroyed the environment, and the need to reform our patriarchal systems to honour and include feminine values of co-operation, conservation, intuition and synthesis.

A distinguished mountaineer, keen skier, hiker and campaigner for non-violence, Arne Naess first articulated the difference between Deep Ecology and 'shallow' environmentalism in 1972, during a lecture given at the World Future Research Conference in Bucharest. Nearly thirty years later, so-called 'shallow' corporate environmentalism still dominates the mainstream, insisting on continued economic growth alongside resource management, techno-fix applications like catalytic converters, and mild lifestyle changes like recycling. By treating symptoms rather than causes, this approach side-steps any serious investigation about the values which underpin the prevailing world-view and perpetuates the notion of 'sustainable development', a concept which Teddy Goldsmith regards as a 'contradiction in terms'.[12]

In contrast, Deep Ecology digs down to the roots of the perceived environmental crisis, searching for a 'fundamental ecological transformation of our socio-cultural systems, collective actions, and lifestyles'.[13] Naess points out that 'Industrial societies are inherently unsustainable and no attempt should be made at temporarily repairing them.'[14] Deep Ecology respects the need not only for biodiversity but also for the abundance of other life-forms. It is not enough just to concentrate on avoiding species extinction; human interference with surrounding ecosystems should be entirely restricted to satisfying 'vital needs'. Within this paradigm, only energy-efficient, non-polluting 'soft' technologies are compatible with a sustainable society, defined by Lester Brown, Director of the Worldwatch Institute, as 'one that satisfies its needs without diminishing the prospects of future generations'.

Bill Devall, a Professor of Sociology at Humboldt State University in California, is another leading exponent of Deep Ecology. Devall frequently uses the term 'ecological self', stressing the 'intimate, personal, sensuous, erotic connection that we have with a specific place'.[15] By cultivating a broader sense of identification with the environment in which we live – the mountains, rivers, seas and trees of the bio-region which ultimately gives us life – Devall believes that the 'ecological self returns us to our primordial human experiences in a natural world'.[16] In this context, our definition of community is extended beyond our human neighbours to include animals, plants, trees, even the micro-organisms which build the soil beneath our feet. 'To say that humans are separate from Nature is to deny the laws of ecology,' says Devall.[17] This understanding has clear political implications, creating the need for long-range strategic planning and thereby transcending the short-termism that has come to characterise the modern left–right political spectrum.

Supporters of Deep Ecology often cite the bottom line which determines the actions of tribal societies – how will the seventh generation be affected? As Vandana Shiva points out, Deep Ecology is not a new idea, but 'the basis on which all sustainable civilisations have evolved'.[18] She refers to the *Upanishads*, one of the ancient Hindu scriptures: 'Every part of creation has a right to live to its full potential.'[19] She also believes that this opens us up to the intuitive side of our being, largely ignored for the last few hundred years because of our preoccupation with reductionist science and the consequent emphasis on the rational, analytic side of the brain: 'But it is more than intuition,' Shiva believes. 'It is a way of knowing in which your relationship, your connection with other species, with the plant, with the soil, with a cow, with a sheep, is so intimate, so deep, that there is instant communication. The ecosystem speaks to you as a whole. It is a pattern that could never be communicated through dissection. But it is the soundest base of knowing the world.'[20] As Shiva points out, tribal healers, shamen and medicine men around the world are able to distinguish the particular properties of a tree, plant or herb, just through their intuitive connection with it. They do not need to break it down to a cellular or molecular level with an array of high-tech equipment in a laboratory. They just know, because that aspect of their being has not been repressed through hundreds of years of conditioning, perpetuated by a mechanistic world-view.

By promoting a spiritual union between the individual and the rest of Nature, Deep Ecology advocates a powerful and subversive political message. As Devall says, 'Supporters of Deep Ecology do not engage in political activism to advance the ego, to gain power for the sake of power over other persons, but to advance and affirm the myriad of beings, the integrity of our broad and deep self.'[21] For most of our politicians, this is simply incomprehensible. The idea of campaigning on behalf of other creatures and non-sentient life-forms, for no personal gain, is so far removed from their own agenda that they completely fail to understand what is being proposed. In addition, these protesters work entirely for free, running campaigns, staging direct actions and organising protests. This is regarded as even more mysterious, that anyone should so whole-heartedly dedicate themselves to a movement which promises no financial reward. This is where the tremendous potential strength of the movement lies. By stepping outside of the old paradigm, it is no longer answerable to those values and is therefore invulnerable. By working as fluid networks rather than rigid hierarchies, the activist element of the movement is impossible to stamp out. You cannot chop the end off a circle.

Deep Ecology has often been misunderstood. After the Seattle protests, much of the mainstream western media condemned the protest as being little more than mindless hooliganism propelled by misanthropic anarchists. The *Observer* seized upon statements made by extremists like Dave Foreman, about the way in which diseases are Nature's way of dealing with over-population, then proposed that 'Gaia has become the basis for sinister beliefs' and described Professor Peter Singer, who advocates legal infanticide, as 'the guru of the "deep ecology" movement.'[22] It is ironic that a movement which was actually founded by a man with staunch Gandhian principles of non-violence, and is trying to solve a crisis which threatens to extinguish all human life, should now be branded as misanthropic.

Despite what some opponents believe, the true essence of Deep Ecology is not about leaving people to starve and die because famine and disease are a necessary part of Gaian self-regulation. That is nothing but a reaction against the understanding that famine and disease are an intrinsic aspect of the whole. That does not imply we do nothing about famine and disease, but that we look at the root causes of the problem rather than constantly patching up the symptoms. Famines are not solved through the distribution of aid. Famines are prevented through the implementation of sustainable agricultural systems. Healthy soil equals healthy food equals healthy people equals healthy society. Toxic soil equals toxic food equals the proliferation of modern cancers. Rather than presenting a fatalistic, nihilistic vision of the universe, Deep Ecology provides us with a new value system and a new political framework which honours the sacred dimension of life. It gives us the impetus to create the world in which we want to live, rather than encouraging a sense of complacency. As Bill Devall says, 'We do not have to live our lives as victims of military-industrial oppression, victims of toxic wastes, victims of doublespeak by politicians and bureaucrats.'[23]

By undermining the anthropocentric paradigm, Deep Ecology enables us to reconnect with Nature at a fundamental level. John Seed, Director of the Rainforest Information Centre in Australia, believes that Deep Ecology completely redefines our conception of the human condition:

> When humans investigate and see through their layers of anthropocentric self-cherishing, a most profound change in consciousness begins to take place. Alienation subsides. The human is no longer an outsider apart. Your humanness is then recognized as being merely the most recent stage of your existence; as you stop identifying exclusively with

> this chapter, you start to get in touch with yourself as vertebrate, as mammal, as species only recently emerged from the rainforest. As the fog of amnesia disperses, there is a transformation in your relationship to other species and in your commitment to them . . . The thousands of years of imagined separation are over and we can begin to recall our true nature; that is, the change is a spiritual one – thinking like a mountain, sometimes referred to as deep ecology.[24]

Social Ecology predates Deep Ecology and has often been in opposition to it. Murray Bookchin traces the principle causes of the environmental crisis to the evolution of society itself and accuses Deep Ecology of trying 'to regale metaphorical forms of spiritual mechanism and crude biologism with Taoist, Buddhist, Christian or shamanistic "Eco-la-la"'.[25] Peter Marshall believes that the divide between the two is 'both destructive and unnecessary'. Although they emphasise different factors as the root cause of the crisis, they both highlight the 'deranged relationship between humanity and nature' and the need for 'a new ecological consciousness and sensibility which recognise humanity to be one species among others on an evolving planet'.[26] Fritjof Capra applauds the way in which Deep Ecology provides 'the ideal philosophical and spiritual basis for an ecological lifestyle and for environmental activism' but also sees the need for Social Ecology to expose the 'fundamentally anti-ecological nature of many of our social and economic structures', based as they are around 'patriarchy, imperialism, capitalism and racism'.[27]

Eco-feminism addresses one of these factors – 'the patriarchal domination of women by men as the prototype of all domination and exploitation in the various hierarchical, militaristic, capitalist, and industrialist forms'.[28] However, this goes much deeper than equal opportunities for both sexes. Eco-feminism reveals the way in which the mechanistic world-view has enshrined masculine values, like competition, aggression and greed, at the exclusion of feminine values, like co-operation, intuition and integration. Some maintain that this has evolved in symbiosis with our own evolution and that, for the last few hundred years, social conditioning has emphasised the rational, analytical and masculine side of the brain, rather than the intuitive and feminine side. This has led to an increasingly individualistic and divisive social hierarchy rather than the inclusive and supportive network of the tribal community. It has also been an intrinsic aspect of reductionist science and our preoccupation with mechanistic explanations at the expense of an overall, holistic interpretation.

There are indications that this is starting to change. Modern scientists, from Albert Einstein and the physicist David Bohm, to Rupert Sheldrake and Fritjof Capra, have approached their work from the perspective of a spiritual understanding. For many, there is the recognition of the limitations posed by the mind, by science and language itself, the basic notation of human thought and communication, when trying to comprehend the entirety of something which is transcendent to it, or within which it is enclosed. Einstein himself admitted that the theory of relativity came to him 'from outside', suggesting that consciousness was not something limited to the human brain.

The final frontier therefore, is consciousness itself. However, a completely new language is required to approach the phenomenon of consciousness since the answers cannot be expressed in dualistic terminology. Objective scientific scrutiny can never explain that which it is dependent upon for its own articulation. It is impossible for a created object to explain that which created it, since consciousness is the substratum of the entire phenomenal world and all that is contained within it. Mechanistic science may explain the functions of certain neural networks within the human brain, but it is simply not equipped to explain how, why, where and what the source of consciousness actually is.

The only language that is suitable for this exploration is the all-inclusive, deeply intuitive and instant apperception of mystical experience. However, our society has developed such a deeply cynical and mistaken view of this dimension to our being that the mystical experience is either discounted as some psychological disturbance equated with schizophrenia, a form of wishy-washy New Age clap-trap, or a genuine but rarefied domain restricted to ascetic saints from ancient times. This is one of the most brutal and saddest misconceptions that we make, since almost everyone, at some stage of their life, has encountered that sense of mystical oneness which defines our connection to the whole universe. Huxley defines the mystical experience as the moment 'in which the subject–object relationship is transcended, in which there is a sense of complete solidarity of the subject with other human beings and the universe in general'.[29] This can be triggered by a beautiful sunset, some sort of epiphany while walking in Nature, or even some tragic personal loss. These experiences may produce radical changes in our perception of the world, dissolving our sense of separation, thus promoting an ecological empathy with the world around us and diminishing our fear of death. The wider social implications of a humanity which respects this dimension to their lives are clearly very profound.

Ironically, institutionalised religion has played just as much of a role as science in denying this sacred dimension to our lives. Medieval mystics, who realised their own divinity, were frequently branded as blasphemers. Any awareness of Nature's omnipresent Spirit, upheld by Paganism, the occult and animistic traditions, has often been denounced as Satanic. Like one endless game of Chinese Whispers, the pure, original message of genuine saints and mystics has been distorted by dualistic, patriarchal religions, producing hierarchical institutions which have perpetuated national conflicts, social inequality and our separation from Nature.

Now, like every aspect of our world-view, this is being modified. As Tarnas observes, the central motivating factor in this transition is the 'tremendous resurgence of the feminine archetype', which is visible in a whole new approach to life:

> Our scientific theories of the human psyche, the new sensibility of how human beings relate to nature and other forms of life on the planet – all of these reflect the emergence of the feminine archetype on the collective scale of the culture which is manifesting as a new sense of connection with the whole. This ideally could result in the *hieros gamos* – the divine marriage – the coming together of the masculine and feminine on many levels: between the human being and nature, between intellect and soul, between men and women. It's an extremely multi-levelled, complex, transformative process we're involved in right now.[30]

The predominance of a patriarchal paradigm therefore, has been blamed for our preoccupation with expanding the 'military-industrial complex', for the concurrent destruction of the global environment, for our loss of connection with a sacred dimension in Nature and for the perpetuation of religions, institutions and social organisations which actively separate us from the reality of what we are. As Tarnas says, 'the church got Sunday and science got the rest of the days of the week.' Consequently, 'that created a dichotomy that eventually became unliveable – a kind of schizophrenia between inner and outer – between the human spirit and the world in which the human spirit finds itself located'.[31] As a result, we find ourselves at a crucial point within our evolution, ushering in a new sense of unity that transcends the old, dualistic paradigm which we inherited from the Enlightenment and which has been consolidated by the ensuing Industrial Age.

The New Economics

Modern economists estimate that, between 1750 and 1850 – the first hundred years of the modern Industrial Age – per capita income in Britain doubled but, for the majority of people, the quality of life declined. The philosopher Alan Watts described the cause of this process as being the 'fatal fallacy of civilisation: the confusion of symbol with reality'. One of the most destructive aspects of this confusion is our perception of money which, as Watts reminds us, 'is a way of measuring wealth but is not wealth in itself'.[32]

Our entire economic system is built around this fundamental flaw, confusing imaginary, conceptual wealth, the financial systems which we have created, with the real, natural wealth which we depend upon, like soil, air and water. Hence we have the absurdities of a system in which our economic indicators increase every time we drive to the shops rather than ride a bicycle, or turn on an air conditioner rather than open the window. These figures merely reflect the rate at which we are turning resources into rubbish and tell us nothing about the way in which our lives benefit. Jerry Mander points out that, while those 'who celebrate technology say it has brought us an improved standard of living, which means greater speed, greater choice, greater leisure, and greater luxury', they overlook the fact that 'none of these benefits informs us about human satisfaction, happiness, security, or the ability to sustain life on earth'.

Perhaps the ultimate challenge facing the environmental movement is to convince the public that the planet can survive, maybe even benefit, without our quality of life being compromised. As we have seen, Herbert Girardet refers to 'the non-negotiable demands of modern life – electricity and mobility'. What we need to embrace, in the developed world especially, is the notion that eco-technologies and new economic frameworks will allow us to have automobiles, televisions and washing machines in a sustainable, ecological society. Part of the psychological defence and denial that many people project towards the green agenda is based on the mistaken assumption that our lives will revert to a dark age of deprivation and suffering. However, the indications are that the reality is quite the reverse.

Most of the developed world is suffering from stress in some form or other and many yearn for a simpler life. The economic system is structured in such a way as to keep us ensnared within the treadmill, ensuring that we all live beyond our means and devote our lives to perpetuating an endless spiral of consumer debt. Those that do manage to step outside the system, or simplify their lives through 'downshifting' to a rural existence, almost invariably discover that they can live on a fraction of what their urban lifestyle demanded and find that their quality of life improves dramatically.

We seem to have forgotten that our survival does not depend on the constant accumulation of material goods and that millions of people around the world continue to live long, happy and stress-free lives without new cars, shopping malls and luxury holidays. Ironically, when we travel to less developed parts of the globe, the overwhelming impression that we usually come away with is just how happy people are living a simple life. Few of us are able to translate that into our own lives. However transitory and shallow its pleasures may be, the lure of materialism is too tempting for the ego to sacrifice. Similarly, we forget the basic truth that, although average life spans are increasing and various technologies appear to have made our lives more comfortable, this does not validate the theory of infinite growth – 'the ability to accelerate a car that is low on gasoline does not prove the tank is full'.[33]

The stark reality is that the extravagant expectations of an affluent modern western lifestyle are devastating the systems that support life on Earth. Around the world, especially in the South, millions of people are being driven from their homes and their ancestral lands by climatic changes caused by excessive consumption patterns practised in the North. As Tony Juniper points out, 'If you're not talking about the redistribution of environmental impacts, you haven't got a global agenda – you've got a northern agenda.'[34] Although northern consumption patterns will have to change dramatically, that does not mean returning to some sort of agrarian peasant lifestyle. We just need the wisdom to see what we actually need to enjoy our time on this planet in a happy and sustainable fashion rather than the stressed-out, dysfunctional and rapacious lifestyles which our current economic system encourages.

Multinational corporations have come to represent all that is financially voracious, socially unethical and environmentally damaging about our economic systems. The visionary new economist David Korten observes how 'An active propaganda machinery controlled by the world's largest corporations constantly reassures us that consumerism is the path to happiness, governmental restraint of market excess is the cause of our distress, and economic globalisation is both a historical inevitability and a boon to the human species.'[35] In fact, believes Korten, 'these are all myths propagated to justify profligate greed and mask the extent to which the global transformation of human institutions is a consequence of the sophisticated, well-funded, and international interventions of a small elite whose money enables them to live in a world of illusion apart from the rest of humanity.'[36] Many would say corporations merely do what we have designed them to do – maximise profits to shareholders at whatever cost. Unfortunately, as Mander notes, this 'takes precedence over community well-being, worker health, public health, peace, environmental preservation, or national security'.

Corporations were originally intended to be public bodies, serving public needs, not the unaccountable institutions which we have today, existing outside the law and the public domain. The 'new economists' propose that corporate interests and the interests of society should be made compatible and synergistic: 'If a corporation persistently seeks to exceed the privileges granted by its charter – such as knowingly selling defective products – or fails to honour its obligations under law – such as consistently violating laws regarding toxic dumping – it is the right and responsibility of citizens, acting through their government, to disband it.'[37] Since all the high street banks invest our money in the 'military-industrial complex' – in the production of weapons, pesticides and genetic engineering – the assumption is that an informed public would dictate some fundamental changes in our economic system through demanding ethical investment and corporate accountability. A corporation pursuing practices which were deemed to conflict with the emerging world-view would quite simply not be allowed to survive.

'New economists' like Korten propose that, during the course of the twentieth century, both communism and capitalism failed to fulfil their ideals: 'Communism vested property rights in a distant state and denied the people any means of holding the state accountable for its exercise of those rights,' while 'capitalism persistently transfers property rights to giant corporations and financial institutions that are largely unaccountable even to their owners'. The alternative is a 'market economy composed primarily, though not exclusively, of family enterprises, small scale co-ops, worker-owned firms, and neighbourhood and municipal corporations'.[38]

There is some evidence that this 'community enterprise economy' is already in its embryonic stages – some 12 million people in the US are now involved with worker-ownership schemes, there are more than 30,000 co-ops, 13,000 credit unions and nearly 100 co-operative banks.[39] To facilitate the transition to this new economy, Korten believes that 'we will need to restore the integrity and proper function of our financial institutions and systems, shift the social and environmental costs of production to producers and the users of their products, eliminate subsidies to big business, localise markets, deconcentrate capital ownership, establish corporate accountability, and restore market competition'.[40] Various economic measures have been suggested to achieve this end, ranging from tighter control on the short-term trading of financial derivatives to new systems for taxation. The systems of global economic governance – the Bretton Woods institutions like the World Bank and the IMF – would be closed down and replaced with UN regulatory bodies which encouraged economic self-reliance, rather than dependence, and released southern economies from their perpetual debt to an international system. Korten also proposes the introduction of a UN Regulatory Agency for Transnational Trade and Investment (UNRATTI) which would regulate transnational companies and effectively 'be nearly the mirror opposite of the GATT–WTO'.[41]

Critics usually dismiss these aims as unrealistic, or lament the return to some from of 'protectionism'. That is not what is being suggested. The emphasis on the local is not to the total exclusion of the global: 'Although we can reduce environmental, technological, and economic interdependence, we cannot eliminate it, nor would we want to. Such interdependence is the fountainhead of the emerging global consciousness that is essential to both our collective survival and our evolutionary potential as a species.'[42] Korten believes that our goal should be to create 'a multilevel system of institutions through which we can reduce unnecessary interdependence'[43] by promoting local control and management of resources, preventing the externalisation of production and consumption costs and encouraging co-operation among local businesses in the search for solutions to shared problems. We have the tools to build this new economy, we just need to implement it.

Some doubt that corporations can be re-structured sufficiently to become part of a sustainable economic order. Since the Industrial Revolution, the role played by corporations has been refined, redefined and entirely removed from the Corporate Charter which gave them birth. Our attitude towards them is built on contradictions. On the one hand, we divest corporations of human ethics and morality, placing them above and beyond the laws which apply to us as individuals. Then, on the other hand, we criticise corporate malpractice as being the extension of the people that the corporation employs. However, the personal view that someone in a corporation may take, regarding the use of sweat-shop labour or the toxic chemicals used in a manufacturing process, is largely irrelevant. The continued existence of the corporation is dependent on profit margins, not personal ethics. Corporations are simply not designed to consider such issues and, when corporate executives are forced to take a stand on social or environmental factors, they do so as part of the posturing required by their public relations department. 'To ask corporate executives to behave in a morally defensible manner is absurd,' says Mander. 'Corporations, and the people within them, are not subject to moral behaviour. They are following a system of logic that leads inexorably toward dominant behaviours. To ask corporations to behave otherwise is like asking an army to adopt pacifism. Form is content.'[44]

By insisting on loyalty, the corporation demands that the individual ego of the employee be subsumed by the collective ego of the company. This has led some to equate corporations with religious cults, and the comparison is not as daft as it might first appear. Like cults, corporations go to extraordinary lengths to foster allegiance to the corporate identity, involving intensive weekend seminars and courses designed to consolidate the individual's belief in the company. This, combined with an overwhelming workload which forces employees to work weekends and evenings as well as the expectations which extend into the few remaining waking hours – taking clients out to dinner – add up to a form of brain-washing, dictated by sleep deprivation, repetitive corporate imagery and the expectation to sacrifice everything, including time with the family that you are working to support.

Like the religious cult, the corporation undermines the individual by requiring standard forms of appearance – usually suits and ties rather than flowing crimson robes, although some corporations dictate even stricter codes of conformity, stretching to types of facial hair and body piercing. Like the religious cult, corporations spend vast sums of money constructing opulent monuments in their own image, sleek steel and concrete temples dedicated to profligate greed. Despite all of this, the individual receives remarkably little recognition for his time and effort. The corporation outlives the sell-by date of its employees and, as Mander observes, seems to possess 'the possibility of immortality'.

Corporations and the capitalist system itself, at least in its current form, fail to deliver what they promise. As Tony Juniper says, 'Capitalism is supposed to generate wealth to solve problems by trickling down and alleviating poverty at the bottom of the ladder. In reality, what is happening is completely the reverse. Wealth is concentrating in the rich, the poor are increasingly marginalised and environmental problems are getting worse.'[45] Korten believes that 'Democracy and market economics are exactly what we should be seeking, because they are the foundation of equitable, self-organising societies', but 'capitalism is the mortal enemy of both', because 'by definition, design and practice, capitalism is a system that concentrates economic power in the hands of the few to the exclusion of the many, creating an illusion in the minds of power holders that it is an engine of prosperity rather than an engine of destruction and upward redistribution.'

Through blind subservience to the principle of 'economic growth', we have allowed money to become our master rather than our servant. Our lives are being controlled by the institutions we invented and which, with global free trade agreements, are increasingly beyond the law. Surely every individual, community and nation on earth should have the right to decide how much it will trade, with whom and on what basis? Rather than regulating trade, financial markets and transnational corporations, the World Trade Organisation is preventing national and local governments from having any say whatsoever in the international flow of goods, labour, services and investments. It is purely a licence for the rich to get richer and for the most ruthless plunderers of the planet to expand their global reach, their ecologically devastating practices, their human rights abuses and their ethical violations. We have unwittingly become enslaved to a runaway system, which was invented by an elite, has been divested of all human accountability, and which most people regard as not only undeniably right but also impossible to change.

A detailed study of the economic principles which can reverse the current trends has been outlined by economists like David Korten and Paul Hawken. Korten has produced an 'Agenda for the 21st century', which shows how corporations can be tamed, trade can be monitored and redistribution can solve the North–South divide. He calls for strict regulations regarding human rights, health, safety and environmental issues; limits to financial speculation, corporate tax evasion and the money laundering activities of transnational banks investing in arms and other major industries which are ecologically damaging; measures to reduce the extreme disparities in per capita resource use and carbon dioxide emissions; an anti-trust regime to reverse the trend towards a global concentration of corporate power in areas like banking, the food system and the media; the elimination of market-distorting export and international transport subsidies, like the absence of any tax on aviation fuel; and mechanisms for dealing with intellectual property rights which restrict access to important pharmaceutical drugs and beneficial technologies in developing countries.[46]

Paul Hawken calls upon us to repeal the Corporate Charter, 'a revocable dispensation that was supposed to ensure accountability of the corporation to society as a whole'.[47] He also highlights the need for our economic system to reflect the true and actual cost of production rather than ignoring social and environmental factors which have always been treated as external and somehow unimportant. When the environmental impacts of producing and packaging a fast-food burger are taken into account, the 'real' cost of the product increases a thousand-fold. The 'real' worth of rainforest in South America, which is being destroyed to expand commercial meat production and the fodder industry which supports it, is hard to calculate, especially when one considers the role that it plays in absorbing carbon dioxide from the atmosphere. Fast food production can hardly be considered economically justifiable when it is contributing to the destruction of a safe and stable climate on which all life depends. When one factors in the fossil fuel use associated with transport, farm machinery and chemical fertilisers, not to mention the manufacture of disposable plastics and styrofoam packaging, the 'real' costs of the food industry as a whole become apparent.

Supermarkets selling organic apples from New Zealand are hardly helping the situation, but a local apple grown in a local orchard and sold through a local box scheme has an 'ecological footprint' which is in keeping with the 'new economics'. Hawken observes that 'In order for a sustainable society to exist, every purchase must reflect or at least approximate its actual cost, not only the direct cost of production but also the costs to the air, water and soil; the cost to future generations; the cost to worker health; the cost of waste, pollution and toxicity.'[48] In the same way that economists draw erroneous conclusions from indicators like GDP, the consumer makes uninformed choices about the impact of buying everything from food and household products to cars and computers, largely because the economic system fails to account for the way in which we are merrily stripping the planet of its biotic capacity. Hence we have the absurdity of a system which encourages Britain to import the same amount of butter that it exports. Short-term thinking leads the British government to decide that solar energy does not make economic sense, despite the fact that photo-voltaic panels on houses could provide 85 per cent of the nation's electrical requirements. Of course, the initial expense of installing this equipment will appear excessive when compared with the current price of oil or gas over a one-year period. When compared with the continued disruption of the global climate and the destruction of entire countries over the next fifty years, solar energy is obviously extremely cheap. The economic models that perpetuate this sort of decision are worse than illogical.

A crucial aspect to restructuring the economic system will be the reinvention of the tax system. Once again, the system we have at the moment is back to front and upside down. We tax the things we regard as providing a positive contribution to society, like income, jobs and creativity, rather than the things which are destroying the planet, like pollution, toxic waste and the exploitation of resources. Hawken suggests replacing the entire tax system incrementally over twenty years through the implementation of Green Fees which are added on to existing products, services and materials so that they reflect their actual costs: 'Eventually the cost of non-renewable resources and industrial modes of production will be more expensive than renewable resources, such as solar energy, sustainable forestry and biological methods of agriculture.'[49] Another concept highlighted by Hawken is 'Negawatts', the ability for industry to harness efficiency, use less energy and thereby generate fewer hydrocarbons in the atmosphere. He points out that this would be 'the first time in the history of industrialism that a corporation has figured out how to make money by selling the absence of something', suggesting that oil companies could invest in energy-efficient eco-technologies within taxpayers' homes, like super-glazed windows, and in return receive a return on their conservation investment through Green Fees, calculated upon the barrels of oil that are saved not consumed: 'Imagine a system where a utility company benefits from conservation, makes money from efficiency, thrives through restoration and profits from sustainability.'[50]

In the same way that the Ecological Age will see a shift from hierarchies to networks, industrial processes will shift from linear to cyclical systems. The current paradigm encourages the accumulation of non-degradeable waste products, both during the production process and at the time when the product is thrown away. Most of us in the western world generate six times our body weight in waste every week, in the form of hazardous and toxic waste water, incinerated ash, agricultural chemicals, plastic packaging and paper.

Michael Braungart, of the Environmental Protection Encouragement Agency (EPEA) in Germany, first made the distinction between 'consumable', 'durable' and 'unsaleable' items. 'Consumable' items are traditionally thought to be just those that we eat and digest. However, breakthroughs in bio-degradeable materials have made it possible for many products, from clothes to plastic containers – which rely on toxic chemicals for their manufacture – to be made from natural polymers. Cotton is currently treated with plasticisers, defoliants and pesticides, while shoes are tanned with chromium, and silk shirts dyed with zinc. As Hawken says, 'We should be designing more things to be thrown away – into the compost heap. A package that turns into dirt is infinitely more useful, biologically speaking, than a package that turns into a plastic park bench.'[51] Like the electric car, which still relies on power generated by fossil fuels, recycling is a classic case of 'shallow' environmentalism, which fails to address the root cause and merely shifts the problem to another area. Much of what we re-cycle creates toxic by-products and consumes considerable amounts of energy: 'Heretical as it sounds, designing for decomposition, not recycling, is the way towards a sustainable future.'[52]

Rather than being sold, 'durable' items, like cars, televisions and fridges, would remain the property of the company that manufactured them and be leased to customers as part of a service. This overcomes the problem of built-in obsolescence, encouraging industry to manufacture products that are designed to last, can be easily upgraded, use recycleable materials and remain within a closed cyclical system rather than a linear one which sends everything into a landfill, where it is of no benefit to anyone.

The last group, the 'unsaleables', include all the toxic materials which cannot be broken down within a natural system – nuclear waste, heavy metals and synthetic chemicals. These would remain the property of the original manufacturer, who would pay rent to store them safely in public utilities. These materials would carry 'molecular markers', which would make them easy to identify and trace to the manufacturer should they be found leaching into the water supply or any part of the food system. This makes manufacturers responsible for the full life-cycle of the materials which they use.

Ecological thinkers like Hawken also encourage us to become more aware of our place in the world, the bio-region where we live, the economic bio-region in which we work. Few of us ever stop to think about where our water comes from, how much waste we are sending to landfills every week, what trees are indigenous to the area in which we live, how much impact our work may be having on people overseas. It has been estimated that the average western adult recognises 1,000 brand names and logos but fewer than ten local plants. Our digital and electronic literacy may be increasing, but our natural, biological awareness is dwindling, regarded as some sort of antiquated pastime.

Contrary to what most mainstream scientists would have us believe, our knowledge about the natural world is actually very limited. The biologist E. O. Wilson estimates that it would take 25,000 person-years to catalogue the species on the planet, aside from the fact that there are only some 1,500 people with the taxonomic ability to do so.[53] There are millions of species out there which can cure diseases and perform crucial biological functions which can help humanity create a sustainable, ecological society. Unfortunately, we are busy obliterating them at an exponential rate, in pursuit of transitory material excess, rather than conserving and studying them for long-term benefits.

We now have the economic models and the eco-technologies which can help to swing the tide. All we need is the vision and the impetus to lie down collectively in front of the economic machine which is raping our planet and stealing our children's future. As Hawken observes, 'Being visionary has always been given a bad rap by commerce,'[54] but without vision our lives lose all sense of purpose, our history is divested of all meaning and our species is destined for extinction. Evolution revolves around quantum leaps, propelled by a minority. The future existence of humanity, and most of the species on this planet, is now dependent upon a quantum leap in our collective vision. We either embrace it, or deny it.

A New Tribal Society for an Ecological Age

There are numerous examples of sustainable tribal societies, from Australia to the Amazon, Alaska to the South Pacific. However, there is not one example of a sustainable industrial society. History shows that expansionist policies of economic domination have invariably collapsed, from the Sumerians to the Mayans to the Romans. Industrial societies don't work. Tribal ones do.

One of those advocating the shift from hierarchies to networks is the writer Daniel Quinn, who has presented his vision for a New Tribal Revolution. Quinn does not propose that we retreat to the forests, trade our suits for fig leaves and build tree-houses. Rather, he suggests that we restructure our institutions, our systems of government and the work-place along tribal principles. Although tribes usually have elders, or even a chief, their role does not confer special benefits upon them. They are just fulfilling a necessary function, maintaining harmony within the community in the same way as the shaman maintains harmony between the tribe and its bio-region, or the men and women who hunt and gather food. Of course, there have been examples of tribes where the leader has developed despotic tendencies and created a hierarchy. The crucial point, however, is that no such society has ever survived.

In our defence of 'civilisation', we tend to regard the tribal network as somehow primitive and inferior. Quinn believes that 'This is why it's so difficult for us to acknowledge that tribalism is not only the pre-eminently *human* social organisation, it's also the only unequivocally *successful* social organisation in human history.'[55] Responding to the notion that this is a naive idealisation of tribal society, he observes that 'the success of humans in tribes is no more an idealization than the success of bison in herds or whales in pods'.[56] Tribal networks have lived in sustainable harmony with the environment for tens of thousands of years. Industrial hierarchies have decimated the planet in three hundred.

Making the switch from hierarchies to networks goes hand in hand with the shift from linear to cyclical thinking. Rather than the pyramidal structures of industrial societies, where power and information are contained within the higher echelons, tribal societies operate in a circular system of consensus decision-making. Each member of the tribe carries out their alloted function as part of the whole and no one person is subservient to another. Similarly, the tribal structure provides 'cradle to grave' security for its members, as opposed to industrial hierarchies where increasing numbers of people are marginalised from their own society through unemployment, ill-health or old age, and suffer intense psychological alienation and lack of self-worth as a consequence. Our society fundamentally fails to address these issues in any sort of satisfactory manner. As with most of our uncomfortable problems, we try to push it under the carpet by throwing money at it, once again confusing material wealth with real security.

An Ecological Age will therefore involve a transition from linear hierarchies to cyclical networks, from a global economy to a community-based economy. Throughout the Industrial Age, we have persisted in drawing straight lines through the circles that surround us. This has manifested itself in everything from our architecture and the urban grid, to our economic system and our notion of time, constraining human energy and consciousness within artificial boundaries. Those living in ecological communities have found that living in dwellings which do not conform to linear constraints immediately has a liberating impact on consciousness, releasing them from the square box mentality that typifies modern urban living. Small businesses, co-operative schemes and community-based projects have already started a new kind of local economy which is in harmony with the surrounding bio-region. Increasing numbers of people are living a new way. As Quinn says, 'no single person is going to save the world' and 'a thousand living a new way won't cause the dominant world order to topple'. However, 'that thousand will inspire a hundred thousand, who will inspire a million, who will inspire a billion – and *then* that world order will begin to look shaky!'[57]

A global tribe is giving birth to the Ecological Age and here are some of the ways in which it works. Although some of these suggestions may apply more to rural areas, many are equally suited to an urban lifestyle. For most people many of these criteria are difficult to meet but just being informed of the issues at stake is a step in the right direction. Contact addresses and numbers are listed in the appendix.

Your local community is your potential tribal network. As a consequence, the more informed choices you can make to support the well-being of that network, the more likely it is to function sustainably and to prosper. Support small local businesses wherever you can, especially those which use local materials and supply local markets. Boycott supermarkets and big chain stores. They promote ecologically damaging practices which have a global impact and destroy local businesses. If you have no option but to use a supermarket, buy local, organic produce as much as possible.

There are now thousands of organic box schemes operating throughout Britain, many of which deliver to London and other urban areas. For as little as £10 a week you can have fresh, organic fruit and vegetables delivered to your door. The Soil Association publishes a directory of these services and their details are in an appendix at the back of this book. Better still, grow your own produce – even a south-facing window ledge can produce the herbs that you need, while urban agriculture and allotment schemes can not only be highly productive but provide contact with the living soil while surrounded by the concrete jungle. There are 300,000 allotments in the UK, covering 12,000 hectares and producing 215,000 tonnes of produce every year worth £561 million.

Visit farm shops, local greengrocers and Community Supported Agriculture schemes as much as possible. Find out where your food comes from and how it is produced. If you live in the country, find out which local farmers are using chemicals and monitor their application. Boycott processed, packaged food. Take your own basket and refuse plastic bags. Register complaints at local supermarkets about their ecologically damaging practices, excessive energy consumption and the way in which small local businesses have suffered.

It is not only with food that we need to make informed choices over our consumption patterns. Organically produced French wine has a very different 'ecological footprint' to commercial bottles from Australia. Beware of spurious 'green', 'organic', 'natural', or 'eco' labels. These are usually a marketing ploy. For example, most 'natural' soaps and shampoos still contain sodium laureth sulphate, a suspected carcinogen. Use public transport as much as possible, as lousy as it may be. Travel less. Ride a bicycle through the park rather than sitting in traffic as you drive to the gym. Move closer to the work-place or bring your work closer to home.

By-pass the financial system by joining one of the many community bartering schemes (LETS). By offering skills and services to the local community your interaction with it multiplies. If at all possible, move your personal savings and your business affairs from high street banks to ethical banks like Triodos or the Co-operative Bank. Failing this, insist on ethical investment within the high street banks which currently invest in the arms trade and a plethora of environmentally damaging practices like genetic modification.

If you work within a large company or organisation, form your own tribal network with like-minded people and promote ethical investment and sustainable practices within the work-place. Ecological practices provide positive results for business itself. Companies like IKEA, Electrolux and Scandic Hotels have integrated the four systems conditions prescribed by the Swedish Natural Step method, thereby reducing their resource use, promoting practices like recycling and increasing their profits.[58] Low-energy light-bulbs reduce overheads as well as energy, as does opening windows rather than turning on air-conditioners. What has previously been regarded as waste could be transformed into an important by-product, increasing efficiency, closing loops and boosting profit margins. (To become more familiar with the principles of 'industrial ecology', I would recommend reading *Natural Capitalism* by Paul Hawken and Amory and Hunter Lovins, listed in the bibliography.)

For a really tangible image of what sustainability means, calculate the 'ecological footprint' of your business, or your personal lifestyle.[59] The footprint reflects the ecological impact of these activities in terms of the average global hectares required to support it, whether it be absorbing waste, carbon dioxide emissions or producing food. The application of this methodology provides some revealing statistics. The US for example, regarded by many as the symbol of everything that a prosperous economy should represent and the role model to which we should all aspire, provides a figure of 9.6 average global hectares to support the average lifestyle. In the UK the figure is 4.6 and in Bangladesh, at the bottom of the list, the figure drops to 0.6. Since the global average for our share of the planet should be about 1.9 global hectares, these figures show that a country like the UK is living beyond its ecological capacity by a factor of nearly three times, the US by a factor of five. When seen in this light, most Northern countries are exposed as parasitic economies, perpetuating their own consumption patterns at the expense of those in the South. As this information spreads, the movement to boycott products from countries like the US will surely gather momentum, precipitating action to create a more equitable economic system and one which respects the carrying capacity of the planet.

Writing letters to local MPs sounds tedious and ineffective but it does work. Tony Juniper told me how FoE have recently pushed fifteen pieces of legislation through Parliament by orchestrating strategic letter-writing campaigns. Subscribe to magazines like *The Ecologist* and *Resurgence* to keep informed of current issues; they often prints names and addresses of relevant MPs to write to in connection with the various campaigns. Join one or more of the environmental pressure groups, vote Green, attend protests and demonstrations, boycott the 'sweatshop brands' like Nike, Disney and The Gap. Buy from small independent retailers and try to find clothes that are produced locally, without the use of chemicals. Look for second-hand televisions, computers, cars and washing machines, or choose energy-efficient models if you buy new ones. Renovate and decorate your house with non-toxic sustainable materials which are produced locally. For example, use British lime-wash rather than oil paints produced overseas. If possible, install renewable energy systems and cut energy use with efficient thermal insulation. Above all, let's try to consume less. Less meat, less petrol, less plastic. It is interesting to note that, during the last war, rations led to an enforced resource efficiency, life expectancy for those at home rose and infant mortality fell. A change in diet meant that people were eating less, but they were eating better. Rather than the excessive consumption we see today, driven by the holy grail of 'consumer choice', a level of scarcity had a positive effect. As Andrew Simms observes, 'For some, less really was more.' Ultimately, we have to remember that every decision about every product that we buy has ecological repercussions and every time we shop we are casting our vote for the future of the planet.

This certainly sounds like a daunting, moralising prescription for how to live and really only skims the surface. The interconnections between what we consume and the impact it has on the planet are inherently complex and, within the current global economy, it is almost impossible to comply with all of the above. However, every time one of us adopts just one of these measures, we collectively take the Ecological Age to a new level of realisation. Even though incremental improvements to a failing system will never make it work, consumer pressure of this kind forces the power brokers at the top of the pyramid to at least entertain the notion of sustainability. As we have seen, this has already produced radical changes in companies manufacturing everything from carpets to photocopiers. Oil companies may still be drilling for oil, but there is the growing recognition that they are actually in the 'energy business' and need to fund research into renewables. In the same way that the Stone Age did not end when we ran out of stone, so the Fossil Fuel Age will not end when we run out of oil – we will make the quantum leap into the Ecological Age, driven by hydrogen fuel cells, solar panels, wind turbines, wave power and biomass.

In the precise instant in which we step outside of the old paradigm, by becoming an active part of the New Tribal Revolution, we cease to be a part of that which is destroying our planet. We immediately become part of a global network which is revitalising local communities and giving birth to a new social, political and economic vision. This is a quiet revolution which is being realised without the use of violence. Many still refuse even to acknowledge it but it is already happening all around us. A new model is emerging from the grass-roots, by its own accord, as part of society's self-organising, self-regulating evolution. This model resembles a web rather than a pyramid. It is in direct opposition to the extraneous, hierarchical notion of power imposed from the top. As Peter Marshall says, 'Having realized that a meaningful life is more important than acquiring wealth or power, a growing number of people are choosing to live lightly on the Earth', and as the old model crumbles and falls away, 'a new society will have developed, already functioning within the shell of the old'.[60] This is the process which we are involved in right now and the challenge that confronts every man, woman and child on the planet – the collective realisation that 'The world has enough for everyone's need, but not everyone's greed', and that 'real wealth is knowing when you have enough'.

The economic system which has plundered the planet in a fraction of our evolutionary time is rapidly approaching breaking point. A runaway train has been set in motion, the drivers have lost control and we are accelerating off the end of the track. It is only a matter of time before the imaginary balls which support the conceptual wealth of a global economy finally drop out of the air. When that happens, the transition to an Ecological Age will have become the only viable alternative. Like most of the mutations and quantum leaps that occur within Nature, it is unlikely to be a smooth ride and will not happen overnight. However, the options that confront us now are simple in the extreme. We can either drown in the disintegration of an obsolete and redundant way of looking at the world, or we can plug into the green web which now encircles the globe. Only then can we get on board and surf the rising tides. Apathy or activism – the choice is ours.

Epilogue

A Spiritual Perspective

Because you are the world, your actions will affect the world you live in, which is the world of your relationships. But the difficulty is to recognise the importance of individual transformation. We demand transformation, the transformation of society about us, but we are blind, unwilling to transform ourselves . . . To go far you must begin near, and the nearest step is the most important one.

J. KRISHNAMURTI[1]

From Ego to Eco: Towards A New Sense of Self

The fact that we have become more preoccupied with brand logos than the preservation of the biotic systems on which our lives depend, suggests that we have somehow forgotten who and what we are and where we came from. As world fisheries collapse around us, rainforests burn to the ground, the ozone layer disappears, whole countries are devastated by climate change and our agricultural systems face one crisis after another, we ignore the reality of what is staring us in the face. The planet is on fire but most of us have yet to notice. Many dismiss the ecological meltdown that surrounds them as being blown out of all proportion by radical alarmists, or because they think doing anything about it is entirely beyond their control. Some still maintain that it is not really happening at all, because of ignorance, psychological defences and spurious scientific data circulated by industries which feel threatened.

Compulsive patterns of consumption have become society's universal drug addiction and we have developed all manner of sophisticated psychological responses to perpetuate our collective denial. We have somehow separated ourselves from Nature to such a degree that we have forgotten just how dependent upon it we are in every moment of our lives. All the material wealth in the world is of little value to anyone if the natural systems which support life can no longer provide food and water for our basic existence. Few of us would ever deny that we evolved from the natural systems that support us but, throughout most of our daily lives, we seem to have forgotten this basic fact. Jed Swift, an American eco-psychologist, believes that it has been 'emotionally and educationally drummed out of us'.[2]

As we have already seen, numerous theories have been developed to explain how, why and when this separation occurred, ranging from the 'original trauma' of the Agricultural Revolution to the dualistic philosophy of Descartes and Newtonian science. The important issue that confronts us now though is not how this sense of separation started, but how we can heal it. How can we redefine our sense of self so that we can make the transition from an ego-centric dualistic perception of the world to an all inclusive eco-centric experience?

Virtually everyone on the planet believes themselves to be the mind–body organism with which they have identified themselves since an early age. We understand ourselves to be this limited, separate, individual entity, which was born to certain parents and one day will die. If someone asks 'Who are you?', we tend to respond with a name and some auto-biographical details about where we live and what sort of work we do. However, if we examine this assumption we find that it is the most basic illusion of all.

What you are is quite clearly not a name. Those are just words. Similarly, if we look closely at the notion of being limited to an organism consisting of a mind and a body, we again fail to locate our original essence. Every cell in our body is replaced every seven years so there is no continuity of matter. If we examine those cells under an electron microscope, we find nothing but vibrating patterns of energy which, upon further scrutiny, prove to be alternating between polarised states of nothingness and beingness, between the noumenal and phenomenal modes of manifestation. Likewise, when the mind is quiet, when there is an absence of thought – in meditation or the state of deep, dreamless sleep – where have we gone? Who or what is it that wakes up and says it slept well or badly?

Basic logic also reveals that we cannot be limited to the mind or the body. For something to be observed, there has be an observer and that which is observed. Since both the body and the mental processes of the mind can be observed, the obvious inference is that we are something transcendent to, but immanent within, both. What we ultimately are, when we strip away the concepts, thoughts and ideas about who we think we are, is pure awareness, the witnessing consciousness itself. Our real nature is that which is prior to thought, conceptualisation and articulation. It is the screen on which the diversity of life is projected. When the images stop rolling, the screen remains the same as it ever was. Everything else in the entire universe is included within, or super-imposed upon, this screen of awareness, which Peter Russell calls 'the canvas of the mind'.[3] Prior to birth, during deep sleep and after death, consciousness is unaware of itself. During the waking state, consciousness, as it functions through all sentient beings, becomes aware of itself. In the human organism, it has the additional capacity for self-reflection, which gives rise to the fears and desires which we ascribe to the ego.

The ego is that which believes itself to be a three-dimensional object, an individual entity engaged in a struggle with an objective world from which it is entirely separate. Ecology suggests that this is a misconception. The human organism is continually interacting with the natural world as part of a fluid and interconnected system. Experiments have shown how the body responds to changes in barometric pressure, often feeling tired just before the onset of rain. Like the planet itself, thousands of biochemical processes are in an endless dynamic flow with external factors, ensuring that the body regulates itself according to environmental conditions. As Ralph Metzner says, 'We are part of Nature; we are in the earth, not on it. We are like cells of the vast living organism that is planet earth.'[4] The human body is a microcosmic cell within Gaia itself. Not only do we contain the same proportion of water as the planet, but our levels of salinity are the same. However, as Metzner observes, 'An organism cannot continue to function healthily if one group of cells decides to dominate and cannibalize the other energy systems of the body.'[5]

Like ecology, quantum physics suggests that there is no physical reality to the egoic structure. Physical reality has been reduced to an energetic background of vibrating particles, oscillating in and out of pure nothingness, the noumenal or potential aspect of consciousness. 'To understand the nature of subatomic matter or light', says psychologist Stanislav Grof, 'you have to accept that they are phenomena which can have characteristics of both particles and waves.'[6] With their Santiago Theory, two Chilean neuroscientists, Humberto Maturana and Francisco Varela, have reached similar conclusions about the illusory nature of the psychological construct with which we identify: 'According to the Santiago Theory, we bring forth the self just as we bring forth objects. Our self, or ego, does not have any *independent* existence but is a result of our internal structural coupling.'[7] For Fritjof Capra, this is 'the crux of the human condition', because 'when we look for an independent self within our world of experience we cannot find any such entity'.[8] Grof accepts that, on a reductionist level, we are 'Newtonian objects, highly developed biological thinking machines', but from a holistic point of view 'we are also infinite fields of consciousness that transcend time, space and linear causality'.[9] The medical scientist Larry Dossey believes that 'we have been labouring under some fairly dismal and erroneous assumptions about ourselves' and 'the most erroneous assumption is that we are separate individuals'.[10]

This alternative view of the world was neatly summarised by the anthropologist and visionary thinker Gregory Bateson, who drew the distinction between two syllogisms. The first syllogism states: 'Men die. Socrates is a man. Socrates will die.' The second syllogism goes like this: 'Grass dies. Men die. Men are grass.' As Bateson acknowledged, the second syllogism strikes one as being plainly illogical, and our reaction is that 'it's the way schizophrenics think, and we should avoid it'.[11] He then identifies the difference between the two. Whereas the Socrates syllogism is concerned with the classification of subjects, identifying Socrates as a man, the grass syllogism is only concerned with 'predicates', with what happens to those subjects. Bateson proposes that the first syllogism is purely a human construct, concerned with the subject of a sentence, and has only been relevant since mankind separated itself from Nature through the invention of language. Previously, organisms in the natural world functioned quite happily with the second syllogism:

> They managed to organize themselves in their embryology to have two eyes, one on each side of a nose. They managed to organize themselves in their evolution. So there were shared predicates between the horse and the man, which zoologists today call homology. And it became evident that metaphor was not just pretty poetry, but was in fact the logic upon which the biological world had been built, the main characteristic and organizing glue of this world of mental processes.[12]

Through our obsession with the individual, with being the subject of our own world, we have superimposed an imagined subjectivity onto patterns and processes which function totally independently of what we think we are. In doing so, we have quite unwittingly divorced ourselves from reality. Modern science is therefore confirming the truth behind the biggest illusion of all – that we are not what we think we are. As activist and writer Joanna Macy observes, by challenging these basic assumptions, we are seeing the gradual emergence of an 'ecological self':

> First, the conventional small self, or ego-self is being impinged upon by the psychological and spiritual effects we are suffering from facing the dangers of mass annihilation. The second thing working to dismantle the ego-self is a way of seeing that has arisen out of science itself. It is called the systems view, stemming from general systems theory of cybernetics. From this perspective, life is seen as composed of self-organizing systems, patterns that are sustained in and by their relationships. The third force is the resurgence in our time of non-dualistic spiritualities.[13]

For thousands of years, Indian yogis, Islamic sufis, Christian mystics, Zen Buddhists and tribal shamen have all pointed to the same basic truth: that the ego has no independent existence; that it is a fictional entity, created by repetitive socio-environmental conditioning. When Self-realisation, Awakening, or Enlightenment occurs, there is the instant apperception that the ego never really existed in the first place. Ramana Maharshi, an Indian saint in the non-dualist tradition of *advaita*, maintained that 'The world is illusory; Brahman alone is real; Brahman is the world.' Brahman is Consciousness, God, Energy, the Self, the Source, the Absolute, whatever name you want to ascribe to that which is beyond name and form, which cannot be expressed, communicated or even talked about without losing its non-dual nature.

Ken Wilber, the acclaimed American transpersonal psychologist, points out that 'This profound realisation is what separates Ramana's genuine Enlightenment from today's many pretenders to the throne – Deep Ecology, Eco-feminism, Gaia revivals, Goddess worship, Eco-psychology, Systems Theory, Web of Life notions – none of which have grasped the first two lines, and therefore, contrary to their sweet pronouncements, do not really understand the third, either.'[14] As Wilber observes, no dogma, teaching or set of concepts can ever be the Truth, they can only point towards it. Truth cannot be contained, it can only happen. This revelation can only emerge in the absence of that which would contain it, understand it, or categorise it. Only with the final dissolution of the ego, and the sense of separation, can the eternal and infinite presence be revealed. Only then does the final understanding dawn, that Consciousness, or Energy, is the Ground of all Being, the substratum of the entire physical universe and ultimately all that there is.

The obvious question that arises is where does freewill fit into this equation. If the ego has no independent existence, how do we make choices in our lives? Again, modern science suggests that our sense of volition is determined by an interaction between our genetic predisposition and the socio-environmental conditioning which is part of a constantly flowing dynamic. Bio-chemical impulses and hormonal changes in the body have a direct impact on our emotional moods. The organism reacts and responds to external events according to the way in which it is constantly being re-programmed by a combination of these factors. Just because you can raise your hand in the air when the thought arises does not validate the notion that the thought is controlled by an independent entity. Neuroscientists like Benjamin Libet have shown that the brain registers a thought nearly half a second before we become conscious of it. The psychologist Susan Blackmore maintains that 'conscious sensation comes too late to play any useful role in actions' and describes the ego as nothing more than 'a construction, created by language'.[15] As we have already seen, the role of the independent, autonomous ego has been removed from the equation. It simply is not there.

Just because most people believe that the ego exists does not validate its existence. As Anatole France said, 'If fifty million people say a stupid thing, it's still a stupid thing.'[16] The ego certainly *seems* to exist, but so does the sea seem to be blue and the sun appear to move through the sky. We are quite happy to accept these illusions for what they are – even though we know them not be true – and this is precisely what the non-dual traditions suggest we do with the ego. Accept that it does not really exist but continue to live life as if it does; accept the fact that, ultimately there is no freewill but continue to live as if there is. As the physicist Neils Bohr pointed out, 'the opposite of one profound truth may well be another profound truth'. Matt Ridley, a geneticist and science writer, observes how

> full responsibility for one's actions is a necessary fiction without which the law would flounder, but it is a fiction all the same. To the extent that you act as in character you are responsible for your actions; yet acting in character is merely expressing the many determinisms that caused your character. David Hume found himself impaled on this dilemma, subsequently named Hume's fork. Either our actions are determined, in which case we are not responsible for them, or they are random, in which case we are not responsible for them. In either case, common sense is outraged and society impossible to organise.[17]

However, as Huxley points out, we should not despair and interpret this as nihilism, since 'nothing in our everyday experience gives us much reason to suppose that the mind of the average sensual man has, as one of its constituents, something resembling, or identical with, the Reality substantial to the manifold world; and yet, when that mind is subjected to certain rather drastic treatments, the divine element, of which it is in part at least composed, becomes manifest, not only to the mind itself, but also, by its reflection in external behaviour, to other minds.'[18]

Therefore, when the fiction of the ego is truly accepted, nothing actually changes. Life goes on just as before. As Macy says, 'This ecological self, like any notion of selfhood, is a metaphoric construct and a dynamic one. It involves choice; choices can be made to identify at different moments, with different dimensions or aspects of our systemically interrelated existence – be they hunted whales or homeless humans or the planet itself.'[19] When the whole notion of an individual, separate existence is entirely and irrevocably dissolved, the distinction between an ego-self and the eco-self dissolves with it, revealing the fact that the entire universe is contained within us.

Reacting *against* the notion of illusory freewill, by interpreting it as nihilistic or complacent, is to miss the point. The instinctive ego response is: 'What's the point of doing anything?' However, if we try to 'do nothing', we soon find that this is quite simply impossible. The body and mind have instinctive, integral energy. The mind chatters. The body becomes restless. There are bodily functions which need to be attended to. Interpreting this concept in this way is an egoistic reaction against it rather than an intuitive understanding. This is only conceptual anyway, limited as it is by the dualistic framework of language. The Truth that it points to is beyond polarities and opposites. As Ramana Maharshi concludes, 'There is neither creation nor destruction, neither destiny nor freewill; neither path nor achievement; this is the final Truth.'

In the 1920s, quantum physics found it impossible to distinguish particles from waves at a sub-atomic level. Heisenberg proposed that the observer cannot be separated from the observed, that 'What we observe is not Nature itself, but Nature exposed to our method of questioning.' Religious traditions that create a division betwen Man and God are dividing Man from Nature, Energy and Consciousness, therefore perpetuating a sense of bondage rather than pointing towards our liberation. This division has been a very useful way for religions to exert power and authority over the population.

Like ecology and quantum physics, the Truth that the Perennial Philosophy points to is that there are no boundaries; All is One, all is God, all is Consciousness. The ego tends to leave itself out of the equation and maintain separation, but the understanding is that the appearance of the ego is itself part and parcel of the whole dynamic. Heaven and Hell, Nirvana and Samsara, are one and the same. Father Bede Griffiths, a Christian monk who lived most of his life in south India, believed that the non-dual tradition of *advaita* was '*the* answer to the problems to humanity', because 'only when we transcend this dualism of the mind and open to the non-dual reality are we free from this conflict and the tragedy of the world'.[20] Swami Vivekananda, an Indian monk who first took this ancient teaching to the Parliament of World Religions in Chicago in 1893, believed *advaita* would become 'the religion of the future enlightened humanity'.

The danger of misunderstanding the Perennial Philosophy is the apathetic assumption that we can be complacent about the ecological crisis when in fact the consciousness of the planet is speaking through us, urging us to do something. Those who feel compelled to do something do so because that is part of the overall functioning of consciousness. Theodore Roszak is among those to have suggested that that may be an intrinsic aspect of Gaian self-regulation, that the 'voice of the earth' is expressing itself in the emerging ecological self. Every day, all around the planet, more and more of us are waking up to the horrors and the absurdities of what we are doing to the planet, the living extension of the body which we identify with.

Perhaps this is the way in which the evolution from ego-centric to eco-centric consciousness is manifesting itself. When the notion of a separate 'skin-encapsulated ego' is abandoned, replaced with a sense of 'ecological self' – which embraces not only our own bio-region but Gaia and the universe itself – then we can make the quantum leap to an Ecological Age. As an expanding proportion of the world population shifts from a limited, self-centred perspective to one which embraces all life, the continued destruction of the planet will face ever increasing opposition. This rising tide is manifesting itself all over the planet, from grass-roots environmental protest in the South to demonstrations against capitalism and globalisation in the North. It can be seen in the proliferation of everything from vegetarianism, women's rights and co-operative banks, to ecological communities, the organic movement and animal welfare groups. The most vocal resistance to the prevailing paradigm is occurring in some of the most affluent parts of the developed world, where the limitations of materialism have been most acutely felt. Those of us who are fortunate enough to be in the position to question the industrial world-view have perhaps the greatest responsibility of all, since the rest of the world is quite literally drowning in our consumption patterns.

The Ecological Age is dawning with a revolution of consciousness which promises to shatter the grandest illusion of all, revealing that what we are is not limited to some fictional psychological construct but is in fact pure consciousness, the matrix within which the ego appears, the eternal and infinite background to the entire cosmos. We are not just a part of Nature, we *are* Nature. We are not only a strand within the 'web of life', we *are* the web of life. Everything in the entire universe – every star, every planet, every cloud, animal, bird, plant and flower – is contained within what we Are. The wider implications of this understanding will clearly have an explosive impact on the sense of human identity, transforming the way in which we view the world, and our position within it, as radically as any previous shift in human history. When the conceptual ego dissolves in the Ground of All Being, the conceptual separation between Man and Nature dissolves with it. This is not a time to feel daunted and depressed by the problems of the world. It is time to spin the green web further and deeper into every cell of our being, time to challenge the conditioned assumptions which have divided us from Nature, time to see the sacred in every part of the living world that surrounds us. It is time for the quiet revolution.

Appendix 1: An Environmental Directory

Biodiversity Action Network (BIONET)

A network promoting effective implementation of the Convention on Biological Diversity (CBD) which was agreed at the 1992 Earth Summit in Rio:

1630 Connecticut Ave. NW 3rd Fl.
Washington, DC 20009
USA

Tel: 202-547-8902
Fax: 202-265-0222
E-mail: bionet@igc.apc.org
Website: www.bionet-us.org

Corporate Watch

UK-based corporate watchdog with links for anti-globalisation movement:

16b Cherwell Street
Oxford OX4 1BG
UK

Tel: 44 1865 791 391
Website: www.corporatewatch.org.uk

EarthAction International

Educates organisations, citizens, journalists, and members of parliaments about important environmental, peace and social justice issues:

30 Cottage Street
Amherst, MA 01002
USA

Tel: 413-549-8118
Fax: 413-549-0544
E-mail: amherst@earthaction.org
Website: www.earthaction.org

EarthDay Network

An alliance of 5,000 groups in 184 countries which inspires a groundswell of grassroots actions in communities around the world:

1616 P Street NW, Suite 200
Washington, DC 20036
USA

Tel: 202 518 0044
Fax: 202 518 8794
Website: www.earthday.net

EarthVoice

The global environmental arm of the Humane Society of the US:

2100 L Street, NW
Washington, DC 20037
USA

Tel: 202-778-6146
Fax: 202-778-6134
E-mail: all@earthvoice.org
Website: www.earthvoice.org

The Ecologist

Ground-breaking UK-based magazine which provides the real story:

Ecosystems Ltd
Unit 18 Chelsea Wharf
15 Lots Road
London SW10 0QJ

Tel: 0207 351 3578
Fax: 0207 351 3617
Website: www.theecologist.org

Envirolink Network

Large US-based network:

5801 Beacon Street, Suite No. 2
Pittsburgh, PA 15217
USA
E-mail: support@envirolink.org
Website:www.networkforchange.com

Friends of the Earth (FOE)

The world's largest environmental network, with affiliates in 63 countries. The US branch addresses environmental economic issues and empowers citizens to address environmental problems in their own communities:

1025 Vermont Ave, NW, Suite 300
Washington, DC 20005
USA

Tel: (202) 783-7400
Fax: (202) 783-0444
E-mail: foe@foe.org
Website: www.foe.org

Fuel Cells 2000

Supports the development and early commercialisation of hydrogen fuel cells, as well as related technologies and fuels for pollution-free, efficient energy generation and storage:

1625 K Street NW, Suite 725
Washington, DC 20006
USA

Tel: 202-785-4222
Fax: 202-785-4313
Website: www.fuelcells.org

Greenpeace USA

US branch of the world's most famous environmental group:

702 H Street NW, Suite 300
Washington, DC 20001
USA

Tel: 202-462-1177
Website: www.greenpeaceusa.org

International Council for Local Environmental Initiatives (ICLEI)

A strategic partner of the Earth Day Network, launched in 1990 as the international environmental agency for local governments:

15 Shattuck Square, Suite 215
Berkeley, CA 94704
USA

Tel: 510-540-8843
Fax: 510-540-4787
Website: www.iclei.org

International Forum on Globalization (IFG)

Public education about the impacts of economic globalization, advocating equitable, democratic and ecologically sustainable economics:

Building 1062, Fort Cronkhite
Sausalito, CA 94965
USA

Tel: 415-229-9350
Fax: 415-229-9340
Website: www.ifg.org

International Society for Ecology and Culture (ISEC)

International organisation concerned with the protection of biological and cultural diversity while promoting local alternatives to the global economy.

PO Box 9475
Berkeley, CA 94709
USA

Tel: 510 548 4915
Fax: 510 548 4916
E-mail: isecca@igc.org
Website: www.isec.org.uk

Ocean Arks International

John Todd's Living Machines:

176 Battery Street
Burlington, VT 05401
USA

Tel: 802-860-0011
Fax: 802-860-0022
Website: www.oceanarks.org

Rainforest Action Network (RAN)

Works to protect rainforests and support the rights of their inhabitants through education, grassroots organising and non-violent direct action:

221 Pine Street, Suite 500
San Francisco, CA 94104
USA

Tel: 415-398-4404
Fax: 415-398-2732
E-mail: rainforest@ran.org
Website: www.ran.org

Rocky Mountain Institute (RMI)

Cutting edge eco-technology research, educational and consulting organization that promotes the efficient and sustainable use of resources:

1739 Snowmass Creek Road
Snowmass, CO 81654
USA

Tel: 970-927-3851
Fax: 970-927-3420
Website: www.rmi.org

Sierra Club

The first environmental group in the US:

85 Second Street, 2nd Floor
San Francisco, CA 94105
USA

Tel: 415-977-5500
Fax: 415-977-5799
Website: www.sierraclub.org

The Natural Step (TNS)

A science-based framework that provides a compass for businesses, communities, government entities and individuals working to redesign their activities to become more sustainable:

PO Box 29372
San Francisco, CA 94129
USA

Tel: 415-561-3344
Fax: 415-561-3345
E-mail: tns@naturalstep.org
Website: www.naturalstep.org

The Wilderness Society

Works to protect America's wilderness and to develop a nation-wide network of wild lands through public education, scientific analysis and advocacy:

900 17th Street, NW
Washington, DC 20006
USA

Tel: 202-833-2300
Fax: 202-429-3958
Website: www.wilderness.org

Union of Concerned Scientists (UCS)

An independent non-profit alliance of 50,000 concerned citizens and scientists across the US:

2 Brattle Square
Cambridge, MA 02238
USA

Tel: 617-547-5552
Fax: 617-864-9405
Website: www.ucsusa.org

World Wildlife Fund (WWF)

US branch of one of the world's largest environmental groups:

1250 24th Street, NW
Washington, DC 20037
USA

Tel: 202-861-8388
Website: www.worldwildlife.org

Worldwatch Institute (WI)

An international strategic partner of Earth Day Network which publishes annual reports on the state of the global environment:

1776 Massachusetts Avenue, NW
Washington, DC 20036
USA

Tel: 202-452-1992
Fax: 202-296-7365
Website: www.worldwatch.org

Appendix 2: Graphs and Tables

TABLE 1 SOME IMPORTANT TRACE GASES IN TWENTIETH-CENTURY HISTORY

Gas	*Human Sources*	*Human Significance*	*Anthropogenic Emissions (%)*[a]	*Concentration in 1900 (ppb)*	*Concentration in 1990 (ppb)*
		OF GLOBAL SIGNIFICANCE[b]			
Carbon dioxide	Fossil fuel burning, deforestation	Greenhouse gas	≈100	290,000	350,000
Methane	Rice fields, livestock, garbage, fossil fuels, mining	Greenhouse gas	≈60	900	1,700
Chlorofluorocarbons	Refrigerants, foams, aerosol sprays	Ozone destroyer, greenhouse gas	100	0	≈3
Nitrous Oxide	Fertilizers, biomass burning, deforestation	Greenhouse gas, ozone destroyer	≈25	285	310
		OF LOCAL AND REGIONAL SIGNIFICANCE[b]			
Sulfur dioxide	Fossil fuel burning, ore smelting	Acid rain	≈65	?	0.3–50
Nitrogen oxides	Fossil fuel and biomass burning	Acid rain, smog	≈65	?	0.001–50
Ozone (in the troposphere)	Vehicle exhaust's interaction with sunshine	Greenhouse gas, smog	50–70	10[c]	20–40[c]

Table compiled by John McNeill for his book, *Something New Under the Sun: An Environmental History of the Twentieth Century*, Penguin Books, 2000.

[a]Anthropogenic emissions are given as a percentage of all emissions (human plus natural) as of about 1990.
[b]The reason some trace gases have global significance while others have local or regional significance is their various 'residence times'. Those that on average remain in the atmosphere only briefly do not disperse around the world, while those that linger longer do. Residence times vary greatly, from a few days (sulfur dioxide) to a century or more (carbon dioxide, nitrous oxide, CFCs).
[c]Concentrations of tropospheric ozone refer only to western Europe.

TABLE 2 THE MEASURE OF THE TWENTIETH CENTURY

Item	*Increase Factor, 1890s–1990s*
World population	4
Urban proportion of world population	3
Total world urban population	13
World economy	14
Industrial output	40
Energy use	13
Coal production	7
Air pollution	≈5
Carbon dioxide emissions	17
Sulfur dioxide emissions	13
Lead emissions to the atmosphere	≈8
Water use	9
Marine fish catch	35
Cattle population	4
Pig population	9
Horse population	1.1
Blue whale population (Southern Ocean only)	0.0025 (99.75% decrease)
Fin whale population	0.03 (97% decrease)
Bird and mammal species	0.99 (1% decrease)
Irrigated area	5
Forest area	0.8 (20% decrease)
Cropland	2

Table compiled by John McNeill for his book, *Something New Under the Sun: An Environmental History of the Twentieth Century*, Penguin Books, 2000.

Developed by Aubrey Meyer and the Global Commons Insititute (GCI), the Contraction and Convergence (C&C) model is perhaps the most simple yet sophisticated framework which tackles the seemingly impossible task of stabilising atmospheric concentrations of carbon dioxide and averting the irreversible trends of runaway climate change. For more detailed information, see *Contraction and Convergence – The Global Solution to Climate Change*, No 5 in the Schumacher Briefings (Totnes, Devon, UK: Green Books 2000)

The first graph shows recorded global surface temperature, which has risen 0.9 degrees Celsius between 1860 and 2000. The top line shows Business-As-Usual (BAU), assuming a 2% increase per year in carbon dioxide and other greenhouse gas emissions. The bottom line shows a total rise of 1.5 degrees Celsius if C&C produced a 60% cut in annual emissions by 2100.

The second graph plots carbon dioxide emissions in parts per million by volume (ppmv) since 1800. The top line represents the worst case scenario of BAU. The bottom line shows a C&C cut of 60%, stabilising CO_2 emissions at 450 ppmv, 70% above pre-industrial levels.

The third graph plots global economic losses from natural disasters (bottom line), which is growing at 10% a year, against a 3% annual growth in global GDP (top line). If the current trends continue as BAU, damages will exceed global GDP by 2065!

The fourth graph plots CO_2 and GDP. Over the last 40 years, CO_2 emissions and global GDP have correlated nearly 100% in a 'lockstep' which must be broken if CO_2 emissions are to stabilise (bottom line) and GDP continue to grow at 3% per annum (top line).

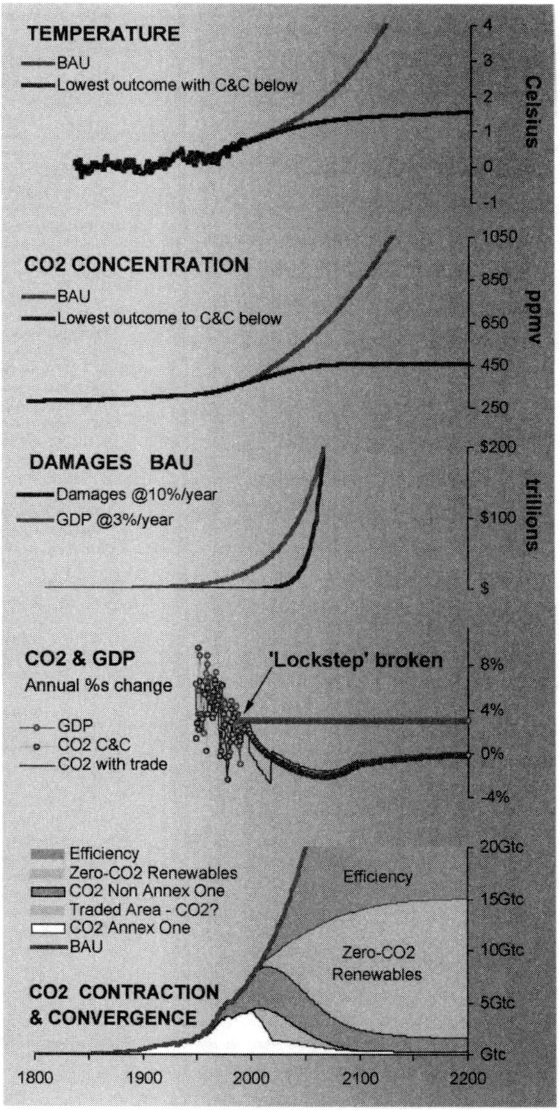

This last graph shows BAU on the top line, with the shaded areas below representing the various components of a possible future scenario where, driven by C&C and depending on factors like increased efficiency and the rate at which fossil fuels are replaced with renewable and zero-emissions technologies, runaway climate change may be averted. The difference between BAU and C&C represents the opportunity for these technologies, worth trillions of dollars per annum – the biggest market in history.

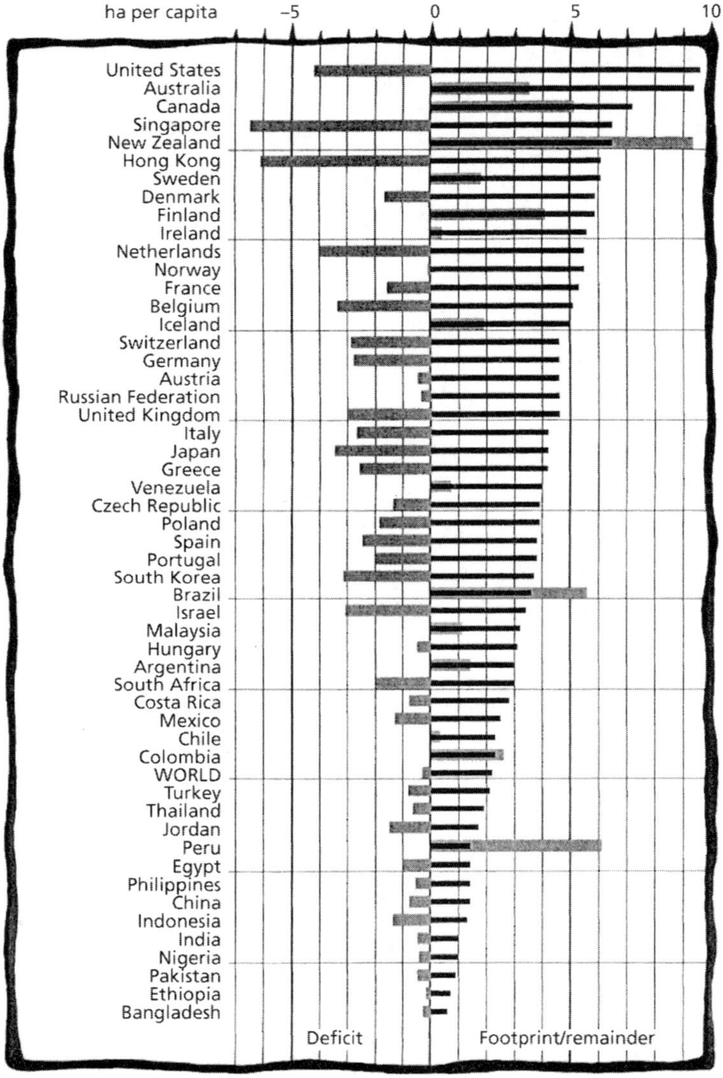

The 'ecological footprint' is an accounting tool that calculates human impacts on the planet, reflecting the amount of bio-productive space required to sustain a particular activity indefinitely. It can be applied to any lifestyle, activity, business, product or manufacturing process, incorporating not just factors like energy, food and resource use but the biological capacity required to absorb full life-cycle impacts like pollution and waste.

The figures on this graph, which is taken from *Sharing Nature's Interest* by Nicky Chambers, Craig Simmons and Mathis Wackernagel, represent the number of global hectares required to support the average lifestyle in each of the countries listed. The black line represents the average per capita footprint. The grey line shows the extent to which each country could meet its own needs within its own bio-productive capacity, including both land and sea. If the grey line extends to the right, the country has a national ecological remainder. If the grey line extends to the left, the country has a national ecological deficit.

Notes

Introduction

1 Quoted in Goldsmith, *The Way: An Ecological World View* (London: Rider 1992), p. 376.

2 Quoted in Porritt, Jonathon, *Seeing Green: The Politics of Ecology Explained* (Oxford: Basil Blackwell 1985), p. 16.

3 Roszak, Theodore, *Ecopsychology: Restoring the Earth, Healing the Mind* (San Francisco: Sierra Club Books 1995), p. 16.

4 McCormick, John, *The Global Environment Movement: Reclaiming Paradise* (London: Belhaven Press 1989), p.viii.

5 Ibid.

6 Ibid.

7 Schwarz, Walter, *Resurgence*, issue 169, March/April 1995, p. 26.

8 Vidal, John, *Resurgence*, issue 184, September/October 1997, p. 42.

9 Henderson, Hazel, in *Towards a New World View: Conversations at the Leading Edge*, ed. Russell E. Dicarlo (Pennsylvania: Epic Publishing 1996), p. 294.

10 Sale, Kirkpatrick, *Resurgence*, issue 192, January/February 1999, p. 23.

11 Vidal, John, *Resurgence*, issue 184, September/October 1997, p. 42.

12 Hawken, Paul, Lovins, Amory B, Lovins, L Hunter, *Natural Capitalism* (London: Earthscan 1999), p. 4.

13 Korten, David, *When Corporations Rule the World* (London: Earthscan 1995), p. 28.

14 Ibid.

15 Hawken et al., *Natural Capitalism*, p. 4.

16 Meyer, Aubrey, *Contraction and Convergence: The Global Solution to Climate Change* (Totnes, Devon: Green Books Schumacher Briefings 2000), p. 29.

17 Ibid., p. 22.

18 For a comprehensive over-view of climate change, see *The Ecologist* report with Vol. 31 No. 9, November 2001.

19 Mander, Jerry, *In the Absence of the Sacred: The Failure of Technology and the Survival of the Indian Nations* (San Francisco: Sierra Club Books 1991), p. 79.

20 Hawken *et al.*, *Natural Capitalism*, p. 52.

21 Harvey, Graham, *The Killing of the Countryside* (London: Jonathan Cape 1997), p. 7.
22 Ibid., p. 104.
23 Ponting, Clive, *A Green History of the World* (London: Penguin 1991), p. 238.
24 Porritt, *Seeing Green*, p. 100.
25 Ponting, *A Green History of the World*, p. 193.
26 Tickell, Sir Crispin, *Resurgence*, issue 163, March/April 1994, p. 7.
27 Leopold, Aldo, *A Sand County Almanac* (Oxford: Oxford University Press 1949), pp. 224–5.
28 Lovelock, James, *Gaia: A New Look at Life on Earth* (Oxford: Oxford University Press 1979), p. 9.
29 Ibid., p. 12.

Part 1 Man vs Nature

1 Quoted in Wall, Derek, *Green History: A Reader in Environmental Literature, Philosophy and Politics* (London: Routledge 1994), pp. 236–7.
2 White Jr, Lynn, The Historical Roots of Our Ecologic Crisis, *Science*, issue 155, March 1967, reprinted in *Machina ex Deo: Essays in the Dynamism of Western Culture* (Cambridge, MA: MIT Press 1968).
3 Ibid.
4 Gore, Al, *Earth in the Balance* (New York: Plume 1993), p. 243.
5 Ecclesiastes (iii. 19).
6 Nash, Roderick, *The Rights of Nature: A History of Environmental Ethics* (Madison: University of Wisconsin Press 1989), p. 90.
7 Quoted in Ponting, Clive, *A Green History of the World: The Environment and the Collapse of Great Civilisations* (London: Sinclair-Stevenson 1991), p. 145.
8 *Resurgence*, issue 185, November/December 1997, p. 49.
9 Nash, *Rights of Nature*, p. 91.
10 Huxley, Aldous, *The Perennial Philosophy* (London: Chatto and Windus 1946), p. 233.
11 Ibid., p. 91.
12 Sheldrake, Rupert, *The Rebirth of Nature: The Greening of Science and God* (London: Bantam 1991), pp. 19–20.
13 Ibid., p. 4.
14 Collingwood, R. G., *The Idea of Nature* (Oxford: Clarendon Press 1945).
15 Ibid.
16 Huxley, *The Perennial Philosophy*, p. 92.

17 Quoted in Ponting, *A Green History of the World*, p. 142.
18 Ibid., p. 76.
19 Tarnas, Richard, *The Passion of the Western Mind: Understanding the Ideas That Have Shaped Our World View* (New York: Ballantine Books 1991), p. 224.
20 Quoted in Collingwood, *The Idea of Nature*, p. 102.
21 Ibid.
22 Quoted in Leiss, William, *The Domination of Nature* (New York: George Braziller 1972), p. 49.
23 Ibid.
24 Ibid., p. 50.
25 Sheldrake, *Rebirth of Nature*, p. 41.
26 Quoted in Thomas, Keith, *Man and the Natural World: Changing Attitudes in England 1500–1800* (London: Allen Lane 1983), p. 18.
27 Quoted in Leiss, *Domination of Nature.*
28 Quoted in Sheldrake, *Rebirth of Nature*, p. 43.
29 Ibid., p. 49.
30 Quoted in Ponting, *A Green History of the World*, p. 147.
31 Quoted in Sheldrake, *Rebirth of Nature*, p. 81.
32 Quoted in Ponting, *A Green History of the World*, p. 148.
33 Quoted in Sheldrake, *Rebirth of Nature*, p. 53.
34 Quoted in Wall, *Green History.*
35 Ibid.
36 Huxley, *The Perennial Philosophy*, p. 93.
37 Ibid., p. 93.
38 Ponting, *A Green History of the World*, p. 300.
39 Ibid., p. 283.
40 Ibid., p. 274.
41 Ibid., p. 330.
42 Ibid., p. 155.
43 Ibid., p. 157.
44 Ibid., p. 151.
45 Ibid., p. 15.
46 Quoted in Porritt, *Seeing Green*, p. 30.
47 Ibid., p. 123.
48 Quoted in Ponting, *A Green History of the World*, p. 159.
49 Huxley, *The Perennial Philosophy*, p. 302.
50 Quoted in Porritt, *Seeing Green*, pp. 50–1.
51 Ibid., p. 59.
52 Quoted in Leiss, *Domination of Nature*, p. 83.

53 Herbert Girardet, personal interview.
54 Quoted in Leiss, *Domination of Nature*, p. 87.
55 Quoted in Leiss, *Domination of Nature*, p. 125.
56 Hawken et al, *Natural Capitalism*, p. 316.
57 Ponting, *A Green History of the World*, p. 358.
58 Thomas, Keith, *Man and the Natural World* (London: Allen Lane), p. 244.
59 Ibid., p. 245.
60 Ponting, *A Green History of the World*, p. 359.
61 Tansey, Geoff and Worsley, Tony, *The Food System: A Guide* (London: Earthscan 1995), p. 33.
62 Quoted in Wall, *Green History*, p. 47.
63 Tansey and Worsley, *The Food System*, p. 33.
64 Wall, *Green History*, p. 44.
65 Ibid.
66 McKibben, Bill, *The End of Nature* (New York: Random House 1989).
67 Ibid., p. 63.
68 Meyer, *Contraction and Convergence*, p. 16.
69 Ponting, *A Green History of the World*, p. 100.
70 Ibid., p. 101.
71 Ibid.
72 Ibid.
73 Sinclair, David, *Shades of Green* (London: Grafton Books 1990), p. 6.
74 Wall, *Green History*, p. 21.
75 Quoted in Thomas, *Man and the Natural World*, p. 243.
76 Quoted in Sinclair, *Shades of Green*, p. 127.
77 Thomas, *Man and the Natural World*, p. 15.
78 Quoted in Thomas, *Man and the Natural World*, p. 27.
79 Ibid., p. 21.
80 Ibid., p. 55.
81 Ibid., p. 27.
82 Ibid., p. 28.
83 Ibid., p. 43.
84 Ibid., p. 167.
85 Ibid.
86 Ibid., p. 278.
87 Ibid., p. 122.
88 Ibid.
89 Ibid., p. 178.
90 Ibid., p. 143.
91 Ibid., p. 144.

92 Ibid., p. 178.
93 Ibid., p. 180.
94 Ibid., p. 259.
95 Ibid., p. 210.
96 Ibid., p. 197.
97 Ibid., p. 213.
98 Ibid., p. 167.
99 Ibid., pp. 167–8.
100 Ibid., p. 168.
101 Quoted in Wall, *Green History*, p. 105.
102 Quoted in Worster, Donald, *Nature's Economy: The Roots of Ecology* (San Francisco: Sierra Club Books 1977).
103 Quoted in Thomas, *Man and the Natural World*, p. 168.
104 Ibid.
105 Quoted in Nash, *The Rights of Nature*, p. 42.
106 Ponting, Clive, *A Green History of the World.*
107 Quoted in Thomas, *Man and the Natural World*, p. 266.
108 Ibid., p. 257.
109 Ibid.
110 From Wordsworth, William, 'Lines Composed a Few Miles Above Tintern Abbey . . .' (1798).
111 Quoted in Thomas, *Man and the Natural World*, p. 257.
112 Ibid., p. 267.
113 Ackroyd, Peter, *Blake* (London: Sinclair-Stevenson 1995), p. 193.
114 From Keats, John, *Lamia* (1819).
115 Ackroyd, Peter, *Blake*, p. 193.
116 Ibid., p. 194.
117 From Blake, William, *Jerusalem*, 'A Vision of Albion' (1804).
118 Quoted in Thomas, *Man and the Natural World*, p. 258.
119 Thomas, *Man and the Natural World*, p. 266.
120 Quoted in Thomas, *Man and the Natural World*, p. 258.
121 Ibid., p. 268.
122 Thomas, *Man and the Natural World*, p. 285.
123 Herbert Girardet, personal interview.
124 Huxley, *The Perennial Philosophy*, p. i.
125 Quoted in Capra, Fritjof, *The Web of Life: A New Synthesis of Mind and Matter* (London: Harper Collins 1996), p. 188.
126 Quoted in Wall, *Green History*, p. 90.
127 From Wilde, Oscar, 'Panthea' (1881).
128 From Swinburne, Algernon Charles, *Hertha* (1871).

129 Quoted in *Self Enquiry* journal (London: Ramana Maharshi Foundation).
130 From Emerson, Ralph Waldo, 'Nature' in *Nature: Addresses and Lectures* (1849).
131 From *The Notebooks of Leonardo da Vinci* (Dover Publications 1975).
132 From Shelley, Percy Bysshe, *Prometheus Unbound* (1820).
133 Quoted in Wall, *Green History*, p. 98.
134 Quoted in Roszak (ed.), *Ecopsychology*, p. 121.
135 For the definitive history of the anarchist tradition, see Marshall, Peter, *Demanding the Impossible: A History of Anarchism* (London: HarperCollins 1992).
136 Quoted in Wall, *Green History*, p. 162.
137 Quoted in Marshall, *Demanding the Impossible*, p. 23.
138 Van Der Post, Laurens, *A Walk with a White Bushman* (London: Chatto and Windus 1986), p. 68.
139 Huxley, *The Perennial Philosophy*, pp. 278–9.

Part 2 In the Land of the Free

1 President George Bush in the run-up to the 1992 Earth Summit in Rio.
2 Quoted in Sheldrake, *Rebirth of Nature*, pp. 58–9.
3 Marsh, George Perkins, *Man and Nature; or, Physical Geography as Modified by Human Action*, 1864, introduction. Edited by David Lowenthal (Cambridge: Harvard University Press 1965).
4 Ibid.
5 McKibben, *The End of Nature*, p. 172.
6 Quoted in Sheldrake, *Rebirth of Nature*, p. 67.
7 Ibid., p. 72.
8 Quoted in Wall, *Green History*, p. 161.
9 Quoted in McKibben, *The End of Nature*, p. 74.
10 Quoted in Marshall, Peter, *Nature's Web: Rethinking Our Place on Earth* (New York: M.E. Sharpe 1996), pp. 348–9.
11 See Cronon, William, *Uncommon Ground: Rethinking Our Place in Nature* (New York: W.M. Norton 1996), p. 83.
12 Quoted in Cronon, *Uncommon Ground*, p. 89.
13 For further analysis of Muir's anthropocentric views in later life, see Marshall, *Nature's Web*, p. 349; Nash, *Rights of Nature*, pp. 40–1; and Cronon, *Uncommon Ground*, p. 72.
14 Quoted in McKibben, *The End of Nature*, p. 62.
15 Foreman, Dave, *Confessions of an Eco-Warrior* (New York: Harmony Books 1991), p. 27.

16 Quoted in Ponting, *A Green History of the World*, p. 260.
17 Ponting, *A Green History of the World*, p. 260.
18 Ibid., pp. 260–1.
19 Ibid., p. 261.
20 See McNeill, John, *Something New Under the Sun: An Environmental History of the Twentieth Century* (London: Allen Lane 2000), pp. 151–4.
21 Quoted in Nash, *Rights of Nature*, p. 63.
22 Leopold, Aldo, *A Sand County Almanac* (Oxford: Oxford University Press 1949), p. 130.
23 Ibid., p. 132.
24 Nash, *Rights of Nature*, pp. 65–6.
25 Ibid., p. 66.
26 Leopold, *A Sand County Alamanac*, p. 129.
27 Ibid., pp. 224–5.
28 Ibid., p. 214.
29 Ibid., p. 178.
30 Ibid., p. 6.
31 Ibid., pp. 104–7.
32 Ibid., p. 107.
33 Ibid.
34 Watts, Alan, *Does It Matter: Essays on Man's Relation to Materiality* (New York: Vintage 1971), p. 22.
35 Mumford, Lewis, *The City in History*. Quoted in Gottlieb, Robert, *Forcing the Spring: The Transformation of the American Environmental Movement* (Washington: Island Press 1993).
36 McNeill, *Something New Under the Sun*, p. 111.
37 Quoted in Sale, Kirkpatrick, *The Green Revolution: The American Environmental Movement 1962–1992* (New York: Hill and Wang 1993).
38 Gottlieb, *Forcing the Spring*.
39 Sale, *Green Revolution*.
40 Gottlieb, *Forcing the Spring*.
41 Ibid.
42 Quoted in Briggs, Shirley A., 'Silent Spring: The View from 1990'. *The Ecologist*, Vol. 20, No. 2, March/April 1990.
43 Quoted in Gottlieb, *Forcing the Spring*, Chapter 3.
44 McCormick, *The Global Environment Movement*, p. 56.
45 Quoted in Gottlieb, *Forcing the Spring*.
46 Quoted in Biehl, Janet, *The Murray Bookchin Reader* (London: Cassell 1997), p. 4.
47 Quoted in Marshall, *Nature's Web*, p. 427.

48 Quoted in Biehl, *The Murray Bookchin Reader*, p. 5.
49 Ibid., p. 5.
50 Ibid., p. 6.
51 Ibid., p. 7.
52 Ibid., pp. 7–8.
53 Ibid., p. 8.
54 Marshall, *Nature's Web*, p. 427.
55 Ibid., pp. 428–9.
56 Roszak, Theodore, *The Making of a Counter Culture* (New York: Doubleday 1969), p. xvii.
57 Quoted in Gottlieb, *Forcing the Spring*.
58 Ibid.
59 Ibid.
60 Ibid.
61 Roszak, *The Making of a Counter Culture*, p. xviii.
62 Herbert Girardet, personal interview.
63 Stevens, Jay, *Storming Heaven: LSD and the American Dream* (London: Paladin Grafton 1989), p. 397.
64 Quoted in Gottlieb, *Forcing the Spring*.
65 Ibid.
66 Ibid.
67 Stevens, *Storming Heaven*, p. 415.
68 Ibid., p. 415.
69 Gottlieb, *Forcing the Spring*.
70 Roszak, *The Making of a Counter Culture*, p. xxvii–xxviii.
71 Ibid., p. xviii.
72 Herbert Girardet, personal interview.
73 Quoted in Sale, *The Green Revolution*.
74 Ibid.
75 Quoted in Gottlieb, *Forcing the Spring*.
76 Sale, *The Green Revolution*.
77 Ibid.
78 Ibid.
79 Quoted in Gottlieb, *Forcing the Spring*.
80 Ibid.
81 Ibid.
82 Quoted in Sale, *The Green Revolution*.
83 McCormick, *The Global Environment Movement*, p. 52.
84 Ibid.
85 Ibid.

86 Ibid.
87 Ibid., p. 54.
88 Brown, Michael and May, John, *The Greenpeace Story* (New York: Dorling Kindersley 1991), p. 8.
89 Ibid.
90 Ibid., p. 9.
91 Ibid., p. 10.
92 Hunter, Robert, *The Greenpeace Chronicle* (London: Picador 1979), p. 21.
93 Brown and May, *The Greenpeace Story*, p. 12.
94 Hunter, *The Greenpeace Chronicle*, p. 35.
95 Brown and May, *The Greenpeace Story*, p. 36.
96 Ibid., p. 15.
97 Ibid., p. 17.
98 Ibid.
99 Ibid.
100 Ibid., p. 18.
101 Ibid., p. 19.
102 McTaggart, David, *Greenpeace III: Journey into the Bomb* (London: Collins 1978), p. 107.
103 McTaggart, *Greenpeace III*, p. 281.
104 Brown and May, *The Greenpeace Story*, p. 33.
105 Ibid., p. 38.
106 Ibid., p. 50.
107 Ibid., p. 53.
108 Ibid., p. 54.
109 Klein, Naomi, *No Logo* (London: Flamingo 2000), p. 380.
110 Ibid., pp. 381–2.
111 Ibid., p. 381.
112 Ibid.
113 Quoted in Schwarz, Walter, *Resurgence*, Issue 169, March/April 1995.
114 Ibid.
115 Quoted in Sale, *The Green Revolution*.
116 Ibid.
117 *Resurgence*, Issue 181, March/April 1997, p. 27.
118 Quoted in Sale, *The Green Revolution*.
119 McNeill, *Something Under the Sun*, p. 29.
120 Gottlieb, *Forcing the Spring*.
121 Quoted in Sale, *The Green Revolution*.
122 Gottlieb, *Forcing the Spring*.
123 Sale, *The Green Revolution*.

124 Gottlieb, *Forcing the Spring.*
125 Quoted in Sale, *The Green Revolution.*
126 Nash, *Rights of Nature*, p. 191.
127 Ibid., p. 191.
128 Quoted in Nash, *Rights of Nature*, p. 193.
129 Ibid., p. 193.
130 Quoted in Gottlieb, *Forcing the Spring.*
131 Sale, *The Green Revolution.*
132 Ibid.
133 Ibid.
134 Ibid.
135 Quoted in Sale, *The Green Revolution.*
136 Barnaby, Frank, The Environmental Impact of the Gulf War, *The Ecologist*, Vol. 21, No. 4, July/August 1991.
137 Quoted in Sale, *The Green Revolution.*
138 Ibid.
139 Wilkinson, Todd, Bushwhacked. Eyes on Washington: An Environmental Guide, *The Amicus Journal*, Spring 2001.
140 Ibid.
141 Quoted in Sayle, Murray. After George W. Bush, the Deluge. *London Review of Books*, 21 June 2001, p. 3.
142 Simms, Andrew, *The Guardian.*
143 Ibid.
144 Quoted in *The Ecologist*, Vol. 31, No. 7, p. 25 (September 2001).
145 Quoted by Brown, Paul, *The Guardian*, 24 July 2001.
146 Brockes, Emma and Borger, Julian, *The Guardian*, 26 July 2001.
147 Fritjof Capra's systemic analysis of international terrorism from personal e-mail.
148 Soueif, Ahdaf, Nile Blues, *The Guardian*, 6 November 2001.
149 Ibid.
150 St Clair, Jeffrey, *The Los Angeles Free Press*, 10 February 2000.
151 Ibid.
152 Ibid.
153 Ibid.
154 Ibid.
155 Ibid.
156 Personal interview.
157 Ibid.
158 Nichols, Mary D. and Young, Stanley, *The Amazing LA Environment* (Living Planet Press 1991).

159 Ibid.
160 Ibid.
161 Ibid.
162 Ibid.
163 Personal interview.
164 Ibid.
165 Ibid.
166 Ibid.
167 Ibid.
168 Ibid.
169 Ibid.
170 Ibid.
171 Ibid.
172 Ibid.

Part 3 Anarchy in the UK

1 *The Ecologist*, Vol. 22, No. 4, July/August 1992.
2 Shoard, Marion, *This Land is Our Land: The Struggle for Britain's Countryside* (London: Gaia Books 1997), p. 12.
3 Ibid., p. 13.
4 Ibid., pp. 13–14.
5 Ibid., p. 20.
6 *The Ecologist*, Vol. 22, No. 4, July/August 1992.
7 Ibid.
8 Ibid.
9 Ibid.
10 Ibid.
11 Sale, Kirkpatrick, *Rebels Against the Future: The Luddites and their War on the Industrial Revolution* (Reading, Massachusetts: Addison-Wesley 1995), p. 2.
12 Quoted in Marshall, *Demanding the Impossible*, p. 97.
13 Ibid., p. 98.
14 Quoted in Shoard, *This Land is Our Land*, p. 37.
15 Quoted in Marshall, *Demanding the Impossible*, p. 100.
16 Ibid., p. 96.
17 Ibid., p. 97.
18 Marshall, *Demanding the Impossible*, Chapter 8.
19 Shoard, *This Land is Our Land*, p. 36.
20 Marshall, *Demanding the Impossible*, p. 97.

21 Shoard, *This Land is Our Land*, p. 38.
22 For the definitive history of anarchism, see Peter Marshall's *Demanding the Impossible.*
23 Quoted in Marshall, *Demanding the Impossible*, p. 13.
24 Ibid.
25 Ibid., p. 15.
26 Ibid., pp. 55–6.
27 Ibid., p. 191.
28 Ibid., p. 210.
29 Quoted in Marshall, *Nature's Web*, p. 300.
30 Quoted in Heilbroner, Robert I, *The Worldly Philosophers: The Lives, Times and Ideas of the Great Economic Thinkers* (New York: Simon and Schuster 1986), p. 77.
31 Quoted in Dobson, Andrew, *Green Political Thought* (London: Routledge 1995), p. 33.
32 Ibid., p. 20.
33 See Ehrlich, Paul R. and Ehrlich, Anne H., *Betrayal of Science and Reason: How Anti-Environmental Rhetoric Threatens Our Future* (Washington: Island Press 1996).
34 Quoted in Marshall, *Demanding the Impossible*, p. 104.
35 Quoted in Marshall, *Nature's Web*, p. 304.
36 Quoted in Heilbroner, *The Worldly Philosophers*, p. 112.
37 Ibid., p. 113.
38 Ibid., p. 116.
39 Quoted in Marshall, *Nature's Web*, p. 312.
40 Quoted in Marshall, *Demanding the Impossible*, p. 174.
41 Quoted in Marshall, *Nature's Web*, p. 313.
42 Wall, *Green History*, p. 9.
43 Quoted in Marshall, *Demanding the Impossible*, p. 175.
44 Marshall, *Nature's Web*, p. 314.
45 Quoted in Marshall, *Demanding the Impossible*, p. 169.
46 Ibid., p. 170.
47 Quoted in Wall, *Green History*, p. 73.
48 Gould, P., *Early Green Politics* (Brighton: Harvester Press 1988).
49 Quoted in Marshall, *Demanding the Impossible*, p. 176.
50 Ibid.
51 Ibid., p. 175.
52 Quoted in Wall, *Green History*, p. 85.
53 Quoted in Dobson, *Green Political Thought*, p. 15.
54 Personal interview.

55 Pearce, Fred, *Green Warriors* (London: Bodley Head 1991), pp. 9–10.
56 Ibid.
57 Ibid.
58 Quoted in Sale, *The Green Revolution.*
59 Goldsmith, Edward, *The Way: An Ecological World View* (London: Rider 1992).
60 Personal interview.
61 Pearce, *Green Warriors*, p. 1.
62 Ibid., p. 3.
63 Quoted in Pearce, *Green Warriors*, p. 9.
64 Quoted in interview by Gerrard, Nicci, *The Observer Review*, 13 August 2000.
65 Ibid.
66 *The Ecologist*, Vol. 30, No. 6, September 2000.
67 Ibid.
68 Ibid.
69 Quoted in Dobson, *Green Political Thought*, pp. 16–17.
70 Dobson, *Green Political Thought*, p. 2.
71 Quoted in Dobson, *Green Political Thought*, p. 9.
72 *The Ecologist*, Vol. 30, No. 6, September 2000.
73 Quoted in interview by Gerrard, Nicci, *The Observer Review*, 13 August 2000.
74 Quoted in Gottlieb, *Forcing the Spring.*
75 *The Ecologist*, Vol. 30, No. 9, December 2000/January 2001.
76 Ibid.
77 Lamb, Robert, *Promising the Earth* (London: Routledge 1996), p. 23.
78 McCormick, *The Global Environment Movement*, p. 143.
79 Sale, *The Green Revolution.*
80 *The Ecologist*, Vol. 30, No. 9, December 2000/January 2001.
81 Ibid.
82 Quoted in Lamb, *Promising the Earth*, p. 33.
83 Ibid., p. 40.
84 Ibid.
85 Ibid.
86 Hawken *et al.*, *Natural Capitalism*, p. 96.
87 Tony Juniper, personal interview.
88 Ibid.
89 Ibid.
90 Ibid.
91 Ibid.

92 Ibid.
93 Capra, Fritjof and Spretnak, Charlene, *Green Politics: The Global Promise* (New York: E.P. Dutton 1984).
94 Ibid., p. 4.
95 Ibid., Preface, pp. xiv–xv.
96 Quoted in Wall, Derek, *Earth First! and the Anti-Roads Movement: Radical Environmentalism and Comparative Social Movements* (London: Routledge 1999), p. 26.
97 Ibid.
98 Ibid.
99 Ibid., p. 33.
100 Quoted in Dobson, *Green Political Thought*, p. 21.
101 Lamb, *Promising the Earth*, p. 11.
102 Ibid., p. 12.
103 Ibid., p. 13.
104 Ibid.
105 Ibid., p. 14.
106 Personal interview.
107 Quoted in Wall, *Earth First! and the Anti-Roads Movement*, p. 81.
108 Ibid., p. 32.
109 Warwick, Hugh, *Resurgence*, Issue 167, November/December 1994, p. 29.
110 Warwick, Hugh, *Resurgence*, Issue 177, July/August 1996, p. 15.
111 Ibid., p. 16.
112 Quoted in Wall, *Earth First! and the Anti-Roads Movement*, p. 21.
113 Ibid.
114 Ibid., p. 36.
115 *The Guardian*, 2 May 2001.
116 Ibid.
117 Wall, *Earth First! and the Anti-Roads Movement*, p. 164.
118 Warwick, Hugh, *Resurgence*, Issue 167, November/December 1994, p. 28.
119 Wall, *Earth First! and the Anti-Roads Movement*, p. 147.
120 Ibid.
121 Warwick, Hugh, *Resurgence*, Issue 177, July/August 1996, p. 16.
122 Collin, Matthew, *Altered State: The Story of Ecstasy Culture and Acid House* (London: Serpent's Tail 1998).
123 Warwick, Hugh, *Resurgence*, Issue 177, July/August 1996, p. 16.
124 Vernon, Roland, *Resurgence*, Issue 164, May/June 1994, p. 4.
125 Ibid.
126 Ibid., p. 5.
127 Kirn, Walter, *Time* magazine, 24 April 2000, p. 43.

128 Klein, Naomi, *No Logo* (London: Flamingo 2000), p. 312.
129 Wall, *Earth First! and the Anti-Roads Movement*, p. 157.
130 Ibid., p. 192.
131 Ibid., pp. 87–8.
132 See Klein, *No Logo*, pp. 318–20.
133 Ibid., p. 321.
134 *The Observer*, 29 July 2001.
135 Ibid.
136 *The Ecologist*, Vol. 31, No. 7, September 2001, p. 41.
137 Ibid., p. 43.
138 Goldsmith, Zac, *The Guardian*, August 2001.
139 *The Guardian*, 27 June 2001.
140 *The Observer*, 29 July 2001.
141 Klein, *No Logo*, p. 4.
142 Ibid., p. 352.
143 Gore, *Earth in the Balance*, p. 39.
144 Monbiot, George, *The Guardian*, 7 August 2001.
145 Helena Norberg-Hodge, personal interview.
146 *The Ecologist*, Vol. 30, No. 9, December 2000/January 2001, p. 25.
147 Ibid.
148 Ibid.
149 Ibid.
150 Quoted in *Forbes* magazine, 24 January 2000, p. 98.
151 Ibid.
152 Ibid.
153 Ibid.
154 Ehrlich and Ehrlich, *Betrayal of Science and Reason* pp. 37–8.
155 Ibid., p. 37.
156 Ibid.
157 Ibid., p. 16.
158 Ibid., pp. 40–1.
159 Ibid.

Part 4 A Green and Pleasant Land

1 Schumacher, E. F., *Small is Beautiful: A Study of Economics as if People Mattered* (London: Abacus 1988), p. 11.
2 See Harvey, *Killing of the Countryside*, p. 133 for more detail.
3 Colborn, Theo, Dumanoski, Dianne and Myers, John Peterson, *Our Stolen Future* (London: Abacus 1997), p. 26.

4 See study in *The Ecologist*, Vol. 30, No. 4, June 2000.

5 Professor John Sumpter, of Brunel University, Middlesex, produced a report which shows a fall in the sperm count of rats attributed to low levels of chemicals found in packaging and food products. He regarded the findings as 'extraordinarily significant' in explaining the dramatic fall in male sperm counts (*Independent*, 19 December 1995). For a complete account of hormone disruptors and oestrogen mimicking compounds within our water supply and the global food chain, see *Our Stolen Future* by Theo Colborn, Dianne and Myers Dumanoski and John Peterson.

6 Professor Richard Lacey, quoted by Vandana Shiva in *Resurgence*, Issue 178, September/October 1996, p. 48.

7 Colborn *et al.*, *Our Stolen Future.*

8 McNeill, *Something New Under the Sun*, p. 28.

9 Badsha, Kartar, Environmental Sickness, Multiple Chemical Sensitivity. *Positive Health*, Issue 71, December 2001, p. 29.

10 Ponting, *Green History of the World*, p. 253.

11 Ibid.

12 McNeill, *Something New Under the Sun*, p. 23.

13 Ibid., p. 25.

14 *Resurgence*, Issue 180, January/February 1997, p. 13.

15 Tansey, Geoff and Worsley, Tony, *The Food System: A Guide* (Earthscan 1995), p. 45.

16 O'Hagan, Andrew, *The End of British Farming* (London Review of Books 2001), p. 53.

17 Bond, Jack W., *How EC and World Bank Policies Are Destroying Agriculture and the Environment* (Holland: AgBe Publishing 1996), p. 39 and Harvey, *Killing of the Countryside*, p. 7.

18 For more detail, see Harvey, *Killing of the Countryside*, Chapter 2.

19 Ibid.

20 *The Observer*, 12 August 2001.

21 Bond, *How EC and World Bank Policies Are Destroying Agriculture and the Environment*, p. 14.

22 Ibid., p. 100.

23 Ibid., pp. 67–8.

24 Ibid., p. 69.

25 *Current Concerns*, No 3/4, April–May 2001 (Zurich).

26 Personal interview.

27 *Current Concerns*, No 3/4, April–May 2001 (Zurich). Source: *Sunday Express*, 8 April 2001.

28 Gunthert, Daniel, *Current Concerns*, No 3/4, April–May 2001 (Zurich).
29 Ibid.
30 Ibid.
31 *The Guardian*, 7 August 2001.
32 Ibid.
33 Harvey, *Killing of the Countryside*, p. 98.
34 Ibid., p. 15.
35 Rifkin, Jeremy, *The Biotech Century* (New York: Tarcher and Putnam 1998), p. 67.
36 Quoted in Anderson, Luke, *Genetic Engineering, Food and Our Environment: A Brief Guide* (Totnes, Devon: Green Books 1999), p. 15.
37 Ibid., p. 11.
38 Sheldrake, *Rebirth of Nature*, p. 52.
39 Blackmore, Susan, *Resurgence*, Issue 177, July/August 1996.
40 *The Guardian*, 18 April 2001.
41 Sexton, Sarah, *Resurgence*, Issue 193, March/April 1999, p. 21.
42 Anderson, *Genetic Engineering*, p. 78.
43 Epstein, Samuel S., Profiting from Cancer: Vested Interests and the Cancer Epidemic, *The Ecologist*, Vol. 22, No. 5, September/October 1992.
44 *Resurgence*, Issue 186, January/February 1998, p. 24.
45 Quoted in Anderson, *Genetic Engineering*, p. 26.
46 Ibid., p. 64.
47 Ibid., p. 68.
48 Viney, Michael, *Resurgence*, Issue 197, November/December 1999, p. 38.
49 Anderson, *Genetic Engineering*, p. 47.
50 See study by Professor Jules Pretty, *Resurgence*, Issue 176, May/June 1996, pp. 7–9.
51 Kimbrell, Andrew, *Resurgence*, Issue 182, May/June 1997, p. 10.
52 Anderson, *Genetic Engineering*, Chapter 4.
53 Ibid., p. 81.
54 Quoted in Warwick, Hugh, *Resurgence*, Issue 187, March/April 1998, p. 21.
55 Quoted in Anderson, *Genetic Engineering*, p. 117.
56 Ibid.
57 *Resurgence*, Issue 185, November/December 1997, p. 31.
58 *Resurgence*, Issue 187, March/April 1998, p. 20.
59 Melchett, Peter, *Resurgence*, Issue 199, March/April 2000, p. 23.
60 Ibid.
61 *The Guardian*.
62 Shiva, Vandana, *Resurgence*, Issue 205, March/April 2001, p. 12.

63 Shiva, quoted in Tansey and Worsley, *The Food System*, p. 22.
64 Simms, Andrew, *Resurgence*, Issue 196, September/October 1999, p. 9.
65 Quoted in Anderson, *Genetic Engineering*, p. 60.
66 Simms, Andrew, *Resurgence*, Issue 196, September/October 1999, p. 9.
67 *Resurgence*, Issue 186, January/February 1998, p. 24
68 O'Hagan, *The End of British Farming*, p. 10 and p. 70.
69 Ibid., p. 11.
70 Sexton, Sarah, *Resurgence*, Issue 193, March/April 1999, p. 23.
71 *Resurgence*, Issue 176, May/June 1996, p. 15.
72 Ibid.
73 *Resurgence*, Issue 181, March/April 1997, p. 6.
74 Ibid.
75 Ibid., p. 7.
76 Quoted in Anderson, *Genetic Engineering*, p. 95.
77 Monbiot, George, *Captive State: The Corporate Takeover of Britain* (London: Macmillan 2000), pp. 270–1.
78 Ibid., p. 273.
79 Harvey, *The Killing of the Countryside*, p. 9.
80 Quoted in Harvey, *The Killing of the Countryside*, p. 108.
81 Quoted in *Resurgence*, Issue 195, July/August 1999, p. 37.
82 Bond, *How EC and World Bank Policies Are Destroying Agriculture and the Environment*, p. 130.
83 Ibid.
84 Ibid., p. 131.
85 Ibid., p. 130.
86 Monbiot, George, *Resurgence*, Issue 205, March/April 2001, p. 16.
87 Ibid.
88 Herbert Girardet, personal interview.
89 Anderson, *Genetic Engineering*, p. 89.
90 Ibid., p. 97.
91 Harvey, *The Killing of the Countryside*, p. 176.
92 Thomas, *Man and the Natural World*, p. 292.
93 Ibid., p. 298.
94 Ibid., pp. 288–9.
95 Ibid., p. 291.
96 Ibid., p. 296.
97 Ibid., p. 298.
98 Ibid., p. 299.
99 Ram Tzu (aka Wayne Liquorman), *No Way: For the Spiritually Advanced* (California: Advaita Press 1990), p. 14.

100 *Resurgence*, Issue 190, September/October 1998, p. 60.
101 Mollison, Bill, *Permaculture: A Designer's Manual* (Tasmania: Tagari 1988).
102 Hart, Robert, *Forest Gardening: Rediscovering Nature and Community in a Post-Industrial Age* (Totnes, Devon: Green Earth Books 1996), p. 52.
103 Ibid., p. 120.
104 Ibid.
105 Jeavons, John, *How to Grow More Vegetables (Than You Ever Thought Possible on Less Land Than You Can Imagine)* (Berkeley, California: Ten Speed Press 1995).
106 Ibid.
107 Quoted in Hawken *et al.*, *Natural Capitalism*, p. 204.
108 Herbert Girardet, personal interview.
109 Fairlie, Simon, *Low Impact Development: Planning and People in a Sustainable Countryside* (Oxfordshire: Jon Carpenter 1996), p. x.
110 Ibid.
111 Ibid., p. xi.
112 Ibid., p. 4.
113 Ibid., p. 6.
114 Ibid., p. 7.
115 Ibid., Foreword.
116 Ibid.
117 Ibid., p. 16.

Part 5 Techno-addicts

1 Sale, *Rebels Against the Future*, p. 4.
2 Quoted in Sale, *Rebels Against the Future*, pp. 15–16.
3 Ibid., p. 28.
4 Ibid., p. 30.
5 Ibid., p. 54.
6 Ibid., p. 57.
7 *The Guardian*, 18 April 2001.
8 Mander, *In the Absence of the Sacred*, p. 4.
9 Quoted in Mander, *In the Absence of the Sacred*, pp. 37–8.
10 Mander, *In the Absence of the Sacred*, p. 4.
11 *Resurgence*, Issue 208, September/October 2001, p. 9.
12 Quoted in Schama, Simon, *Landscape and Memory* (London: Fontana 1996), p. 13.
13 Mander, *In the Absence of the Sacred*, p. 48.

14 Ibid., p. 77.
15 Ibid., p. 78.
16 Ibid., p. 42.
17 Huxley, *The Perennial Philosophy*, p. 261.
18 Mander, *In the Absence of the Sacred*, p. 26.
19 Schumacher, *Small is Beautiful*, p. 124.
20 Glendinning, Chellis, Technology, Trauma and the Wild, in Roszak (ed.), *Ecopsychology*, p. 47.
21 Ibid., p. 52.
22 Ibid.
23 Ibid., p. 54.
24 Ibid., pp. 44–5.
25 Shepard, Paul, Nature and Madness, in Roszak (ed.), *Ecopsychology*, pp. 37–8.
26 Quoted in Durning, Alan Thein, Are We Happy Yet? in Roszak (ed.), *Ecopsychology*, p. 70.
27 Quoted in Mander, *In the Absence of the Sacred*, p. 55.
28 Ibid., p. 57.
29 Ibid., p. 63.
30 Ibid.
31 Ibid., p. 51.
32 Quoted in Ferkiss, Victor, *Nature, Technology and Society: Cultural Roots of the Current Environmental Crisis* (New York and London: New York University Press 1993), p. 178.
33 Mander, *In the Absence of the Sacred*, p. 71.
34 Quoted in Mander, *In the Absence of the Sacred*, p. 70.
35 *Resurgence*, Issue 174, January/February 1996, p. 9.
36 Hawken *et al.*, *Natural Capitalism*, p. 51.
37 Griffiths, Jay, *Resurgence*, Issue 174, January/February 1996, p. 9.
38 Ibid.
39 Russell, Peter, *Resurgence*, Issue 177, July/August 1996, p. 25.
40 Huxley, *The Perennial Philosophy*, p. 274.
41 Quoted in Hawken *et al.*, *Natural Capitalism*, pp. 15–16.
42 Todd, John, in *Gaia: A Way of Knowing*, ed. William Irwin Thompson (San Francisco: Lindisfarne Press 1987), pp. 133–4.
43 Hawken *et al.*, *Natural Capitalism*.
44 Ibid., p. 138.
45 Ibid., p. 79.
46 Ibid., p. 80.
47 Ibid., pp. 139–41.

48 Ibid., p. 199.
49 Ibid., p. 203.
50 Quoted in Anderson, *Genetic Engineering*, p. 103.
51 Quoted in Mander, *In the Absence of the Sacred*, p. 179.
52 Quoted in Goldsmith, *The Way*, p. 317.
53 Ibid., pp. 317–18.
54 Schumacher, *Small is Beautiful*, p. 11.
55 Ibid., p. 13.
56 Ibid., pp. 106–7.
57 Ibid., p. 26.
58 Ibid., pp. 30–1.
59 Ibid., pp. 47–8.
60 Ibid., p. 50.
61 Ibid., p. 126.
62 Ibid., p. 128.
63 Ibid.
64 Ibid.
65 *Resurgence*, Issue 174, January/February 1996, p. 11.
66 Ibid., p. 11.
67 McNeill, *Something New Under the Sun*, p. 310.
68 Hawken *et al.*, *Natural Capitalism*, p. 23.
69 McNeill, *Something New Under the Sun*, p. 311.
70 Ibid.
71 Ibid.
72 Hawken *et al.*, *Natural Capitalism*, p. 23.
73 Ponting, *Green History of the World*, p. 330.
74 Hawken *et al.*, *Natural Capitalism*, p. 23.
75 McNeill, *Something New Under the Sun*, p. 310.
76 Hawken *et al.*, *Natural Capitalism*, p. 27.
77 Ibid., p. 29.
78 Ibid., p. 25.
79 Ibid., p. 26.
80 Ibid.
81 Ibid., p. 27.
82 Ibid.

Part 6 Conclusion: Towards an Ecological Age

1 Quoted in Porritt, *Seeing Green*, Preface.
2 Tarnas, Richard, in *Towards a New World View: Conversations at the*

Leading Edge, ed. Russell E. DiCarlo (Pennsylvania: Epic Publishing/Floris Books 1996), p. 41.

3 In DiCarlo (ed.), *Towards a New World View*, Chapter 1.
4 Ibid., Chapter 26.
5 Ibid., Chapter 24.
6 Ibid., Chapter 20.
7 James Lovelock, personal interview.
8 Ibid.
9 Ibid.
10 Capra, *The Web of Life: A New Synthesis of Mind and Matter* (London: HarperCollins 1997), p. 46.
11 Capra, *The Web of Life.*
12 Teddy Goldsmith, personal interview.
13 Drengson, Alan and Inoue, Yuichi (eds.), *The Deep Ecology Movement: An Introductory Anthology* (Berkeley: North Atlantic Books 1995).
14 *Resurgence*, Issue 168, January/February 1995, p. 26.
15 Drengson and Inoue (eds.), *The Deep Ecology Movement*, Chapter 9.
16 Ibid.
17 *Resurgence*, Issue 199, March/April 2000, p. 19.
18 Ibid., p. 16.
19 Ibid.
20 Ibid., p. 17.
21 Devall, Bill, *Resurgence*, Issue 155, November/December 1992, p. 19.
22 *The Observer*, 28 November 1999, p. 21.
23 Devall, Bill, *Resurgence*, Issue 155, November/December 1992, p. 19.
24 Quoted in Macy, Joanna, *World as Lover, World as Self* (Berkeley: Parallax Press 1991), p. 34.
25 Quoted in Marshall, *Nature's Web*, p. 424.
26 Marshall, *Nature's Web*, p. 428.
27 Capra, *Web of Life*, pp. 6–9.
28 Ibid., p. 9.
29 Huxley, Aldous, *Moksha: Aldous Huxley's Classic Writings on Psychedelics and the Visionary Experience*, ed. Michael Horowitz and Cynthia Palmer (Vermont: Park Street Press 1999), p. 221.
30 Tarnas, Richard, in DiCarlo (ed.), *Towards a New World View*, p. 44.
31 Ibid., p. 47.
32 Watts, Alan, *Does It Matter*, p. 5.
33 Hawken *et al., Natural Capitalism*, p. 310.
34 Tony Juniper, personal interview.
35 Korten, *When Corporations Rule the World*, p. 12.

36 Ibid., p. 12.
37 *Resurgence*, Issue 163, March/April 1994, p. 17.
38 Korten, *When Corporations Rule the World*, p. 312.
39 Ibid., p. 312.
40 Ibid., p. 313.
41 Ibid., Chapter 24: Agenda for Change.
42 Ibid., p. 320.
43 Ibid.
44 Mander, *In the Absence of the Sacred*, p. 137.
45 Tony Juniper, personal interview.
46 Korten, *When Corporations Rule the World*, Chapter 24: Agenda for Change.
47 Hawken, Paul, *Resurgence*, Issue 163, March/April 1994, p. 17.
48 Ibid.
49 Ibid., p. 18.
50 Ibid.
51 Ibid.
52 Ibid.
53 Ibid., p. 19.
54 Ibid.
55 Quinn, Daniel. *Beyond Civilization: Humanity's Next Great Adventure* (New York: Harmony Books 1999), p. 191.
56 Ibid., p. 12.
57 Ibid., p. 152.
58 For more information about the Natural Step Organisation, contact Andre Heniz at TNS International, Wallingatan 22, SE 111–24, Stockholm, Sweden, or visit www.naturalstep.org
59 This inspirational methodology was first conceived by Mathis Wackernagel and William Rees in their book *Our Ecological Footprint: Reducing Human Impact on the Earth* (Gabriola Island, BC: New Society Publishers 1996) then followed by Wackernagel with Nicky Chambers and Craig Simmons in *Sharing Nature's Interest* (London: Earthscan 2000).
60 Marshall, Peter, *Resurgence*, Issue 205, March/April 2001, p. 27.

Epilogue – A Spiritual Perspective

1 From a talk in Bangalore, 1948. Quoted in Blau, Evelyne, *Krishnamurti: 100 Years* (New York: Stewart, Tabori and Chang 1995), p. 100.
2 Quoted in *Whole Life Times*, April 2000 (Los Angeles).
3 *Resurgence*, Issue 177, July/August 1996, p. 25.

4 Roszak *et al.*, *Eco-psychology*, pp. 66–7.
5 Ibid.
6 Grof, Stanislav, in DiCarlo (ed.), *Towards a New World View*, p. 124.
7 Capra, *Web of Life*, p. 287.
8 Ibid.
9 Grof, Stanislav, in DiCarlo (ed.), *Towards a New World View*, p. 124.
10 Dossey, Larry, in DiCarlo (ed.), *Towards a New World View*, p. 152.
11 Bateson, Gregory, Introduction to Thompson, William Irwin (ed.), *Gaia: A Way of Knowing*, (San Francisco: Lindisfarne Press 1987), pp. 45–6.
12 Ibid., p. 46.
13 Macy, *World as Lover, World as Self*, pp. 185–6.
14 Wilbur, Ken, Foreword to *Talks with Ramana Maharshi* (California: Inner Directions 1999).
15 *Resurgence*, Issue 177, July/August 1996, p. 28.
16 Quoted in Liquorman, Wayne, *Acceptance of What IS – A Book About Nothing* (California: Advaita Press 2000), p. 20.
17 From Matt Ridley's *Genome*, quoted in *The Advaita Inquirer*, summer 2001, newsletter for the Advaita Fellowship, Redondo Beach, California.
18 Huxley, *The Perennial Philosophy*, introduction.
19 Ibid., p. 192.
20 *Resurgence*, Issue 160, September/October 1993, p. 34.

Select Bibliography

Anderson, Luke. *Genetic Engineering, Food and Our Environment: A Brief Guide* (Totnes, Devon: Green Books 1999)

Biehl, Janet. *The Murray Bookchin Reader* (London: Cassell 1997)

Bond, Jack W. *How EC and World Bank Policies Are Destroying Agriculture and the Environment* (Holland: AgBe Publishing 1996)

Brown, Michael and May, John. *The Greenpeace Story* (New York: Dorling Kindersley 1991)

Capra, Fritjof and Spretnak, Charlene. *Green Politics: The Global Promise* (New York: E.P. Dutton 1984)

Capra, Fritjof. *The, Web of Life: A New Synthesis of Mind and Matter* (London: HarperCollins 1997)

Colborn, Theo, Dumanoski, Dianne and Myers, John Peterson. *Our Stolen Future* (London: Abacus 1997)

Collingwood, R. G. *The Idea of Nature* (Oxford: Clarendon Press 1945)

Cronon, William. *Uncommon Ground: Rethinking Our Place in Nature* (New York: W.M. Norton 1996)

DiCarlo, Russell E. (ed.). *Towards a New World View: Conversations at the Leading Edge* (Pennsylvania: Epic Publishing 1996)

Dobson, Andrew. *Green Political Thought* (London: Routledge 1995)

Drengson, Alan and Inoue, Yuichi (eds.). *The Deep Ecology Movement: An Introductory Anthology* (Berkeley: North Atlantic Books 1995)

Ehrlich, Paul R. and Ehrlich, Anne H. *Betrayal of Science and Reason: How Anti-Environmental Rhetoric Threatens Our Future* (Washington: Island Press 1996)

Evernden, Neil. *The Social Creation of Nature.* (Baltimore: John Hopkins University Press 1992)

Ferkiss, Victor. *Nature, Technology and Society: Cultural Roots of the Current Environmental Crisis* (New York: New York University Press 1993)

Foreman, Dave. *Confessions of an Eco-Warrior* (New York: Harmony Books 1991)

Glacken, Clarence J. *Traces on the Rhodian Shore: Nature and Culture in Western Thought from Ancient Times to the End of the Eighteenth Century* (Berkeley: University of California Press 1990)

Goldsmith, Edward. *The Way: An Ecological World View* (London: Rider 1992)

Gore, Al. *Earth in the Balance* (New York: Plume 1993)

Gottlieb, Robert. *Forcing the Spring: The Transformation of the American Environmental Movement* (Washington: Island Press 1993)

Hart, Robert. *Forest Gardening: Rediscovering Nature and Community in a Post-Industrial Age* (Totnes, Devon: Green Earth Books 1996)

Harvey, Graham. *The Killing of the Countryside* (London: Jonathan Cape 1997)

Hawken, Paul, Lovins, Amory B and Lovins, L Hunter. *Natural Capitalism* (London: Earthscan 1999)

Heilbroner, Robert. *The Worldly Philosophers: The Lives, Times and Ideas of the Great Economic Thinkers* (New York: Simon and Schuster 1986)

Henderson, Hazel. *Creating Alternative Futures.* (Bloomfield: Kumarian Press 1996)

Huxley, Aldous. *The Perennial Philosophy* (London: Chatto and Windus 1946)

Huxley, Aldous. *Moksha: Aldous Huxley's Classic Writings on Psychedelics and the Visionary Experience*, eds. Michael Horowitz and Cynthia Palmer (Vermont: Park Street Press 1999).

Jeavons, John. *How to Grow More Vegetables (Than You Ever Thought Possible on Less Land Than You Can Imagine)* (Berkeley, California: Ten Speed Press 1995)

Klein, Naomi. *No Logo* (London: Flamingo 2000)

Korten, David. *When Corporations Rule the World* (London: Earthscan 1995)

Lamb, Robert. *Promising the Earth* (London: Routledge 1996)

Leiss, William. *The Domination of Nature* (New York: George Braziller 1972)

Leopold, Aldo. *A Sand County Almanac* (Oxford: Oxford University Press 1949)

Lovelock, James. *Gaia: A New Look at Life on Earth* (Oxford: Oxford University Press 1979)

Macy, Joanna. *World as Lover, World as Self* (Berkeley: Parallax Press 1991)

Mander, Jerry. *In the Absence of the Sacred: The Failure of Technology and the Survival of the Indian Nations* (San Francisco: Sierra Club Books 1991)

Marsh, George Perkins. *Man and Nature; or, Physical Geography as Modified by Human Action*, 1864. Ed. David Lowenthal (Cambridge: Harvard University Press 1965)

Marshall, Peter. *Demanding the Impossible: A History of Anarchism* (London: HarperCollins 1992)

Marshall, Peter. *Nature's Web: Rethinking Our Place on Earth* (New York: ME Sharpe 1996)

McCormick, John. *The Global Environment Movement: Reclaiming Paradise* (London: Belhaven Press 1989)

McKibben, Bill. *The End of Nature* (New York: Random House 1989)

McNeill, John. *Something New Under the Sun: An Environmental History of the Twentieth Century* (London: Allen Lane 2000)

Merchant, Carolyn. *The Death of Nature: Women, Ecology and the Scientific Revolution* (San Francisco: Harper and Row 1983)

Merchant, Carolyn. *Radical Ecology: The Search for a Livable World* (New York: 1992)

Meyer, Aubrey. *Contraction and Convergence: The Global Solution to Climate Change* (Totnes, Devon: Green Books Schumacher Briefings 2000)

Mollison, Bill. *Permaculture: A Designer's Manual* (Tasmania: Tagari 1988)

Nash, Roderick. *The Rights of Nature: A History of Environmental Ethics* (Madison: University of Wisconsin Press 1989)

Nichols, Mary D. and Young, Stanley. *The Amazing LA Environment* (Living Planet Press 1991)

O' Hagan, Andrew. *The End of British Farming* (London Review of Books 2001)

Pearce, Fred. *Green Warriors: People and Politics Behind the Environmental Revolution* (London: Bodley Head 1991)

Ponting, Clive. *A Green History of the World: The Environment and the Collapse of Great Civilisations* (London: Sinclair-Stevenson 1991)

Porritt, Jonathon. *Seeing Green: The Politics of Ecology Explained* (Oxford: Basil Blackwell 1985)

Quinn, Daniel. *Beyond Civilization: Humanity's Next Great Adventure* (New York: Harmony Books 1999)

Ram Tzu (aka Wayne Liquorman). *No Way: For the Spiritually Advanced* (California: Advaita Press 1990)

Rifkin, Jeremy. *The Biotech Century* (New York: Tarcher and Putnam 1998)

Roszak, Theodore. *The Making of a Counter Culture* (New York: Doubleday 1969)

Roszak, Theodore (ed.). *Ecopsychology: Restoring the Earth, Healing the Mind* (San Francisco: Sierra Club Books 1995)

Rothenberg, David. *Hand's End: Technology and the Limits of Nature* (Berkeley: 1993)

Sale, Kirkpatrick. *The Green Revolution: The American Environmental Movement 1962–1992* (Hill and Wang 1993)

Sale, Kirkpatrick. *Rebels Against the Future: The Luddites and their War on the Industrial Revolution* (Reading, Massachusetts: Addison-Wesley 1995)

Schama, Simon. *Landscape and Memory* (London: Fontana 1996)

Schumacher, E. F. *Small is Beautiful: A Study of Economics as if People Mattered* (London: Abacus 1988)

Sheldrake, Rupert. *The Rebirth of Nature: The Greening of Science and God* (London: Bantam 1991)

Shoard, Marion. *This Land is Our Land: The Struggle for Britain's Countryside* (London: Gaia Books 1997)

Sinclair, David. *Shades of Green* (London: Grafton Books 1990)

Stevens, Jay. *Storming Heaven: LSD and the American Dream* (London: Paladin Grafton 1989)

Tansey, Geoff and Worsley, Tony. *The Food System: A Guide* (London: Earthscan 1995)

Tarnas, Richard. *The Passion of the Western Mind: Understanding the Ideas That Have Shaped Our World View.* (New York: Ballantine Books 1991)

Thomas, Keith. *Man and the Natural World: Changing Attitudes in England 1500–1800* (London: Allen Lane 1983)

Thompson, William Irwin (ed.). *Gaia: A Way of Knowing* (San Francisco: Lindisfarne Press 1987)

Van Der Post, Laurens. *A Walk with a White Bushman* (London: Chatto and Windus 1986)

Wall, Derek. *Green History: A Reader in Environmental Literature, Philosophy and Politics* (London: Routledge 1994)

Wall, Derek. *Earth First! and the Anti-Roads Movement: Radical Environmentalism and Comparative Social Movements* (London: Routledge 1999)

Watts, Alan. *Does It Matter: Essays on Man's Relation to Materiality* (New York: Vintage 1971)

White Jr, Lynn. The Historical Roots of Our Ecologic Crisis, *Science*, Issue 155, March 1967, reprinted in *Machina ex Deo: Essays in the Dynamism of Western Culture* (Cambridge, Massachusetts: MIT Press 1968)

Worster, Donald. *Nature's Economy: The Roots of Ecology* (San Francisco 1977)

Index